JAMES CALLAGHAN
An Underrated Prime Minister?

EDITED BY
Kevin Hickson & Jasper Miles

Biteback Publishing

First published in Great Britain in 2020 by
Biteback Publishing Ltd, London
Selection and editorial apparatus copyright © Kevin Hickson and Jasper Miles 2020.

ISBN 978-1-78590-633-6

10 9 8 7 6 5 4 3 2 1

A CIP catalogue record for this book is available from the British Library.

Set in Bulmer

Printed and bound in Great Britain by
CPI Group (UK) Ltd, Croydon CR0 4YY

CONTENTS

ACKNOWLEDGEMENTS

FIRST AND FOREMOST, THE editors would like to thank the contributors for their time in writing for the book. All are in their own right authorities on the subjects on which they write, from the fields of politics, journalism and academia. At any time, we would have been very grateful, but we are especially so due to the unique circumstances in which we found ourselves in the first half of 2020.

We would also like to thank the publisher, Biteback, particularly Molly Arnold and Olivia Beattie. It is pleasing that they have once again allowed us to publish with them.

The book appears on the fortieth anniversary of Jim Callaghan's retirement from a long career on the frontline of British politics. Anyone who served for so long is likely to have amassed critics as well as supporters and the range of views on Callaghan are expressed in this volume. We very much believe in opinion diversity and allowing the reader to decide for themselves what the verdict should be on Callaghan.

On a personal note, we would like to thank our families and friends for their ongoing support.

Kevin Hickson and Jasper Miles
Wistaston and Brough
August 2020

NOTES ON CONTRIBUTORS

Jonathan Aitken was a Conservative MP from 1974 to 1997. His numerous books include *Margaret Thatcher: Power and Personality* (2014), *Pride and Perjury* (2000) and *Nixon: A Life* (1993).

Martin S. Alexander is Emeritus Professor in the Department of International Politics at Aberystwyth University and has written prominent works on British and French defence policy.

Kevin Bean is a Fellow of the Institute of Irish Studies at the University of Liverpool.

Duncan Brack was the Liberal Democrats' first Policy Director, and between 2010 and 2012 a special advisor in the Department of Energy and Climate Change. Professionally he is now an independent environmental policy researcher and an Associate Fellow of Chatham House. He also edits the *Journal of Liberal History* and has edited several books on Liberal and Liberal Democrat history.

Mark Garnett is Senior Lecturer in Politics at the University of Lancaster, where he teaches and researches on British politics and contemporary political history, especially in relation to the Conservative Party and think tanks.

Wyn Grant is Emeritus Professor of Politics at the University of Warwick. He has written extensively on economic policy, agricultural policy and pressure groups.

Eric Grove was Professor of Naval History at Salford University and then Liverpool Hope University. He previously taught at Dartmouth and Greenwich Naval Colleges and the University of Hull. He has published numerous works on British naval policy.

Pauline Hadaway has completed her PhD at the University of Manchester and has worked in various posts in the arts and education in Northern Ireland.

Simon Hannah is a writer, active trade unionist and member of the Labour Party. His book, *A Party with Socialists in It: A History of the Labour Left*, was published in 2018. His most recent book is *Can't Pay, Won't Pay: The Fight to Stop the Poll Tax* (2020).

Roy Hattersley was Secretary of State for Prices and Consumer Protection under James Callaghan and was deputy leader of the Labour Party between 1983 and 1992. He has published extensively on British history and politics.

Kevin Hickson is Senior Lecturer in British Politics at the University of Liverpool. He has had published fifteen books and numerous journal articles on various aspects of British politics and contemporary political history. His most recent books are *Britain's Conservative Right since 1945* (2020) and (as joint author) *Peter Shore: Labour's Forgotten Patriot* (Biteback, 2020).

R. Gerald Hughes is Reader in the Department of International Politics at Aberystwyth University and has published extensively on diplomatic and military history and the history of intelligence.

David (Lord) Lipsey is a Labour peer. He was special advisor to Tony Crosland and then worked in 10 Downing Street for James Callaghan. His memoirs, *In the Corridors of Power*, were published by Biteback in 2012.

Jane Martin is Professor of Social History of Education and Director of the DOMUS Centre for Interdisciplinary Research in the Histories of Education and Childhood at the University of Birmingham. She has published widely, including *Making Socialists: Mary Bridges Adams and the Fight for Knowledge and Power, 1855–1939*, and is currently researching Caroline Benn and the campaign for comprehensive education. She is editor of the Routledge journal *Educational Review*.

Jasper Miles is joint author of *Peter Shore: Labour's Forgotten Patriot* (Biteback, 2020) and has taught at Queen Mary, University of London and Goldsmiths, University of London.

Austin Mitchell was Labour MP for Great Grimsby between 1977 and 2015. He was previously an academic and a presenter for Yorkshire television. His memoirs, *Confessions of a Political Maverick*, were published by Biteback in 2018.

Philip (Lord) Norton is Professor of Government and Director of the Centre for Legislative Studies at the University of Hull and a Conservative peer. He is widely recognised as a leading authority on the British constitution, having published thirty-four books and many articles on the subject.

David (Lord) Owen served as Foreign Secretary between 1977 and 1979. He became a founding member and later leader of the Social Democratic Party and is now an independent social democrat peer. He has published numerous books.

Neil Pye teaches British Politics at the University of Liverpool and is a former Labour Party councillor. He specialises in the post-war history of the Labour Party, the rise and fall of Militant-led Labour in Liverpool, and currently researches the metro mayors and devolution in the north-west of England.

Dominic Sandbrook is Visiting Professor at King's College London, a columnist for the *Daily Mail* and a book critic for the *Sunday Times*. Apart from his BBC television series, he is best known for his series of books about Britain since the 1950s, the most recent of which is *Who Dares Wins: Britain 1979–1982* (2019).

Eric Shaw is Honorary Research Fellow in the Division of History and Politics at the University of Stirling and has published extensively on the Labour Party. His latest book is *The People's Flag and the Union Jack: An Alternative History of Britain and the Labour Party* (2019) with Gerry Hassan.

Kristan Stoddart was Reader in International Politics at Aberystwyth University and has published numerous books including *The British Nuclear Experience: The Roles of Beliefs, Culture and Identity* (2014) with John Baylis.

Mark Stuart teaches and writes on British politics. His books include biographies of John Smith and Douglas Hurd.

Andrew Taylor is Emeritus Professor of Politics at the University of Sheffield. He has published widely on British politics. His most recent book, *What About the Workers?*, examining the Conservative Party's relations with the organised working class, was published in 2020 by Manchester University Press.

Harry Taylor is a political director and former Labour councillor. He is joint author of *Peter Shore: Labour's Forgotten Patriot* (Biteback, 2020). His biography of Victor Grayson is forthcoming.

Polly Toynbee is a columnist at *The Guardian* and was previously Social Affairs editor at the BBC. She has written numerous books, most recently *The Lost Decade: 2010–2020 and What Lies Ahead for Britain* (2020) with David Walker.

Ben Williams is Tutor in Politics at the University of Salford. He has written *The Evolution of Conservative Party Social Policy* (2015) and is joint editor (with Kevin Hickson) of *John Major: An Unsuccessful Prime Minister?* (Biteback, 2017).

PREFACE

Roy Hattersley

I MADE MY MAIDEN SPEECH on the afternoon of Thursday 5 November 1964 and – the ordeal being over – I remained, as courtesy required, on the green benches of the House of Commons for the rest of the day's debate on the Queen's Speech. Consumed by a combination of anxiety about the quality of my performance and relief that it was over, I let what remained of the session pass over my head – except for one brief comment on the conduct and character of the Chancellor of the Exchequer. 'The Right Honourable Gentleman for Cardiff South East', said Michael Foot, 'does everything on purpose.' The observation was not, I think, intended as a compliment. But during the twenty years that followed, I grew to realise that 'doing everything on purpose' was one of the attributes that made Jim Callaghan a good Prime Minister and might, had he spent longer in Downing Street, have made him a very good one.

Michael Foot was not alone in thinking that Jim Callaghan preceded each decision, great and small, by a careful calculation of which outcome was best for him. Colleagues made bitter jokes about his evolution from Leonard, through James, to Jim as he sought to polish his image as a man of the people, and they recited lists of occasions on which he had supported people and causes not, it was argued, based on their merits, but because it was in his political interest to break faith with his natural friends and political allies. The crucial part he had played in frustrating Barbara Castle's proposals for trade union reform was said to be unforgivable and was certainly unforgiven.

Neither the record nor the subsequent reputation prevented Jim Callaghan from being elected Labour leader in a contest between the most distinguished list of candidates in the history of the party's elections. By defeating Roy Jenkins, Tony Crosland, Denis Healey, Tony Benn and Michael Foot, Callaghan prevented his detractors from suggesting that he had won by default. His victory over far more exciting contenders was a triumph for the less colourful virtues – care, caution, the avoidance of unnecessary risks and the methodical planning of the way ahead. Jim Callaghan became leader of the Labour Party because a majority of Labour Members of Parliament believed that when he became Prime Minister of Great Britain and Northern Ireland, he would do everything on purpose. And so he did. Even the two disastrous decisions which brought his government to its undistinguished end – the failure to call an election in the summer of 1978 and the refusal to muster the votes which would have defeated Margaret Thatcher's 'vote of confidence' in 1979 – were taken after days of careful deliberation.

Jim Callaghan began his premiership as he meant to go on. He had inherited from Harold Wilson the economic crisis which, in the autumn of 1976, was to culminate in the application for an IMF loan and the massive reduction in public expenditure which was its price. Within forty-eight hours of taking office, the new Prime Minister had come to an agreement with the Chancellor of the Exchequer, which guaranteed that Denis Healey could prescribe whatever remedial measures were necessary without the fear that they would be rejected by the Cabinet. The Chancellor would give the Prime Minister early warning of his intentions and – assuming they contained nothing to which he took violent exception – the Prime Minister would support the Chancellor to the death.

And so it turned out. So, negotiations for an IMF loan began. The cuts in public spending that were necessary for their completion were identified. The Cabinet split into three factions and debated the Chancellor's proposals in six separate meetings without achieving any sort of consensus. To my surprise, the Prime Minister was strangely silent, giving me – a Secretary of State for six weeks – hopes that he might throw his weight behind moderation. Tony Crosland broke the bad news to me on the evening before the Cabinet's seventh discussion of the proposed spending cuts. 'It's tomorrow,' he said, and responded to my obvious bewilderment with a sort of apology. 'I thought you realised. Jim was always going to support Denis. He just waited for the right moment. Tomorrow he'll say we have to agree, or all resign.'

From that moment onward, I became a student of the Jim Callaghan Cabinet management techniques. His most impressive stratagem was what Denis Healey called the 'Pyrrhic Defeat' – having a decision that he had always supported forced upon him. Not once during his three years in Downing Street was he forced to accept a policy or proposal with which he disagreed. He won all the arguments by fair means if possible and foul if there was no other way. When I suggested that the metrication Bill was so unpopular that I should be allowed to postpone it for a year, he expressed his surprise that I was intimidated by the massed ranks of greengrocers and ladies' hairdressers and my proposal was lost in the laughter. Fred Peart, the Minister of Agriculture – persuaded by his civil servants to press for a renegotiation of monetary compensation amounts, a fiendishly complicated formula for adjusting payments under the Common Agricultural Policy – read his brief to the Cabinet without, it was painfully clear, understanding a word of it. 'Explain all that again,' commanded the Prime Minister. 'We all like hearing you talk.' The monetary compensation amounts remained unchanged.

Although he chaired Cabinet meetings with the benign air of an indulgent uncle, in private conversation Jim Callaghan was often brusque to the point of rudeness. He became particularly prickly when the subject was related to the one issue which aroused in him a quite unnecessary feeling of insecurity. Surrounded – in both the Cabinets in which he served and the Cabinet which he led – by men of remarkable academic distinction, he felt, and often expressed, regret that he had left school at the age of seventeen. In the autumn of 1978, he asked me which new Members of Parliament I thought worthy of promotion into government. Without hesitation, I suggested Bryan Gould, a young New Zealander who had left the Foreign Office to represent Southampton. Callaghan suggested that I was biased because Gould was, like me, educated at Oxford and responded to my denial by suggesting, 'well, Cambridge'. Reminded that I had not got within matriculation distance of either university, he brought the conversation to a grinding halt. 'Nobody is going to get into the government who treats me as if I have just come down from the trees.'

Jim Callaghan was invariably generous and supportive to me in times of domestic as well as political difficulty. The worst treatment I ever received at his hand was the brushing aside of some of my more reckless proposals as if only an idiot would suggest such nonsense. Indeed, I felt so comfortable with his leadership that, in the summer of 1978, I not only defied his instructions but wrote an impertinent letter telling him that I was doing so.

Dear Prime Minister,

At the last Cabinet before the summer break, you told ministers that you did not want our advice about the date of the election. I, of course, accept your instruction. However, had you wished for advice, I would have strongly urged you to hold the election this autumn.

I received no reply.

At a little after six o'clock on the morning of Thursday 7 September 1978, I was woken by a telephone call from Tom McCaffrey, the Prime Minister's press officer. Jim Callaghan, he told me, would broadcast to the nation that evening. I was to represent the government in the debate which followed. Asked to speculate on what the Prime Minister would say, McCaffrey replied, 'Didn't you write to him last week?' He then assured me that all would be revealed at the Cabinet meeting later that day.

By the time the Cabinet assembled, the news that the Prime Minister was to broadcast was public. So ministers did not even try to hide their impatience as he read a long statement on the encouraging state of the economy, the success of Britain's membership of the European Union and the amicable relations that the United Kingdom enjoyed with what we had learned to call 'third countries'. The statement being completed, Jim Callaghan added in what sounded like an afterthought.

'I wrote to the Queen this morning. You'd better know what I said.'

Most of the letter to the Queen – which the Prime Minister read out from start to finish – was, as far as I could tell, identical to the statement with which he had entertained the Cabinet. But it ended with an additional sentence. 'I therefore do not propose to ask you to dissolve Parliament this autumn.' The gasps and suppressed nervous laughter were interrupted by a comment which I have come to regard as vintage Callaghan.

'You can discuss it if you want to. But I doubt if you will persuade me to write again, saying that I have changed my mind.'

In fact, the Prime Minister had taken advice – from ministers who, he knew, wanted to postpone the election. They had been consulted after the collection of information from a variety of opinion polls had convinced him that the most likely outcome of an autumn poll was a Labour majority of between ten and half a dozen. And Jim Callaghan had grown tired of governing on a shoestring, with every Bill held back until the number of Labour MPs who were too sick to vote had been counted, and every division in doubt until the result was announced. So he had made the decision to gamble on the spring.

Perhaps he should have expected that Labour's compact with the unions would collapse during the coming winter and that attempts to enforce pay restraint would end in weeks of strikes and stoppages. But that was the industrial background against which Margaret Thatcher moved her vote of no confidence in the Callaghan government in March 1979. Even then, Labour could have survived. But the Prime Minister forbade the seduction of a trio of Ulster Unionists with the offer of a pipeline from Scotland to the Six Counties and vetoed a plan to bring to Westminster by ambulance a dying Labour backbencher who, upon being 'nodded through' the division lobby, would have tied the vote and thus prevented the passage of Mrs Thatcher's lethal resolution. I realise now – though at the time I was only bewildered – that Jim Callaghan had decided that his government had run its natural course and that although he did not welcome defeat, he did so little to prevent it because he was ready to rest. It would be wrong to say that he lost 'on purpose'. But he certainly accepted it with the calm that could only have come from a contented acceptance which was so near to it that Michael Foot was vindicated.

FOREWORD

Lord Owen

Prime Minister Harold Wilson and Foreign Secretary Jim Callaghan worked closely together during the 1975 Common Market referendum campaign and stated publicly that though they were recommending staying in, they would implement the referendum result if it were to the contrary. During the referendum campaign, according to the official history, a senior civil servant, Patrick Nairne, wrote to Callaghan that in the event of a 'No' vote there would be no need to hurry into a withdrawal. Callaghan contradicted him in the most powerful terms, saying it would be necessary to start repealing the 1972 Act very soon thereafter.

Wilson hoped to be able to retire soon after the referendum, but events kept delaying his departure. Eventually Harold Lever telephoned Callaghan, at Wilson's request, on Boxing Day 1976 to let him know privately that Wilson planned to resign in March. Roy Jenkins told me a few days later that he had been given the same message. After the first ballot, Jenkins withdrew; on the second ballot I voted for Denis Healey and only on the third ballot on 5 April 1976 for Jim Callaghan, who beat Foot by 176 to 137 votes and became Prime Minister.

In forming his government, Callaghan was aware that Jenkins had told Wilson in January 1976, even before the ballot, of his wish to become President of the European Commission. So he kept Roy as Home Secretary and refused his wish to become Foreign Secretary. Sensing an impending financial crisis, Callaghan decided not to replace Denis Healey with Tony Crosland and instead appointed him as Foreign Secretary. I continued as Minister of Health while Barbara Castle was brutally replaced as Secretary of State for Health and Social Security. Much to my astonishment, Callaghan's official biographer, Kenneth Morgan, reveals that Callaghan had even then considered appointing me Foreign Secretary. Tragically, Tony Crosland died in February 1977 following a severe brain haemorrhage and much to my surprise, as his deputy, Callaghan asked me to become Foreign Secretary. From the first moment he was always considerate and thoughtful. He told me he was considering appointing Judith Hart as my deputy and when I suggested Frank Judd he agreed; few other Prime Ministers would have acted in this way.

It was Callaghan's handling of the IMF crisis that made me first recognise his considerable strengths as Prime Minister. On his first day in office Callaghan was told that sterling, which stood at an exchange rate of $1.86 and falling, might drop by 10–15 per cent. On 12 April Healey told him that the Bank of England had spent $2 billion in support of sterling over the preceding fifteen months. By the autumn, an IMF loan depended on public expenditure cuts which Healey wanted to accept. In one-on-one conversations, which Healey knew about, Callaghan talked to Helmut Schmidt, Henry Kissinger, President Ford and H. Johannes Witteveen, the Dutch head of the IMF. After these conversations, Callaghan understood there was no escaping the IMF package; but with skill and patience he let everyone in the Cabinet feel they had been part of the discussions and there were no resignations when, on 9 December, Healey announced the IMF loan of £3.9 billion.

The main diplomatic achievement of Callaghan's premiership was paving the way for the enlargement of the EEC by helping eventually to admit Greece, Spain and Portugal as members. Callaghan called a special all-day Cabinet meeting on 29 July 1977 which defined an anti-federalist position with the EU – a Cabinet meeting described by Tony Benn in his diaries as 'one of the most remarkable Cabinets I have ever attended'.[1]

Increasing the powers of the European Parliament required unanimity, but the late-night pressuring of UK ministers to sign up was rendered impossible by making it a prior condition that primary legislation had to be passed through the UK Parliament. The other significant accompaniment to direct elections to the European Assembly was that, for the first time, a majority in any UK Cabinet accepted genuine proportional representation for a national election. It was a hard-fought victory agreed by the Cabinet before the Lib–Lab Pact was solidified. The pact sadly carried only a pledge that the Prime Minister would use his best endeavours to carry it through Parliament – which he did, but it failed, only succeeding in 1999.

An example of how Callaghan managed Cabinet can be found at its meeting on 21 September 1978, when he flicked a note across the Cabinet table saying, 'Come and have lunch.' We walked back to Parliament through St James's Park and Jim motioned to Ken Stowe, his private secretary, to hang back so that we could talk privately about Denis Healey. He then brought up the issue of the European Monetary System and his concern about two speeches that Healey had made recently, one of which appeared to have argued that we should join the Exchange Rate Mechanism, and the other that we should not. Jim reiterated his view that the party would not wear entry to the ERM and that it would have to wait until after the election. I suggested the possibility advanced recently to me by a very clever diplomat, Michael Butler, of joining the EMS but not the ERM. Jim pondered this for a moment and then asked me what Denis's attitude might be. I said he could be persuaded. Then, Jim, ever fertile in man-management, suggested that I get Butler to square the Treasury officials, who could then sell this somewhat ingenious approach to Denis, who could bring it to Cabinet as his idea. Jim would before this square Peter Shore. At the Cabinet, first Healey and then Callaghan argued that we needed a zone of monetary stability and that we should commit ourselves to helping to achieve this, but without any obligations restricting our own freedom to manage the sterling exchange rate as we thought fit. I was doubtful whether any of the other Cabinet members, except Harold Lever and Peter Shore, understood what was happening and that we would not join the ERM, the element of the EMS to which Peter was most adamantly opposed, but we would join the monetary system.

As Foreign Secretary and Prime Minister, Callaghan did a lot with the German SPD in the Socialist International network to ensure Mário Soares became Portuguese Prime Minister following the Carnation Revolution which overthrew the previous Prime Minister, Caetano. It was uncertain for a while whether Portugal would end up as a democracy. Callaghan found unconventional money and, with German funds from the SPD, they successfully manoeuvred so that an election in 1976 elected Soares as Prime Minister. Between 1977 and 1978, Helmut Schmidt and Callaghan both confronted Giscard d'Estaing, eventually demanding a personal assurance that if they agreed Greece could come in first, France would not block Portugal and Spain entering the European Community later. To those on Labour's left who question Callaghan's socialism, there can be no doubt about his full-hearted commitment to it internationally.

His biggest failure as Prime Minister came over his handling of trade union militancy. The crisis unfolded on 12 December 1978 over the refusal of left-wing Labour MPs in the Tribune Group to support the imposition of sanctions against Ford Motor Company for awarding a 17 per cent wage increase to their members. This was a

very personal issue for Callaghan. He had fixed the 5 per cent limit
for wage increases without consulting Denis Healey and his personal
authority was on the line. Here is my account, handwritten late at
night. Very little is known or recorded of the discussions. The original is in my archives in Liverpool University and referred to by John
Shepherd in his book on the Winter of Discontent entitled *Crisis?
What Crisis?*

This account reveals the flaws which led to the government's fall.

12 December 1978

Went to No. 10 with Denis Healey, Fred Mulley and PM to discuss nuclear issues. 10.45 abandoned meeting; discussed political situation.
Called in Michael Foot and then Michael Cox, the Chief Whip. Denis
arguing for making the vote a vote of confidence – it appeared the
issue had not been discussed before. Michael Foot against. PM and
Michael had seen in the House Left MPs, Ron Thomas etc. – came
back certain some would abstain.

Issue complex. 18 or more Members away in Luxembourg. Cledwyn
[Hughes] in Lagos. Arthur Irvine ill, number uncertain. Michael Foot
v. sure we could win vote of confidence next day. Irish would abstain.
Scot Nats uncertain. Welsh Nats c. us. Gerry Fitt uncertain. ?Geraint
Howells. Question of vote in January not on new register? Extent of
damage on old. Jim moving towards making it a matter of censure. Fed
up. Decided to meet at 12.45 to discuss report of the Whips.

12.45 Michael Cox reported marginal chance of winning if we
made it a vote of confidence – uncertain about delegation at European
Parliament.

PM against a deal with Scottish Nats not prepared to name Assembly election date. ? limit of September. No Jim. I argued to be more
open. Michael had sounded Enoch. No chance of Irish voting with us.
Might be able to stop? Fred Mulley quiet – Denis and Jim still keen

to make it vote of confidence. Keep party united, felt if we won could hold sanctions policy afterwards.

I doubted this, spoke a little, main anxiety was to keep Jim in a mood which would not send him off to the farm.

Decided to meet at 3 p.m. Fred and PM lunch with Chiefs of Staff. I lunched with Harry Walston. Even he against sanctions, shook me a little, wholly relaxed about losing – perhaps outside people couldn't give a damn. Denis all along a hawk on Sanctions. This had worried me before; not sure I could possibly trust his judgement and when allied Roy Hattersley very doubtful.

Fred Mulley told me he said to Jim after lunch, 'stick with Michael'. [illegible] advice. I wanted a decision which was Jim's – one he could live with when he shaved next morning, not foisted on him.

Met at 3 in PM's room in House [of Commons]. Denis firmly in favour of confidence [vote]. I knew we couldn't by then get Cledwyn back [from Lagos]. Final straw Michael Cox thought the Council delegation were in Brussels – went out to confirm. Yes, said Jack Diamond. 5 minutes later came in. They were in Luxembourg! This was final straw. I didn't have any confidence in Whips. We could make it a vote of confidence and screw it up by having our people stranded in Luxembourg. Jim wavered. Roy Hattersley and Joel Barnett called in. Roy backed Denis. Joel yes to confidence if we could win but could we win? I kept quiet watching Jim. Suddenly he moved decisively to Michael's viewpoint and in doing it put strong psychological pressure on Michael to deliver the Left. Very critical was I think his [Jim's] wish to go on as a duo – to separate now after all these months was wisely thought to be too damaging. Gamble to make it confidence. Option to call an election in January, February, March or April open if one went for a confidence vote next day.

Impression was these two had bound themselves in together – almost touching. History will show. Writing at 11.38 [in the evening]. I feel we were right.

It was Callaghan's choice that morning; only he personally could have made it a vote of confidence. To do so would have meant confronting the Tribune Group, and Michael Foot and a few other Cabinet ministers might have resigned. Had a vote of confidence been lost, I believe we would have gone on to win the ensuing January general election. But if we had won, in my view, had Callaghan risked all – had he decided there would be a vote of confidence that morning – the Winter of Discontent would never have been anything like as bad as it was. Essentially, Callaghan decided not to fight. We lost that night but won a vote of confidence next day. But the genie was out of the bottle. The left had won – and Callaghan's authority just slipped away. In the Winter of Discontent, we were unable even to bury the dead and still Jim would not call a vote on a state of emergency, telling Cabinet he asked himself to do so every night but wondered the next day if it would make any difference.

His words to me after Mrs Thatcher won the vote of no confidence that precipitated the election by one vote on 28 March 1979 were, 'Will you be alright in Plymouth?' Not the voice of someone who anticipated victory. He was graceful in defeat.

As Prime Minister he entirely fulfilled the old adage that 'office maketh the man'. As the head of the UK government, he drew on his trade union past and his extensive experience in Parliament since 1945, keeping a minority government going against all the odds, and brought into No. 10 a new respect for the office that had been diminished under Wilson and Heath.

NOTES
1   T. Benn, *Conflicts of Interest: Diaries 1977–80* (London: Arrow, 1991), p. 201.

INTRODUCTION

Kevin Hickson and Jasper Miles

FORTY YEARS AGO, JAMES Callaghan stepped down as leader of the Labour Party. It brought his thirty-year tenure on the Labour front bench to an end. After serving as a junior minister under Clement Attlee, he rose up the ranks in Labour's long period of opposition between 1951 and 1964. Uniquely, he served in all three of the senior positions in government prior to becoming Prime Minister (Chancellor of the Exchequer, 1964–67; Home Secretary, 1967–70; and Foreign Secretary, 1974–76). Critics said that he had not served with distinction in any of them and that his general approach to politics was unprincipled, primarily concerned about securing his position within the party and wider Labour movement. However, later interpretations would stress Callaghan's achievements in all three posts.[1]

After Labour lost the 1979 general election, Peter Jenkins was one of the few who remarked favourably about Callaghan. He wrote that Callaghan had tried 'with good sense and good humour to grapple with intractable difficulties … His Prime Ministership deserves an honourable epitaph. He did not abdicate. He did not cheat or deceive. He was brought down by forces beyond his control.'[2] However, many commentators within and outside the party were critical. Attention focused – naturally enough – on the nature of the new Conservative administration under Margaret Thatcher. While Callaghan defended his government's record – notably at the 1979 Labour Party conference – within the Labour Party, the left took control and interpreted the Wilson–Callaghan governments as not only a failure but an outright betrayal of the hopes and beliefs of the grassroots. The Labour moderates hardly jumped to defend the government's record, with the breakaway Social Democratic Party (SDP) seeking to show that they offered something different from the Labour Party. Whereas Callaghan was a man under the control of the trade unions, they had no such sectoral interests.

Nor did the passage of time come to the aid of the Callaghan premiership. The long period of opposition led to a feeling that Labour could not get back into power and commentators questioned whether Callaghan was going to be Labour's last Prime Minister. Even at the height of Thatcherism and the social dislocation that it entailed, criticism of the Callaghan premiership and his supposed lack of political nous continued. A review of his autobiography, which was published in 1987, stated: 'Mr Callaghan completed his political career by putting off a general election, fixing an unrealistic pay limit and leading his troops into the swamps of devolution, where they were duly massacred'.[3] At successive general elections, the Conservatives sought to revive images of the Winter of Discontent in the minds of the electors – even as late as 1997, although by this stage more out of desperation. New Labour, in an attempt to show that the party was thoroughly 'modernised', sought to separate itself from the party's past and denigrated its own history, especially that of the 1970s. Firm associations with the failure of government persist, and perhaps always will, despite the attempt of historians to reappraise the record of that government as a whole and Callaghan specifically.

On becoming Prime Minister in 1976 at the age of sixty-four,

Callaghan had fulfilled a boyhood dream, having been enthused as a child by the deeds and speeches of previous statesmen such as Pitt, Palmerston, Gladstone, Disraeli and Lloyd George. In the Cabinet Room, he sat in the Prime Minister's chair 'as of right and not by invitation', understanding that he was 'a trustee of the past as well as someone who had to try and carry the nation forward into the future'.[4] He spoke of being a bridge between government and the people. However, he immediately faced an economy that was already in difficulties. He presided over two events which define the way his government is viewed to this day – the IMF crisis of 1976, when Britain appeared on the verge of bankruptcy; and the 1978–79 Winter of Discontent, when the trade unions appeared to be beyond the rule of law. The more forgotten period in between can be regarded as more successful, as the economy began to recover. Indeed, public support for Callaghan's government increased, leading to widespread speculation that there would be an autumn election in 1978. This is one of the great 'what ifs' of history – could Callaghan have won that election, and what would have become of 'Thatcherism' if he had done so? On such short-term calculations do long-term trends rest.

Callaghan was firmly shaped by his background, having come from a proud naval family: his father had served aboard the royal yacht. Growing up, Callaghan attended the Baptist church. The *Sunday Times* felt that the religious teachings left a lasting impact, and while he read Shaw, Wells, Laski and Marx, he preferred 'quotations from the Bible and hymns to lines from the literary giants'.[5] His family experienced severe poverty following the death of his father at a young age. He was forced to leave education at seventeen and enter work, unable to afford the costs of attending university. He rose through the ranks of the trade union movement before seeing active service in the Royal Navy in the Second World War. In 1945 he was elected to Parliament for a seat in Cardiff and quickly became a junior minister. It was the beginning of a long and prominent career in frontline politics. Elsewhere, he had a close relationship with the Police Federation, was thought of as anti-permissive in relation to the liberal social reforms of the 1960s, and was a strong monarchist, believing the Queen to be one of the few people he could talk to frankly. This inspired both affection and a protective instinct in Callaghan.[6]

The story points to several sources of Callaghan's distinctive approach to politics – rooted in the working class and strongly patriotic. Ambitious without being flamboyant. Practical rather than intellectual. Small-c conservative rather than permissive. Respectful of British institutions and history. Before leaving the House of Commons, he lamented the latter's treatment: 'we seem constantly ready to emphasise all the things we've done which were discreditable'.[7] Writing in 2020, Callaghan's comment appears even more prescient. In sum, this distinctive approach to politics helped him cultivate an image as 'honest', 'lucky', 'sunny' and 'avuncular', of common sense and sound, non-doctrinaire judgement. For some, this made him Labour's Stanley Baldwin. For others, at the time and subsequently from both the left and the right of the party, his traditional approach to politics generally, and the Labour Party specifically, embodied a bygone era.

This book is a timely reappraisal of the record of Jim Callaghan as Prime Minister. There is no editorial line, no single view which is imposed on the authors. Opinion diversity – seemingly under threat in some quarters, including in institutions whose purpose is to foster independent thought and critical thinking – is not only valued but encouraged. Some of the chapters are more favourable to Callaghan and some more critical. The final judgement of how to rate Callaghan is left to the reader. Some will continue to criticise for his various failures, perceived or real – the weakness of the British economy, his lack of vision, the dominant position of the trade unions, the tactical blunders which led to eighteen years of opposition for his party. Others may well stress the achievements – his instinctive understanding of the opinions of the working class, his steering of the economy through an extremely difficult period, his desire to maintain the welfare state and a more just society, the sense of decency in public life and the sense of duty to one's country.

STRUCTURE OF THE BOOK

In addition to the opening remarks from two distinguished members of Callaghan's Cabinet, the book is divided into three main sections. The first section seeks to place the Callaghan premiership within its historical context. Harry Taylor discusses the social and cultural framework, particularly the sense of pessimism which prevailed at that time and how that contrasted with the much more optimistic mood of a decade before. Kevin Hickson examines Callaghan's understanding of democratic socialism and how that fitted (or perhaps didn't fit) into the nature of the Labour Party's political thought at that time. Mark Stuart studies the nature of Callaghan's handling of Cabinet and the organisation of 10 Downing Street, arguing that he was much less of a Cabinet man than is often perceived. Philip Norton analyses the particularly rebellious nature of parliament which was seen in those years. Eric Shaw then examines the wider Labour Party, stressing the opposition from within the party towards Callaghan and the growing problem of entryism. Finally, Mark Garnett evaluates the general election campaign of 1979, showing how Callaghan, through necessity, adopted a more presidential style, with more focus on the leader than the party. These chapters show the sheer scale of the challenges Callaghan faced. Any reasonable assessment of his premiership must make allowance for the complexity of the situation in which he sought to govern.

The second section examines the policies of Callaghan's government. Wyn Grant explores the crucial economic policy events of

those years, particularly the IMF crisis of 1976 and subsequent developments. Andrew Taylor examines the equally critical industrial
relations policy which culminated in the Winter of Discontent. Ben
Williams discusses the often-neglected social policy record of that
government. Jane Martin goes on to evaluate education policy, upon
which Callaghan had a direct impact with his Ruskin College speech
in the autumn of 1976. Neil Pye grapples with the record on devolution and local government, which, despite the ultimate failure of
devolution to Scotland and Wales, did have more success in terms
of inner-city policy. Kevin Bean and Pauline Hadaway examine a
further issue to which Callaghan gave considerable attention, Northern Ireland, showing how his desire to address social and economic
inequalities was continually thwarted by the communal divisions and
political conflicts that he sought to resolve. Jasper Miles discusses
Callaghan's approach to European integration in the period immediately after Britain joined the EEC and membership was confirmed
in the 1975 referendum, finding much on which to agree with his
handling of these matters. The final chapter in the second section
explores Callaghan's handling of foreign and defence issues.

The third and final section consists of commentaries from a range
of perspectives. David Lipsey reflects on his time working for Callaghan in 10 Downing Street between 1977 and 1979. Austin Mitchell
offers further reflections from the vantage point of being a newly
elected MP following the Grimsby by-election on 28 April 1977. Both
of these pieces show considerable admiration for Callaghan. The
following three pieces approach Callaghan from different ideological and party-political perspectives. Jonathan Aitken offers his perspective as a new backbench Conservative MP. Duncan Brack then
examines the relationship between the Liberal and Labour parties,
especially in the Lib–Lab Pact of 1977–78. Simon Hannah discusses how the Labour left viewed Callaghan, both in government and
then in opposition after 1979. The final two pieces, by prominent

journalists, place Callaghan in a longer-term perspective. Polly Toynbee is highly critical of Callaghan, whose opposition to the 'In Place of Strife' proposals in 1969 led to the defeat of what she regards as reasonable measures to curb the excesses of trade union action – a failure which led ultimately to the Winter of Discontent, Callaghan's downfall and the destruction of the trade unions as a powerful force within the realm under Thatcher. In contrast, Dominic Sandbrook offers a more favourable interpretation of Callaghan, arguing that his instincts were in tune with the underlying conservatism (with a small 'c') of the working class, and that until and unless Labour reconnects with that conservatism, it will never regain power.

NOTES

1   For a highly critical account see P. Kellner and C. Hitchens, *Callaghan: The Road to Number 10* (London: Littlehampton, 1976). For a much more positive interpretation see K. Morgan, *Callaghan: A Life* (Oxford: Oxford University Press, 1997). For a previous balanced assessment of the 1974–79 government as a whole see A. Seldon and K. Hickson (eds), *New Labour, Old Labour: The Wilson and Callaghan Governments, 1974–1979* (London: Routledge, 2004).

2   'Epitaph for a Prime Minister', *The Guardian*, 30 March 1979.

3   'Happy go lucky Jim', *London Daily News*, 23 April 1987.

4   J. Callaghan, *Time and Chance* (London: Collins, 1987), pp. 394–5; 'James Callaghan: The top dog who preferred honesty', *The Guardian*, 3 June 1985.

5   'How Sunny Jim's light dimmed for Labour's faithful', *Sunday Times*, 15 March 1985.

6   'The men who knew her: James Callaghan', *Sunday Times*, 1 April 1986.

7   'James Callaghan: The top dog who preferred honesty', *The Guardian*, 3 June 1985.

PART ONE
CONTEXTS

1

A DECADE OF EXTREMES: THE SOCIAL AND CULTURAL CONTEXT

Harry Taylor

The press is just full of crises, anarchy, chaos, disruption
– bitterly hostile to the trade union movement. I have
never seen anything like it in my life.[1]
TONY BENN, JANUARY 1979

THE 1970S IS PERHAPS the decade of the British twentieth century that has suffered most unjustly from historians and popular reflection. If you ask someone born from the 1980s onwards what they associate with the 1970s, they will probably tell you industrial unrest, crisis, violence, uncollected rubbish and unburied dead. It's a decade portrayed in stark contrast to its predecessor, the 1960s, which, we are constantly told, 'swung', with a lot of friendly folks talking about peace and love. The '60s was the decade of technocrat Harold Wilson's 'white heat', the Beatles and the Rolling Stones, when England even won the World Cup. The '70s was the decade of hapless Jim Callaghan's 'Crisis? What crisis?', the angry explosion of punk via the Sex Pistols, football hooliganism and violent racist skinheads. The '60s and the '70s, so our national consciousness tells us, were two very distinct decades: one of hope and one of despair. The Britain of Wilson's 1966 general election victory bore little or no resemblance to the Britain of 1976 when Callaghan inherited the keys to 10 Downing Street. But as with most popular recollections, though, it isn't true, and the fact that it is continually perpetuated corrupts our vision of ourselves as a country and our approach to contemporary politics. This chapter aims to build a picture of the '70s as one of political and cultural extremes, but one that was very much a natural progression from the issues of the previous decade.

On the face of it, to look back to the election of Richard Nixon in 1968 and Edward Heath in 1970 is to see the abrupt end to the hopes of the '60s which ushered in a more fractious era, of the ramping up of the Vietnam War and British industrial unrest. But in reality, the '70s were merely a continuation of the 1960s – the real 1960s, that is, not the caricature we're sold by cheap Channel 5 television programmes. The hopes and politics of those in the late '60s lived on and in some cases thrived in the 1970s, but so too did the politics of hate. One only need look at Enoch Powell's 'Rivers of Blood' speech from 1968 and how that hung like a spectre over the British political discourse of the 1970s. It had single-handedly ensured the survival and growth of a new grouping on the British right, the National Front, and radicalised race as a political issue.[2] On the other side, the revolutionaries were drawn towards Trotskyism after the failure of the Soviet Union to live up to their theoretical concept of a socialist society. But they were the same faces in the 1970s as they were in 1968, just a little older and better versed in the theories of Marxism. Football hooliganism and industrial unrest, both the so-called 'English Disease', depending on your perception, were already significant points of concern by the late 1960s. If anything, the surprising thing about the 1970s is that old political ideas, and in some cases old politicians, were resurrected by those seeking answers to new problems.

A FASCIST RENAISSANCE?

Revolutionary Marxism (in the form of Trotskyism) and British fascism both enjoyed a strange revival in the 1970s that made them a fashion accessory to some and an imminent threat to the British political order to others. On an episode of the Thames Television *Today* programme in 1975, an elderly but buoyant Sir Oswald Mosley gave a confident interview covering his controversial political past and his vision of Britain's future. Mosley was enjoying something of an Indian summer. Robert Skidelsky (now a crossbench peer) had recently published a sympathetically selective and surprisingly well-received biography of the former leader of the British Union of Fascists which prompted re-spected reviewers and historians to question whether Mosley was really that bad after all.[3] Now Mosley, for nearly four decades his very name associated with treason, was on primetime British television, confident, eyes flashing and warning the viewers about a coming crisis in Britain. Alluding to an earlier discussion, Mosley was asked:

> Interviewer: ...you gave me the impression that you still believed the call might come for you, do you really believe that?
>
> Oswald Mosley: Oh yes, I'm much better now than I've ever been in my life.
>
> Int: Better at what?
>
> OM: Better at politics ... I feel my whole life has been a training for what can now come.
>
> Int: Who on earth would ask you?
>
> OM: I have not yet seen anybody else in the present situation who can meet the crisis which is coming ... When things go wrong it's

a bigger risk to let the muddle grow to a disaster than to have a man of action.[4]

Mosley's whole political outlook since he resigned from the Labour government in May 1930 was that a colossal crisis was just around the corner and that the British people would turn to him in their hour of need. The thing about Mosley's prediction in 1975 was that for once, he wasn't the only one foreseeing the imminent economic and political collapse of Britain. Worryingly, there were even some outside the ageing fascist's close-knit band of supporters who thought a Mosley-type figure was needed to lead Britain out of the coming crisis, and they were people with serious sway in '70s Britain.

Not long after the Mosley interview, the musician David Bowie told the *New Musical Express* in October:

There will be a political figure in the not too distant future who'll sweep this part of the world … You've got to have an extreme right front come up and sweep everything off its feet and tidy everything up … It'll do something positive, at least, to cause a commotion in people and they'll either accept dictatorship or get rid of it.[5]

This wasn't a one-off, either, and he told a press conference, 'I believe Britain could benefit from a fascist leader.' In April 1976, Bowie told a *Playboy* interviewer:

I believe very strongly in fascism. The only way we can speed up the sort of liberalism that's hanging foul in the air at the moment is to speed up the progress of a right-wing, totally dictatorial tyranny and get it over as fast as possible. People have always responded with greater efficiency under a regimental leadership. A liberal wastes time saying, 'Well, now, what ideas have you got?' Show them what to do, for God's sake. If you don't, nothing will get done.[6]

In May he was photographed at London's Victoria Station standing in an open-top Mercedes-Benz wearing a black shirt and giving
what appeared to be a Nazi salute.[7] His defenders said it was all ar-
tistic irony and/or too much cocaine, but it's questionable whether
Bowie's rank-and-file fans recognised the nuance.[8] Nevertheless,
fascist imagery very quickly became fashionable in the burgeoning
punk scene. Sid Vicious of the Sex Pistols, whose mother was a '60s
hippie, wrote the song 'Belsen was a Gas' and regularly appeared on
stage wearing a swastika T-shirt, and as punk left the art colleges and
came to the street, the journalist Mary Harron reflected, 'There was
violence in the air. There was violence in the streets ... Backstage at
the 100 Club, I saw these little teenage girls with swastikas, and my
reaction was, "to us it's a cartoon, here this is being done for real".'[9]

The year 1976 also saw the release of a sensational biography of
Oswald Mosley's sister-in-law Unity Mitford, a close confidante of
Adolf Hitler who dreamed of peace between Britain and Germany.[10]
The day Britain declared war on Germany, she shot herself. Jon
Savage records the effect of the book and the wearing of the swastika
in *England's Dreaming*:

> Unity's appearance in the media made it clear that much had been left
> out of the accepted history of the thirties: for a while, the British had
> shown a distinct penchant for fascism ... Fascism seemed a possible
> British archetype, an inversion of the image that had been rammed
> down everybody's throats in hundreds of lying war movies: history
> could have gone either way ... The wearing of the swastika served
> notice on the threadbare fantasy of Victory, the lie of which could be
> seen on most urban street corners. That this fantasy was now obsolete
> was obvious to a generation born after the war and witness to Eng-
> land's decline.[11]

Before the explosion of punk, fascism was already fashionable among sections of British youth. Surprisingly, it is the skinhead movement that is generally regarded as being the harbinger of fascism on Britain's working-class streets and the football terraces. Surprising because the skinheads grew out a late 1960s scene that adored Jamaican reggae and soul music and nothing could seem more contradictory than a racist skinhead.[12]

The most famous skinhead in Britain in the 1970s was Joe Hawkins, despite him living only as a character in a series of pulp fiction novels. One of the best-selling authors in 1970s Britain was James Moffat, who published under the pseudonym Richard Allen. Allen authored eighteen volumes of British cult fiction that spanned the ever-evolving British working-class youth scene. They were violent, explicit and incredibly popular. The first of his books, published in 1970, introduced Joe Hawkins to British youth. *Skinhead* (New England Library, 1970) was the first skinhead book of all time and sold thousands of copies, while the uproar caused by its content only further encouraged sales. It also persuaded Allen to keep the story of Joe Hawkins going: in 1971 the sequel, *Suedehead*, joined *Skinhead* in the top ten paperback charts and also sold over a million copies.[13] Allen's pulp novels became 'such a part of popular culture that they were even on the syllabus for English Literature school exams!'[14] Skinhead historian George Marshall saw the appeal:

> If Joe's not between the sheets with some bird, he's putting the boot into some poor bastard, out there paki-bashing, planning a robbery or something similar. How he found time to kill a copper beats me, but you could count on old Joe to come up trumps before the end of every thin novel.[15]

The racial element is clear, and things got so bad that talks were held between representatives of the British and Pakistani governments to discuss the 'p***-bashing' on Britain's streets. For the assailants, the term 'p***' was a catch-all that included Indians, Bengalis and anyone with a South Asian appearance. And according to Marshall, an anti-racist skinhead,

> The colour of their skin made them easy scapegoats for the problems facing a country that might have won the war, but had obviously lost the peace. Asians were seen as competition for jobs and housing, at a time when jobs in heavy industries were being lost and traditional working-class communities were under attack by town planners intent on throwing up high-rise flats. That, together with the fact that they didn't fight back, made them a ready target for a smack in the mouth.[16]

But for George Marshall, to be a skinhead was not to fulfil the caricature of a fully paid-up far-right activist:

> Many a young skinhead might have claimed old Enoch as a hero, but the nearest most got to organised politics was being handed tea and biscuits by the Young Liberals at Skegness one bank holiday. Most skinheads were too young to vote anyway, but Labour would no doubt have been the most popular choice. P***-bashing and p***-rolling, as mugging Asians was often called, was certainly no part of an extreme right plot.[17]

Nevertheless, Powell's politics were clear and though he distanced himself from the National Front, the party were keen to associate themselves with the views of a former Cabinet minister. A good number of skinheads seemed to agree with Powell's narrative, whether or not they were active in the NF. During the 1970 general election a squad of forty skinheads offered to form a personal bodyguard for Powell.[18]

The association of skinheads with racial violence and football hooliganism and later the abundant use of the swastika in punk imagery, not to mention the music itself, was just a contributory factor to the sense of a great unease among the youth of Britain in the 1970s. Their futures didn't seem as certain as those of the previous generation, while many of their parents were becoming increasingly concerned with the political extremism finding oxygen on the left as well as the right.

A TROTSKYITE REVIVAL?

If Sir Oswald Mosley and fascism in general enjoyed a renaissance in 1970s Britain, then so too did Leon Trotsky. Trotsky had been the outstanding figure of the Russian Revolution but fell victim to Stalin's ruthless seizure of power after the death of Lenin. Between his expulsion from the Soviet Union and his murder by a Stalinist assassin in 1940, Trotsky led his small, scattered band of followers to spread his message of international socialism through world revolution. The 1970s saw two major books, a stage play and a film dealing with Trotsky's life and theories which reignited interest in the murdered Bolshevik leader. The first was *Trotsky: A Documentary* by Francis Wyndham and David King, released in 1972 by Penguin/Allen Lane. The book was a great success and sold out its 25,000 print run in Britain. There followed a major film, *The Assassination of Trotsky*, directed by Joseph Losey and starring Richard Burton as Trotsky and Alain Delon as the Stalinist assassin, Ramón Mercader. The screenplay was written by Nicholas Mosley, the first son of Sir Oswald Mosley and his first wife, Cynthia Curzon, and adapted to a book of the same name which also sold well.[19] The stage play, *The Party*, is dealt with later in the chapter.

After the Second World War, three men appeared in Britain who would lead its disparate strands of Trotskyism for four decades: Yigael Glückstein, Isaac Blank and Thomas Gerald Healy. Glückstein would use the alias Tony Cliff and eventually form the Socialist Workers Party; Blank would change his name to Ted Grant and become the ideological force behind the Militant Tendency, while

Gerry Healy formed the Workers Revolutionary Party (WRP). Although all three are worth mentioning in some detail for their own impact on the 1970s, it was Gerry Healy and the WRP that captured the extremism and sectarianism of the decade near perfectly.

Gerry Healy was born in Galway, Ireland. He grew up to be a short man with an even shorter temper who could counter no deviation from his own conception of pure Trotskyism. At times, the WRP was the biggest Trotskyist group in Britain, and Healy was certainly its most surreal character.

The seed of Healy's fame in the 1970s was planted in the late 1960s via living-room discussions with well-connected middle-class and affluent accountants, solicitors, actors, film directors and producers in London. He gave regular Friday night lectures to these audiences, and Alex Mitchell, then a reporter on the *Sunday Times* who later fell under the spell of Healy, described one such Friday night:

> Healy's summary of the grievous betrayals of Harold Wilson's Labour government, the cowardice of the leaders of the Trades Union Congress (TUC), the current sterling crisis and the devaluation of the pound, was a tour de force. Highly intelligent men and women with degrees from Oxford, Cambridge, London University, the London School of Economics and other institutions of higher learning sat mesmerised by the analysis delivered by this unprepossessing figure with a round, almost hairless head, no neck and tiny legs ... he wore rimless glasses which added to the coldness of his physical being and he appeared to have neither eyebrows nor lips. His mouth was a sharp wound located between his button nose and jutting chin. His teeth were never visible, even when he laughed. Yet what flowed from the cavity was powerful and gripping.[20]

In 1973 the National Theatre Company presented *The Party* by Trevor Griffiths. Both Griffiths and the National's literary manager who commissioned the play, Kenneth Tynan, had regularly attended Healy's Friday night talks, and it was quite obvious that *The Party* was based around them. The lead character was the Glaswegian Trotskyist, John Tagg, based clearly on Gerry Healy. Quite incredibly, Sir Laurence Olivier was cast to play Tagg, and Britain's leading stage actor set himself the task of learning the theories of Marxism to fulfil the role. At the end of Act One, Olivier had to deliver a twenty-minute monologue on revolutionary politics, which was word-for-word Healy and sent shivers down the spines of many in the audience:

> The party means discipline. It means self-scrutiny, criticism, responsibility, it means a great many things that run counter to the traditions and values of the Western bourgeois intellectuals. It means being bound in and by a common purpose. But above all, it means deliberately severing yourself from the prior claims on your time and moral commitment of personal relationships, career, advancement, reputation and prestige. And from my limited acquaintance with the intellectual stratum in Britain, I'd say that was the greatest hurdle of all to cross. Imagine a life without *success*. The intellectual's problem is not vision, it's commitment. You enjoy biting the hand that feeds you, but you'll never bite it off. So those brave and foolish youths in Paris now will hold their heads out for the baton and shout their crazy slogans for the night. But it won't stop them from graduating and taking up their positions in the centres of ruling class power and privilege later on.[21]

The Party received mixed reviews and was unfairly given a more limited run than expected before it even had its opening night. Some felt the British establishment could not have such revolutionary stirrings poured forth from the stage. Nevertheless, it showed a willingness by leaders of Britain's cultural life to give oxygen to political extremism. Despite Healy and Olivier not exactly hitting it off together backstage, Healy certainly seemed to attract actors to the WRP, including

Vanessa Redgrave and Frances de la Tour, who played Miss Jones in *Rising Damp*. Redgrave, their most glamorous supporter, won an Oscar for best actress in 1978 and gave a controversial acceptance speech in which she attacked 'Zionist hoodlums' for trying to disrupt a documentary she had filmed on Palestine. She had campaigned for Labour and Harold Wilson in the 1964 and 1966 general elections, but by the late 1960s believed that capitalism had to be overthrown. She stood in the two 1974 general elections, where she polled 760 votes (1.7 per cent) in February and 572 votes (1.5 per cent) in October. In February, the WRP had beaten the International Marxist candidate, but in the October contest the National Front polled five times the WRP vote.

The BBC television cameras captured Redgrave's losing speech to a packed Newham Town Hall on the night of the October 1974 election. It gives a flavour of the rhetoric of the WRP that attracted the ire of the press:

> Friends and comrades,
>
> We stood, the only party to stand all ten candidates in this campaign on a socialist programme, the only programme to answer this crisis, the only programme to meet the needs of the working class in this crisis... [slow clapping starts to build in hall]
>
> ...the working class must take over the means of production without compensation under workers' control. The working class must now prepare for the greatest battle in the whole of its history ... the working class must now build a mass revolutionary party to take power and carry out a socialist programme. Our party will stand with the working class indissolubly through the crisis. Thank you very much. Goodnight.[22]

It was probably the first use of the word 'indissolubly' in a televised political speech and what followed seems to sum up the 1970s perfectly. Harry Bauckham, Mayor of Newham, had waited patiently through Redgrave's speech while her rival candidates walked off the stage. He gently tapped Redgrave on the arm to indicate he needed to wrap up proceedings and, after she left the microphone, Bauckham, immaculate in evening dress and his chain of office, told the crowd and the viewers at home, '…would you please mind how you drive, if you've been drinking.' The fiery rhetoric of Redgrave with her unmistakably upper-class accent contrasted with the polite manners of Mr Bauckham, a working-class Labour councillor with a sense of humour.

The results for Redgrave showed that the working class had not been seduced by the twin assault of the glamour of Redgrave and the theory of Healy. Instead they stuck overwhelmingly with Reg Prentice, a figure of the Labour Party right who faced a two-pronged assault from Trotskyists: those of the WRP and those within his own local Labour Party, aligned to Militant. Prentice's biographer, Geoff Horn, describes the changing face of the Labour Party membership in the East End constituency:

> Prentice's moderate approach clashed with a new generation of Labour activists who injected a more left-wing tone at local party meetings. He might well have suspected that this tone reflected a more extreme form of left-wing doctrine gaining ground in the Party. Haworth (former Secretary to the Parliamentary Labour Party) recalled Prentice going round to the house of some of the newer members during the election campaign, and reacting with visible shock when he saw a photo of Lenin in the corner of the room.[23]

Some accused Prentice of paranoia, but his instinct was right, as John Clark, then a Labour Party member in Newham North East, recalled: 'Quite a lot of us voted for Vanessa Redgrave. I certainly did. I think not everybody would confess to it but quite a lot of people did.'[24]

Perhaps it's of little surprise that by the end of the decade Prentice had joined the Conservative Party.

Yet again the working class had let down those who sought to speak for and lead them. The Newham North East result shows in microcosm that for all the newspaper columns sensationalising the threat from the Trotskyists, and indeed the fascists, the British people were loath to deviate into the uncharted waters of political extremism. As seems to be the preserve of Trotskyist groups, the WRP spent most of its time attacking rival Trotskyist organisations after it failed miserably at the ballot box, and at its height had no more than 3,000 members.[25]

WAITING FOR COLONEL BLIMP

There was another more surprising group that was making plans for the takeover of Britain should the country collapse in a political or industrial crisis: the generals. As far-fetched as it now may seem, there was a conspiracy among some members of the British establishment to bring down Harold Wilson's government in 1968, with Lord Mountbatten as the suggested figurehead of the new regime. In 1974 the founder of the SAS, Sir David Stirling, was revealed in a leaked report to be building what some called 'a private army' to support – overthrow, according to your view – the government during a period of industrial unrest. Stirling's operation was named GB75 and funded by millionaire arms dealer Geoffrey Edwards.[26] The project seemed preoccupied with Tony Benn and it's clear that even if the organisation was set up to 'support' the Labour government, one of its prices may have been the sacking of Benn.[27] Stirling was no Pinochet, though, despite what the hysterical elements of the left-wing press tried to make out, and when he stood down little was heard of the project again.

A man who did seem to want to emulate Pinochet's takeover of Chile in Britain was General Sir Walter Walker. He had fought in Burma, Malaya and Borneo. He specialised in brutally putting down communist guerrillas and had experience of mobilising volunteer forces. What Britain needed, according to Walker, was:

> ...dynamic, invigorating, uplifting leadership. A true leader who inspires trust and confidence, who puts love of country before all else ... who puts country before career; the national interest before party politics; who has the moral courage to expose and root out those who try to rot us from within and hold us to ransom by anarchy, blackmail and brute force.[28]

The quote is taken from a letter Walker had published in the *Daily Telegraph* which attracted considerable attention and responses from people volunteering for this new force and sending donations. It is strangely reminiscent, in some ways, of the monologue delivered by John Tagg, played by Sir Lawrence Olivier, in *The Party*. One can also see that such talk would have played to Sir Oswald Mosley's ego and that he would have seen in himself the 'true leader' that General Walker spoke of. But Walker's enterprise fizzled out, with many seeing him as delusional or dangerous, and he never received the serious backing from industry, the military or the Conservative Party that he expected.

CONTINUITY

This chapter demonstrates that for all the press hysteria of imminent political collapse, and for all the hopes of the likes of Sir Oswald Mosley and Gerry Healy that the great crisis of capitalism was upon us, Britons had little time for conspiracies and extremists. But the industrial unrest at the close of the decade, the so-called 'Winter of Discontent', seemed to resonate with the public to such an extent that they saw in it their fears of extremism, conspiracy, crisis and collapse which had lingered throughout the decade realised.

The surprising thing for someone looking back on a decade in which they did not live is how facts differ from the accepted popular narrative. Nothing highlights this more than Jim Callaghan and the 1979 general election. Callaghan consistently polled ahead of his opponent, Margaret Thatcher, when the public was asked who would make the best Prime Minister. He also polled as more popular than the Labour Party as a whole, demonstrating a sizeable personal respect for Callaghan among the British electorate. What was it about Jim Callaghan that the British public evidently liked?

Jim Callaghan was five years older than his predecessor Harold Wilson, seemed a good deal more relaxed (Callaghan saw none of the conspiracies Wilson did) and had a soothing, reassuring manner. Callaghan had little time for the intellectual side of Labour politics, had no higher education and had served in the Royal Navy in the Second World War. Like Ernest Bevin before him, Callaghan had worked his way up through the trade union movement and was a working-class (small-c) conservative. With such attitudes he seemed in step with the swathes of sensible, socially conservative and patriotic Britons who had spent a decade refusing extremism when offered.

Despite the barrage of Conservative Party propaganda since, there was no great rush to Margaret Thatcher by a nation demanding change from an extremist Labour government. As we've seen, Callaghan polled better in the personal ratings and he had vetoed policies he thought too left (the nationalisation of the banks, a ban on foxhunting, abolishing the House of Lords) from going into Labour's election manifesto. Even the *Sunday Telegraph* was moved to write of Callaghan that he was 'the most accomplished purveyor of comfortable conservatism our politics has seen in many a long year'.[29] In fact,

1979 was the very opposite of 1945, with Labour as the conservative choice to steady the ship and the Conservatives as those proposing to rip up the post-war settlement and belief in state intervention, for example the sale of council houses.

Ultimately, though, the caution and conservatism that the public admired prevented Jim Callaghan from calling an election in 1978 that he would very likely have won. As Andrew Thorpe observes, by autumn 1978 Callaghan had 'proved a much better premier than many observers had expected'.[30] Even when the country did descend into industrial unrest, the Army was nowhere to be seen. The two strikes most feared – the water workers and electrical power workers – never materialised and the country was never brought to a halt. Despite the active imaginations of General Walker and Sir David Stirling, the British Army was too stretched between Northern Ireland and its bases in Germany to think about taking power.

When election defeat came for Labour in 1979, it could have been much worse without Jim Callaghan. It was no epic victory for Margaret Thatcher. The Conservatives won just 43.9 per cent of the vote, the lowest (bar Wilson in 1974's elections) for any ruling party since the war. At 76 per cent, the turnout was down; hardly the numbers one would expect to see from a country clamouring for change. Labour even increased their vote from 1974 by 75,000 votes nationally. The Conservatives had won power on the back of securing the votes of those who had previously voted Liberal and for the National Front. It was no 1945.

NOTES

1   T. Benn, *Conflicts of Interest: Diaries 1977–80* (London: Arrow, 1991), p. 433.
2   H. Taylor '"Rivers of Blood" and Britain's Far Right', *Political Quarterly* (2018), vol. 89, no. 3, pp. 385–91.
3   R. Skidelsky, *Oswald Mosley* (New York: Holt, Rinehart & Winston, 1975).
4   Interview with Sir Oswald Mosley, *Today*, Thames Television, 1975: https://www.youtube.com/watch?v=293eHsrjp1A

5 'The life and death of Victor Jara – a classic feature from the vaults', *The Guardian*, 18 September 2013: https://www.theguardian.com/music/2013/sep/18/victor-jara-pinochet-chile-rocks-backpages

6 D. Sandbrook, *Seasons in the Sun: The Battle for Britain, 1974–1979* (London: Penguin, 2013), pp. 342–3.

7 A. W. Turner, *Crisis? What Crisis? Britain in the 1970s* (London: Aurum, 2008), pp. 220–21.

8 It is important to state that nowhere did Bowie mention race. The author has it on good authority that Bowie later made a substantial donation to the anti-Nazi movement (private information).

9 J. Savage, *England's Dreaming* (London: Faber & Faber, 1991), p. 240.

10 D. Pryce-Jones, *Unity Mitford: A Quest* (London: Weidenfeld & Nicolson, 1976).

11 Savage, *England's Dreaming*, p. 241.

12 With the exception of Eric Clapton, a man who made his career from covering and copying the Blues music of black America. One of the original guitar heroes of the '60s as a member of The Yardbirds, John Mayall & the Bluesbreakers and Cream, Clapton ranted about immigration and gave his support to Enoch Powell's repatriation policy to an audience at a gig in Birmingham in August 1976.

13 'New from S. T. Publishing', catalogue (1996).

14 G. Marshall, *Spirit of '69: A Skinhead Bible* (S. T. Publishing, 1994), p. 54.

15 *Ibid.*, p. 54.

16 *Ibid.*, p. 36.

17 *Ibid.*, p. 36.

18 *Der Spiegel*, June 1970, quoted in *ibid.*, p. 37.

19 N. Mosley, *The Assassination of Trotsky* (London: Michael Joseph, 1972).

20 A. Mitchell, *Come the Revolution* (Sydney: NewSouth Publishing, 2011), p. 202.

21 T. Griffiths, *Trevor Griffiths – The Party* (London: Faber & Faber, 1974), pp. 52–3.

22 Footage of Vanessa Redgrave, BBC News, 1974: https://www.youtube.com/watch?v=dEnGIoqs420

23 G. Horn, *Crossing the Floor: Reg Prentice and the Crisis of British Social Democracy* (Manchester: Manchester University Press, 2013), pp. 108–9.

24 *Ibid.*, p. 109.

25 Sandbrook, *Seasons in the Sun*, p. 303.

26 *Ibid.*, p. 139.

27 *Ibid.*, p. 139.

28 *Ibid.*, p. 137.

29 Sandbrook, *Seasons in the Sun*, p. 786.

30 A. Thorpe, *A History of the British Labour Party*, 4th edn (London: Palgrave, 2015), p. 207.

2

THE CONSERVATISM OF LABOUR: JAMES CALLAGHAN AND IDEOLOGY

Kevin Hickson

WHEN JIM CALLAGHAN REFLECTED in his memoirs on one of his first acts as the new Prime Minister in 1976 – the sacking of Barbara Castle – he remarked that she was too ideological. She thought that he lacked ideology.[1] This pejorative conception of ideology contrasts sensible, rational and pragmatic politicians – usually of the broad centre ground of British politics – with those who let their judgement be clouded by their fixed principles, usually of the firm left or right of the political spectrum kind. To his critics, the same act was held up as Callaghan's tendency to bear grudges, since his relationship with Castle had been severely strained during the Cabinet debates over her 'In Place of Strife' proposals in 1969, when Callaghan had been the champion of the trade unions.

To argue that a self-avowed pragmatist clearly motivated by ambition and perhaps some malice was himself ideological may strike the observer as a foolhardy claim. However, since all politicians are ideological then it would seem an appropriate stance to take after all. For ideology should not be seen in its pejorative sense but rather as something to be objectively studied. Ideology is here understood as a set of interconnected values which act as a guide to political action.[2] At any given moment there is a dominant set of beliefs and assumptions which form the prevailing ideology and rival ideas which seek to challenge and ultimately replace them. Some politicians usher in radical change, such as Clement Attlee in 1945 or Margaret Thatcher in 1979. Others go along with the prevailing orthodoxy, moulding it in a particular direction.

The significance of Callaghan, it will be argued, is that he sought to preserve a certain form of political ideology – the social democratic framework which had prevailed in the UK since the end of the Second World War – at the time of its sharp decline. His task was not therefore a radical one of ushering in change but a defensive one of preserving the status quo. Callaghan was a most appropriate person for this essentially conservative task since he was, as we will see, a conservative. I do not mean to imply that he was a Conservative in any sense; clearly this would be an absurd suggestion.[3] Callaghan was firmly rooted in the traditions and institutions of working-class politics and British democratic socialism. However, he was within that tradition a conservative rather than a progressive, recognising that the working class had its own traditionalist temperament. Indeed, there was a more general conservative sentiment in the country among all classes, and Callaghan articulated their concerns.

The chapter will begin by outlining the nature of the Labour Party's political thought up until Callaghan's day and the tensions between the progressive and conservative tendencies within it. We will then go on to outline Callaghan's own instinctively conservative disposition. It will thus show that far from being an unprincipled pragmatist, Callaghan had a clear set of guiding principles – albeit ones best understood as intuitive rather than intellectual.

LABOUR'S POLITICAL THOUGHT

Prior to the Second World War, Labour's political thought was fluid. As it sought to come to terms with a constitutional framework which predated its existence and the emergence of British democracy, it rejected more revolutionary ideas and attached itself firmly to the parliamentary route to socialism. However, the failures of the two short-lived governments of 1924 and 1929–31 led to further introspection and the search for an economic theory which allowed for both the existence of private property and state intervention. The ideas being proposed by John Maynard Keynes appeared to be that middle way, especially once Labour secured a majority in 1945 and quickly implemented its manifesto commitments. Even the defeat in 1951 – when Labour secured more votes than the Conservatives but fewer seats – did not dampen its loyalty to the constitutional state, rejecting not only direct protest but even reforms to the electoral system. The pendulum would eventually swing back – even if it took thirteen years – and further socialism could be implemented through the existing constitution. Debates between left and right within the party took place within this framework and rested largely on the pace with which 'socialism' should be implemented and what its precise form should be – especially the extent of public ownership and whether or not to retain nuclear weapons.

Callaghan initially started off as someone more sympathetic to the left of the party. Following his election to Parliament in the 1945 landslide, he associated with some of the more radical backbenchers in what became known as the Keep Left group, being a signatory to a critical letter they sent to Clement Attlee.[4] However, even at that time his ambition was clear; he never fully engaged with the left and effectively deserted them after becoming a junior minister. In opposition from 1951 he moved further to the right of the party, especially so as Nye Bevan – who became the figurehead for the left after his resignation as health minister in 1951 – was seen as a divisive figure helping Labour to lose successive elections. In the debates between the Gaitskellites and the Bevanites, he was associated with the former – although never one of the inner circle. Whereas some leading figures on the right took an overtly intellectual approach to politics, Callaghan associated with the institutions of the organised working class, the trade unions – labourist rather than socialist or revisionist.

The radical left inside and outside the party would regard 'labourism' in a wholly negative light; the trade unions were reformist organisations, busily engaged in reforming capitalism by incremental means rather than seeking to replace it with socialism and improving the lot of their members relative to other sections of the working class. This commitment to labourism was an explanation for why the Labour Party had failed to introduce socialism. However, it was an essential feature of Callaghan's political values. The radicals had failed to understand the nature of the working class, which was not interested in revolution but rather gradual improvement in the conditions of their daily lives. Callaghan was rooted in the working-class movement and believed that the trade unions were a patriotic and responsible force within Britain. It was their irresponsibility – or rather the irresponsibility of the more radical union leaders and shop stewards – in the Winter of Discontent which not only led to the fall of the Callaghan government but seemingly, too, to the collapse of Callaghan's whole approach to politics.

Elsewhere, I have argued that the Labour Party's political thought is best categorised as fivefold.[5] The first two were the 'Old' and 'New' left. The Old or Bevanite left was committed to the attainment of socialism by parliamentary means – believing that what was needed was a more radical leadership within Parliament. However, the experiences of Labour in government in the 1960s and 1970s led to a belief that Labour could only introduce socialism if it embraced extra-parliamentary activity. This idea stemmed from the work of

Ralph Miliband[6] and was influential on the new Labour left in the early 1980s under the direction of Tony Benn. Callaghan was clearly opposed to the New Left. He was highly critical of Benn within the Cabinet and even more so after the 1979 defeat. Callaghan opposed the Alternative Economic Strategy, which had emerged in opposition between 1970 and 1974, culminating in *Labour's Programme 1973*, calling for a more radical agenda including extensive economic protectionism and widespread public ownership. But his dislike of Benn's politics also stemmed from what Callaghan regarded as his disloyalty. Although Benn remained a member of the Cabinet throughout the period of Labour government, he was known to be writing a diary which would eventually be published, and also known to be associating with critics of the government on the back benches and within the wider party. After the election defeat, Benn publicly denounced the government within which he had served for its alleged betrayal of the grassroots of the party.[7] Labour needed to 'democratise' – including electing the leader and deputy leader, mandatory reselection of MPs and giving the annual conference the final say over policy. Callaghan, who had decided to stay on as leader for a year in opposition, had to suffer the brunt of the chorus of betrayal.

If Callaghan had little in common with the Bennites, he had come to have a better relationship with Michael Foot. Foot had been a staunch Bevanite, loyal even after his hero's U-turn on nuclear disarmament at the 1957 Labour Party conference. Foot remained a prominent agitator on the back benches during the Wilson government of 1964–70, and in the early to mid-1970s became a staunch critic of European integration, leading him to be on the opposing side of the 1975 referendum from Callaghan. In 1976, Foot stood against Callaghan, winning the first round before eventually being runner-up. He was clearly the leading figure on the parliamentary left, but by this time had come round to the view that he ought to be serving in government. Despite important policy differences, Foot placed great emphasis on loyalty. This was best demonstrated during the IMF crisis of 1976, when Foot could have opposed the cuts and led the left faction, but instead faithfully supported Callaghan in the belief that the issue had the potential to bring down the government. He did likewise in the Winter of Discontent, when he may have been expected to have more sympathy for the trade unions.

The right was also divided between the 'old' or Gaistkellite right and, later, New Labour. Unlike the left, which can be defined in terms of its commitment to unshakeable socialist principles, the right saw the need to adjust to social and economic change. But whereas some saw New Labour as merely a modern-day manifestation of the Gaitskellite revisionists, others stressed a fundamental divide be-tween the two over their conception of equality.[8] Callaghan, as we have seen, was associated by the late 1950s with the revisionists. On the dawn of the election of New Labour in 1997, Callaghan appeared on the BBC election coverage, clearly delighted that his party had returned to power after eighteen years in the wilderness.[9] However, his enthusiasm for New Labour was never absolute – in the run-up to the election he expressed his dislike of what he regarded, justi-fiably, as New Labour's trashing of the party's history. He felt that there were a 'number of myths about the way we behaved which have been promulgated by the Conservative government and which some-how our own people … have come to accept' and that he looked 'to history to put it right'.[10] Watching that coverage from 1997 again recently one is struck – with the benefit of hindsight – how the seeds of destruction within the New Labour project were already there. A seemingly spontaneous demonstration of euphoria at the arrival of Tony Blair in Downing Street had been carefully choreographed. Alastair Campbell was visible throughout proceedings. Meanwhile, back in the studio, Callaghan, alongside Neil Kinnock, reminisced about the good and bad times the party had seen.

Callaghan's position can be further contrasted with the three other figures from the 'right' of the party who stood for the leadership in 1976. In particular, his position contrasted with that of Roy Jenkins. Jenkins had also started out as a defender of the Gaitskellite project but had, over the course of the 1960s, emerged as the champion of a more liberal form of social democracy. This can be seen, above all, in three aspects. Firstly, when the issue of European integration emerged in the 1960s, Jenkins was a staunch supporter. He had resigned from the shadow Cabinet in the early 1970s over the issue and was Labour's strongest advocate for entry. He took an active part in the 1975 referendum in the 'Yes' campaign. After the leadership contest, he had hoped to become Foreign Secretary, but when Callaghan refused – on the grounds that he was too pro-European and would split the party – he decided to withdraw from British politics and became President of the European Commission.[11] He would come to the view that the Labour Party was no longer capable of advancing the 'progressive' cause and that a new centre/centre-left party was needed. Secondly, on social issues, he had a different outlook to Callaghan. He had been a liberal reforming Home Secretary, giving at least tacit support to a range of causes such as homosexual and divorce law reform. In contrast, Callaghan – who succeeded Jenkins as Home Secretary in 1967 – had a more conservative outlook. Finally, Callaghan and Jenkins disagreed on constitutional reform, where the former defended the broad parameters of the traditional constitution but the latter supported radical constitutional reform in a more pluralistic direction. For Jenkins's supporters, the 1976 leadership contest was a bitter blow. Not only had their hero been defeated but the party had chosen the least intellectual and most conservative of the candidates. David Marquand, who had been a Jenkinsite MP and then senior advisor to him at the European Commission, lamented at the end of the decade that the Labour Party had become conservative and proletarian and that a new party was needed. As a progressive party for middle-class radicals it had 'outlived its usefulness'.[12] When the SDP was formed there was never any doubt that Callaghan would not join them. For him it would have been an act of disloyalty to the party he had supported since he was a boy.

In contrast, Callaghan did have better relations with Tony Crosland. Although Crosland had also been a liberal-minded reform-er – arguing in his major book, *The Future of Socialism* (1956), that the economic problems of laissez-faire capitalism had nearly been resolved and that there was a need for more 'gaiety' in public life – he was already close to Callaghan by the time of Gaitskell's premature death in 1963. Indeed, concerned about the suitability of George Brown for the leadership for personal reasons, Crosland had encour-aged Callaghan to stand against Harold Wilson and effectively ran his campaign.[13] Had the right been able to agree on a single candidate, they may well have won the leadership contest. However, Wilson won comfortably on the second round after Callaghan had been eliminat-ed. Crosland and Callaghan had then been on opposing sides over devaluation of the pound when Callaghan was Chancellor. Crosland was subsequently publicly critical of Wilson and Callaghan's attempt to preserve the parity of sterling.[14] However, this issue was not to lead to a lasting breach between the two of them. In the early 1970s, with the European issue at its height, Crosland expressed his agnosticism on the issue. This led to a parting of the ways between Crosland and Jenkins. Indeed, some saw a growing populism in Crosland's ideas at this time, not just on Europe but other issues too.[15] His ideas were closer to Callaghan at this time than they were to Jenkins. In fact, it can reasonably be argued that Callaghan and Crosland were closer to the views of Gaitskell than Jenkins was by this time, with Jenkins appearing to have abandoned democratic socialism completely. After Crosland had been eliminated in the first round of the 1976 leadership contest, his support switched to Callaghan. Despite a major differ-ence of opinion between the two over the IMF cuts, their relationship had remained on good terms until Crosland's death in February 1977.

Denis Healey was also largely on good terms with Callaghan. They had been Gaitskellite allies, but were also rooted in pragmatism. They had served in the Wilson government together and were ambivalent on the European question in the early 1970s. Neither was associated firmly with the social reforms of the 1960s yet neither opposed them. Similarly, they had a middle-of-the-road view on European integration, seeing it neither as a threat to national independence as the opponents of membership did, nor a panacea as the Jenkinsites did. If not motivated primarily by European integration, nor social liberal reforms, then to Healey and Callaghan the aim of democratic socialism was to bring about economic and welfare policies which would better the position of working-class members of society. Neither liberalism nor socialist dogma appealed to them – Healey defined his socialism as a determination to improve the lot of the working class.[16] Everything else was theory. Callaghan would not have dissented from this definition of British socialism, characterised by its pragmatism and empiricism.

Despite the differences between Foot, Healey, Crosland and Callaghan, one thing which united them – and which distinguished them from Jenkins to the right and Benn to the left – is the emphasis on party unity and public demonstrations of loyalty to the leadership. This is the fifth strand of Labour Party thought, the party centrists. The centrists believed that the party was the only vehicle that could bring about improvements in the material conditions of the working class. This meant the laborious task of persuasion, building up democratic representation in the House of Commons and legislating for reform. Extra-parliamentary activity was justified in so far as it assisted these objectives, but in the hands of the radical left damaged them. It also meant dismissing the fatalism of the social democrats, who lacked emotional commitment to the Labour Party, as well as the hard-headed realism that under first-past-the-post the choice was limited to which of two parties ultimately formed the government.

CALLAGHAN'S CONSERVATISM

Callaghan's rejection of more theoretical approaches to politics – whether from the left or the right of the party – is due to his conservative approach. He was a small-c conservative in his politics. More honest Conservatives recognised this. John Biffen talked of the conservatism of Labour,[17] while Peregrine Worsthorne thought Callaghan to be much more in the mould of the English ruling class than Margaret Thatcher was and expressed his admiration for Callaghan's political traits of experience, authority and reassurance.[18] According to Hennessy, Callaghan's values 'remained fixed at around 1948 … a kind of composite Clem Attlee and Ernie Bevin by another means'.[19] Callaghan's only statement of political principles was made in 1948.[20] Dick Leonard had described him as 'Labour's Conservative'.[21] This can be seen in all aspects of his conservatism – cultural, constitutional, economic, social and philosophical.

Although Callaghan represented a South Wales seat throughout his parliamentary career, his cultural reference points were British, if not English. He was, as has already been discussed, rooted in the working class. His upbringing in a naval and church-going family was to stay with him throughout his life. Callaghan was staunchly patriotic. This stemmed partly from his early childhood memories of his father but also from wartime service in the Navy. According to his biographer, 'they lent his every instinct a deep, almost unquestioned patriotism'.[22] Although he had seemingly abandoned any kind of religious worship in his early adult life, with those who knew him thinking he was agnostic,[23] he clearly recalled his experiences of the Baptist church and his devout mother in his memoirs.[24] He would cite passages from the Bible and sing hymns especially in times of stress.[25] As Kenneth Morgan put it, 'Without doubt Callaghan approached life from a traditional moral standpoint.'[26] Commentators would mention the apparent ease with which he communicated with the working-class residents of his constituency. Part of his reason for rejecting the politics of Tony Benn is that he did feel more rooted in the working class, seeing them as they were rather than in an idealised way.[27] He recognised that they were far from the Marxist stereotype.

His constituency was very much urban and industrial, yet Callaghan also had a love of the rural landscape. In 1967 he managed to become a partner in a working farm, which he eventually came to own outright. During his premiership he liked to go to the farm as often as possible. According to Dominic Sandbrook, scenes of Callaghan on the farm reinforced his image: 'Pictures of Farmer Jim trudging across his fields to inspect his cattle, a tweed hat jammed on his head, reinforced his avuncular, reassuring image, the soul of small-c conservatism in a changing world.'[28]

After retiring from politics he spent more and more time on the farm. He expressed his enjoyment of agricultural work, which gave a better sense of satisfaction than politics, where one was often dealing with intangible problems and rarely seeing the end of what one had started; whereas in farming the results of one's labour were readily apparent, especially at certain times of the year such as lambing season.[29] Some critics have pointed to the tendency of Labour leaders to move to the countryside as a reason why Labour had never succeeded in forming a counter-narrative to the Conservative evocation of the rural idyll.[30] However, such an argument fails to take account of the fondness for rural life which existed in working-class communities, whether it be in the maintaining of allotments or the demand for the right to roam.

Other institutions were also praised by Callaghan. An example of such was the Scouts. In a select committee hearing in 1985, Austin Mitchell asked Callaghan how ministers should behave towards civil servants. Callaghan said that they must be loyal, polite and courteous. When Mitchell said that sounded like a 'Boy Scout code', Callaghan replied, 'What is wrong with the Boy Scouts?'[31] A similar regard was extended not only to the Royal Navy but to all of the armed forces.

Callaghan admired the British Commonwealth. His most significant role in opposition in the 1950s was as shadow Commonwealth
Secretary. In this role he toured widely and made close contacts with
several countries.[32] This led him to believe he could resolve the problem of minority white government in Rhodesia. He also was slow to
come round to membership of the EEC, based in part on his concern
that it would undermine Britain's relations with other Commonwealth countries.

Callaghan's cultural conservatism led on to a conservative approach to the constitution.[33] This attitude was widely held in Old
Labour, which saw the first-past-the-post electoral system and the
wider Westminster model of British politics as the best way to achieve
British socialism. Proposed liberal reforms to the constitution would
reduce the possibility of doing so, whether it be an electoral system
which would make coalition more likely, the creation of rival bodies
to the House of Commons or increasing the power of the judiciary.
Hence, when the Liberal Party demanded electoral reform in return
for a pact in 1977–78, Callaghan said that this would be a step too far.[34]
He was also insistent on ruling out a commitment to House of Lords
reform in the 1979 manifesto. Callaghan also inherited pressures for
legislative devolution to Scotland and, to a lesser extent, Wales. Although he persevered with this, he had no personal enthusiasm for
the idea. This was in tune with a large proportion of his own backbenchers who opposed devolution as either pandering to the politics
of nationalism, or else eroding the sovereignty of the Westminster
Parliament. Above all, Callaghan admired the British monarchy. He
respected the Queen specifically, regarding her as the only person in
whom he could confide as well as receiving useful advice based on
her already considerable reign. He also liked and respected Prince
Philip, and was keen to have traditional street parties to celebrate the
Queen's Silver Jubilee in 1977.[35]

On the economy – as both Chancellor and Prime Minister – his innate conservatism was also readily apparent. He, along with Harold Wilson and George Brown, had ruled out devaluation in 1964 until it was eventually forced on him in 1967. When he returned as Prime Minister he deliberately allowed the Cabinet to discuss at great length the IMF crisis without revealing his own position.[36] Although his own experience as Chancellor had led him to distrust the Treasury, he was always likely to come down on the side of his Chancellor, Denis Healey, in 1976, believing that the cuts were necessary not only to bring public expenditure under control but also to placate the financial markets. The reality of the national and international constraints on action outweighed the more idealistic arguments of his political opponents. But Callaghan also recognised the problems that the reserve nature of sterling had caused the pursuit of Labour's economic aims in the 1960s and 1970s and sought to address this issue, with observers praising his grasp of technicalities.[37] Again, this approach can be seen as consistent with Callaghan's wider conservatism – an emphasis on pragmatism over idealism and solving short-term problems rather than having a longer-term strategy.

Callaghan's conservatism extended to social attitudes. This is not to say that he was a reactionary figure, since he had accepted the reforms of the 1960s as civilising, but that he expressed certain attitudes which showed that he was far from in the vanguard of progressivism. Again, he was not alone within the Labour Party at that time. Numerous Labour MPs represented Catholic areas and many recognised that the desire for reform from sections of the party outran public opinion, and especially working-class opinion. This is seemingly a far cry from today's Labour Party, which is much more in tune with socially liberal attitudes than it was in Callaghan's day.

Callaghan had a strong sense of morality, drawn from his childhood experiences in which the Baptist church had played an important role. His principles led him to adopt public positions on particular issues or to express certain opinions in private. This included a more conservative approach towards immigration than some in the Labour Party wished to see, such as the introduction of the 1968 Commonwealth Immigrants Act. Some saw this as racist, as it was aimed at stopping a particular community – the Kenyan Asians – from entering Britain. His instincts led him to be dismissive of the idea of multiculturalism. He said in 1977 that he wanted 'immigrants to marry UK natives, "decent white Britons", and let us have a coffee-coloured community, but one single community, not this inflow of different cultures into a so-called "multicultural society"'.[38]

However, Callaghan was not a reactionary on the issue, denouncing Enoch Powell's 'Rivers of Blood' speech in the same year and introducing legislation to outlaw racial discrimination in the UK. Further legislation followed in 1976 setting up the Commission for Racial Equality.

Law and order was a further issue on which Callaghan focused. He had been the parliamentary spokesman for the Police Federation in the 1950s. Following this he had maintained close links with the police including during his time as Home Secretary. In 1974, Callaghan expressed the opinion that he admired the Conservative manifesto's tougher law-and-order policy and 'wished we had anything as good as this in ours'.[39] However, he was, again, no reactionary figure. He had presided over the final elimination of the death penalty in Britain at the end of the 1960s and had also set up investigations into corruption within the police.

He was instinctively sceptical of what was then prevalent in youth culture. 'For all his empathy for young people, the rebelliousness of the young, not just their methods of violent disruption, but their long hair, untidiness, and dabbling in drugs, were alien to him.'[40] He held a similarly conservative approach to feminism as Morgan states: 'Aspects of feminism he found hard to take ... (fearing) for the impact upon society of broken homes, single mothers, divorce, and unrestrained sexual emancipation.'[41] As Morgan asserts, 'in this he probably reflected the views of the majority of the party and the nation'.[42]

An issue on which Callaghan expressed private reservations – and which highlights his socially conservative attitude – was homosexuality. Bernard Donoughue, the head of Callaghan's policy unit, reflects on Callaghan expressing surprise that such people existed. When told that they not only existed but that several of his own MPs were gay, he again expressed his surprise. It seems that he only 'discovered' homosexuality late in his career. 'They say we are all suppressed homosexuals. But it puzzles me. There have always been so many attractive girls,' Callaghan is reported as saying.[43] Moreover, he then pleaded with his interlocutors not to repeat such stories of homosexuality in front of his wife: 'You won't tell those stories in front of Audrey, will you? She would be very shocked.'[44]

Callaghan was also strongly focused on education. He had told Harold Wilson following devaluation in 1967 that he wished to be moved to the post of Education Secretary due to his interest in the idea, but instead was made Home Secretary. On assuming the premiership in 1976 he identified education policy as one of his priorities, culminating in his Ruskin College speech in October. The details of this are discussed in a later chapter, but the relevant point here is that Callaghan expressed conservative views on this area of policy also. Concerned that the professionals had effectively taken a monopoly over the making of education policy and that the views of parents and employers were being ignored, he called for a return to more traditional teaching values and methods. This upset the liberal educational establishment and led on to education reforms under Margaret Thatcher.

The final element of Callaghan's conservatism was philosophical – a sense of pessimism. Callaghan had at least come into power with a sense of optimism: 'Don't tell me that this country can't succeed. Of course it can.'[45] However, by the time he left office any sense of optimism had gone. Callaghan's first election to Parliament in 1945 had coincided with the dawn of the new social democratic consensus. His time as Prime Minister marked its final collapse. Callaghan recognised this, believing it – in the end – to be inevitable. Although his government limped on, there was a feeling of decay. In 1978 he had refused to call an election in the belief that it would not bring about a Labour majority, and that he had seen enough of minority government, with its need to stitch together temporary alliances in order to win votes and the inability to act more decisively. He appeared reluctant to accept the need to bring in seriously ill MPs or reach deals with the likes of the Ulster Unionists for the decisive 'no confidence' vote in 1979. Callaghan had appeared to have given up. In the 1979 election he commented privately that there was a 'sea change' occurring and that nothing could be done about it.[46] Thus came to an end both Callaghan's premiership and the post-war consensus.

In many ways Callaghan marked the end of Labour's conservatism. On the issues over which he differed from Roy Jenkins, the Labour Party moved over time in the direction of Jenkins – pro-Europeanism, constitutional reform and cultural liberalism. For a while, at least, Jenkins seemed to have a significant influence on Tony Blair, although Blair never delivered on the progressive model which Jenkins wished to see. Since 2010, the Labour Party has, if anything, moved even further in a 'progressive' direction, despite the calls by advocates of so-called 'Blue Labour' to embrace a more conservative approach. The extent of this change from Callaghan's time can be seen by the overwhelming pro-European stance during and since the 2016 referendum and Labour's general attitude to social and cultural change. Pressures exist for a fresh attempt to revive the idea of a 'progressive alliance', given the scale of the 2019 general election defeat, with an electoral pact between Labour, Liberal Democrats, Greens, and Scottish and Welsh nationalists. If this succeeds it will mark a further shift away from Callaghan's approach, and a deviation from the instincts of a good deal of Labour's traditional voters. It may be safely argued that the progressives won the day within the party, but they have not done it any electoral favours.

NOTES

1   J. Callaghan, *Time and Chance* (London: Collins, 1987), p. 402.

2   In doing so, it draws on the theoretical approach of M. Freeden, *Ideologies and Political Theory: A Conceptual Approach* (Oxford: Oxford University Press, 1998).

3   The extent to which the Conservative Party has been a force for conservatism since 1945 has been repeatedly questioned – see K. Hickson, *Britain's Conservative Right since 1945: Traditional Toryism in a Cold Climate* (Basingstoke: Palgrave, 2020).

4   K. Morgan, *Callaghan: A Life* (Oxford: Oxford University Press, 1997), p. 66.

5   M. Beech, K. Hickson and R. Plant (eds), *The Struggle for Labour's Soul: Understanding Labour's Political Thought Since 1945* (London: Routledge, 2004) and M. Beech, K. Hickson and R. Plant (eds), *The Struggle for Labour's Soul: Understanding Labour's Political Thought Since 1945*, 2nd revised edn (London: Routledge, 2018).

6   R. Miliband, *Parliamentary Socialism: A Study in the Politics of Labour* (London: George Allen & Unwin, 1961).

7   For coverage of the speech see 'Cast into the Wilderness', *Labour: The Wilderness Years*, BBC, 3 December 1995: https://www.youtube.com/watch?v=3XrO72C1WQo

8   Most prominently Roy Hattersley.

9   For coverage of the 1997 general election see 'BBC 1997 General Election (2017 Broadcast)', BBC, 1 May 1997: https://www.youtube.com/watch?v=D28zwi6-DpQ

10 P. Hennessy, *The Prime Minister: The Office and Its Holders since 1945* (London: Allen Lane, 2000), pp. 394–5.

11 J. Campbell, *Roy Jenkins: A Well-Rounded Life* (London: Vintage, 2015), p. 464.

12 Quoted in Campbell, *ibid.*, p. 509.

13 S. Crosland, *Tony Crosland* (London: Coronet, 1982), p. 116.

14 C. A. R. Crosland, *Socialism Now and Other Essays*, D. Leonard (ed.) (London: Jonathan Cape, 1974).

15 See S. Meredith, *Labours Old and New: The Parliamentary Right of the British Labour Party 1970–79 and the Roots of New Labour* (Manchester: Manchester University Press, 2008).

16 D. Healey, *The Time of My Life* (London: Penguin, 1990), p. 472.

17 J. Biffen, 'The Conservatism of Labour', in M. Cowling (ed.), *Conservative Essays* (London: Cassell, 1978).

18 P. Worsthorne, 'Too Much Freedom', in Cowling, *ibid.* See also the interview with Worsthorne on the eve of the 1979 no confidence vote: *Today*, BBC, 28 March 1979: https://www.youtube.com/watch?v=ZqzIZVJOQdk

19 Hennessy, *The Prime Minister*, p. 379.

20 J. Callaghan, 'The Approach to Social Equality', in D. Munro (ed.), *Socialism: The British Way* (London: Essential Books, 1948).

21 Quoted in Morgan, *Callaghan*, p. 759.

22 *Ibid.*, p. 759.

23 B. Donoughue, *Downing Street Diary: Volume Two – With James Callaghan in No. 10* (London: Pimlico, 2009).

24 Callaghan, *Time and Chance*, pp. 19–36.

25 Donoughue, *Downing Street Diary*, p. 399.

26 Morgan, *Callaghan*, p. 759.

27 The 'noble savage', as Joe Ashton put it, *Labour: The Wilderness Years*.

28 D. Sandbrook, *Seasons in the Sun: The Battle for Britain, 1974–1979* (London: Penguin, 2013), p. 461.

29 'Michael Cockerell on James Callaghan', BBC, March 1976: https://www.youtube.com/watch?v=pF0ZTZYS0FE

30 J. Paxman, *The English: A Portrait of a People* (London: Penguin, 1999), pp. 163–4.

31 Hennessy, *The Prime Minister*, p. 392.

32 Callaghan, *Time and Chance*, pp. 118–46.

33 Hennessy, *The Prime Minister*, p. 392.

34 Callaghan, *Time and Chance*, pp. 455–6.

35 Sandbrook, *Seasons in the Sun*, p. 630.

36 K. Hickson, *The IMF Crisis of 1976 and British Politics* (London: I. B. Tauris, 2005).

37 Morgan, *Callaghan*, p. 754.

38 Donoughue, *Downing Street Diary*, p. 152.

39 Sandbrook, *Seasons in the Sun*, p. 392.

40 Morgan, *Callaghan*, pp. 760–61.

41 *Ibid.*, p. 761.

42 *Ibid.*

43 Donoughue, *Downing Street Diary*, p. 435.

44 *Ibid.*, p. 436.

45 Sandbrook, *Seasons in the Sun*, p. 465.

46 Morgan, *Callaghan*, p. 697.

3

CALLAGHAN AND CABINET

Mark Stuart

ESSENTIALLY, THERE ARE TWO main ways of running the Labour Party: grabbing it by the scruff of the neck in the manner of Hugh Gaitskell, Neil Kinnock and Tony Blair, or balancing competing wings of left and right, as typified by Clement Attlee, Harold Wilson and James Callaghan. During the International Monetary Fund (IMF) crisis of 1976, Callaghan ran his Cabinet in a collegiate way; so much so that every senior minister felt that they had had their say and, remarkably, no one resigned. However, as this chapter will show, Callaghan's apparent openness during the IMF crisis was actually born out of necessity and did not reflect a general willingness to reveal the inner workings of Cabinet government. Moreover, Callaghan's way of running Cabinet was otherwise modelled more on a strong presidential style of leadership more akin to Margaret Thatcher and Tony Blair.

CABINET

The formation of Callaghan's Cabinet in April 1976 might have been expected to reflect the need to balance the left and right of the party. However, the overall impact of the changes was to strengthen the position of the right. Despite Denis Healey and Tony Crosland, two key figures in the contest from the right, both performing poorly (polling only thirty votes and seventeen votes respectively in the first round of the contest), they were nevertheless rewarded with two of the three main offices of state in the shape of the Treasury and the Foreign Office. Whereas it made sense for Callaghan to keep Healey as Chancellor with a budget looming, the choice of Crosland for the Foreign Office was something of a surprise. Roy Jenkins, who polled fifty-six votes in the leadership contest, would have considered accepting the Foreign Office had he been offered it, but Callaghan judged Jenkins's pro-European views to be a source of potential division inside the party, and instead Jenkins chose to take up the Presidency of the European Commission which had been promised to him by Harold Wilson. As soon as Jenkins left to take up his appointment, he was replaced at the Home Office by Merlyn Rees, who had nominated Callaghan for the leadership, preserving the dominance of the right of the party in all three main offices of state.

Michael Foot's move from Employment to Leader of the House of Commons might at first sight be interpreted as important in the context of preserving party unity. Foot, who had finished a clear second in the Labour leadership contest, carried immense weight with the left of the party and the wider Labour movement, notably the trade unions. His loyalty to Callaghan would prove instrumental to the government holding onto power in increasingly difficult circumstances. However, Foot's move was at his own behest. Moreover, Foot's influence over Callaghan did not extend as far as convincing him to keep Barbara Castle, another key left-winger, in Cabinet. Callaghan and

Castle personally loathed one another, all the more so after Callaghan had blocked Castle's 'In Place of Strife' proposals in 1969. Thus, Castle's Cabinet career came to an end, and with the publication of her diaries, she would become one of Callaghan's most bitter critics.

It has often been pointed out that on assuming office in the spring of 1976 Callaghan became the first Prime Minister to have occupied all three main offices of state in the shape of the Chancellor of the Exchequer (1964–67), Home Secretary (1967–70) and Foreign Secretary (1974–76). However, despite such unrivalled experience, in none of these roles had Callaghan particularly excelled himself. Like Winston Churchill, his previous stints of ministerial office had been at best inauspicious, yet, also like Churchill in 1940, all Callaghan's political skills came together during a moment of national crisis.[1]

To point out that Callaghan found himself in a difficult position in 1976 is an understatement. On the one hand, he had to deal with the harsh measures expected by the IMF, which had already placed undue pressure on the fledgling socialist government in Portugal led by Mário Soares.[2] On the other hand, he had to secure a package of cuts which would be acceptable not only to the Cabinet but also to the wider trade union movement, and all this set against a backdrop of a non-existent majority in the House of Commons. Callaghan would also have been particularly mindful of the fact that Labour MPs had already defeated the Wilson government in a White Paper proposing cuts in public expenditure in March 1976. Only a vote of confidence the following day had secured support for the measure.[3] Had the Treasury simply presented Cabinet with a take-it-or-leave-it set of cuts in its usual clunking-fist manner, then the Labour government could have fallen in a spirit of acrimony. A different approach was required, and Callaghan was ideally suited to pursue it.

Firstly, as a former trade union official from the inter-war period, Callaghan had been socialised in a culture of consultation, where ideas were endlessly hammered out in smoke-filled rooms by union executives. As Tony Benn commented many years later, 'Jim was an old trade unionist who believed that you ought to discuss.'[4] What is often missing from existing accounts of the IMF crisis (but not from the chapter on the economy elsewhere in this book) is how Callaghan remained in close touch throughout this period with both Len Murray, the General Secretary of the Trades Union Congress (TUC), and Jack Jones, the powerful General Secretary of the Transport and General Workers' Union,[5] as well as the National Executive Committee, the ruling body of the Labour Party, and the Parliamentary Labour Party (PLP). So, Callaghan's frequent comments in Cabinet during the crisis about the need to preserve party unity were not shallow homilies, but were instead rooted in a deeper understanding of the Labour movement, of which he was an authentic member.

Secondly, Callaghan had watched his old hero Clement Attlee run his Cabinets full of big beasts in a collegiate manner and had learned the right lessons. Like the Cabinet of 1945–50, Callaghan faced senior ministers who were extremely powerful figures in their own right. Moreover, Callaghan's Cabinet members were uniquely experienced in economic affairs, Peter Shore later pointing out several years later that around the Callaghan Cabinet table were sat at least three ex-Chancellors, four ex-presidents of the Board of Trade and one ex-Secretary of State for Economic Affairs.[6] It would therefore have been near-impossible for the Treasury simply to have bounced a decision on such an economically literate set of senior ministers. Instead, Callaghan allowed his Cabinet to scrutinise every single aspect of the Treasury's plans. It was one of the rare moments in the postwar period when the Treasury was truly held to account by Cabinet. But such high levels of scrutiny and interminable discussion had an added benefit for Callaghan, highlighted succinctly by Dr Bernard Donoughue, Callaghan's senior policy advisor in No. 10: 'Ministers have discussed the cuts so often, they come to think they have agreed them.'[7]

Thirdly, Callaghan had often watched his predecessor, Harold Wilson, endlessly balancing competing forces in Cabinet, though sometimes without any clear sense of political direction. Callaghan was different. Rather than being tactical almost for its own sake (a common accusation levelled at Wilson), he had a clear idea of what he wanted to achieve from the very start – a deal which fell short of what the IMF was demanding, but one which would still reassure the jittery financial markets, and yet keep his fragile government in power.

And yet, despite being boxed in politically, Callaghan's natural inclination was for strong, decisive leadership. According to Bernard Donoughue, Callaghan was by nature a realist, in favour of taking difficult decisions sooner rather than later, telling a special Cabinet in August 1975 in his capacity as Foreign Secretary, 'Let us do the tough things now and get them out of the way.'[8] Such an attitude of mind always made him more likely to back his Chancellor Denis Healey's tough stance on public expenditure cuts.

In July 1976, as outlined in Chapter 7 on economic policy, matters came to a head when sterling came under sustained and severe pressure, forcing the Chancellor to arrange a stand-by credit facility with the IMF. After seven exhaustive Cabinet meetings stretching over two weeks, an initial package of cuts was agreed. Only Tony Benn actively considered resignation at this point, telling Callaghan that he would need to consult his Bristol South East constituency party. According to Bernard Donoughue, who was present, Callaghan called Benn's bluff by saying, 'Tony, why don't you make up your own mind? And if you do stay in Cabinet but continue campaigning against a collective Cabinet decision, you will be sacked immediately.'[9] Again, while the prevailing consensus is that Callaghan was collegiate, he also had a certain steel about him, exercising strong, decisive leadership in his handling of Benn.

Tony Benn headed up a group of five other senior ministers (comprising Michael Foot, the Leader of the House of Commons, as well as Stan Orme, John Silkin, Albert Booth – all from the left of the party – as well as Peter Shore, a sole figure from the right) whose Alternative Economic Strategy, as outlined in the economic chapter, envisaged the creation of a so-called 'siege economy', with the imposition of high import tariffs and currency controls.[10]

Callaghan's second group of opponents in Cabinet proved a tougher nut to crack, headed by Anthony Crosland, the Foreign Secretary, and Harold Lever, chancellor of the Duchy of Lancaster, and supported by Roy Hattersley (prices and consumer protection) and Shirley Williams (education). Crosland felt that Britain was too big to fail and that the cuts agreed in July were sufficient, arguing that new cuts would have a disastrous impact on investment.[11] The Foreign Secretary therefore strongly urged the Chancellor to call the IMF's bluff.

However, there were two problems with the Croslandite grouping. Firstly, they were not united. Ultimately, Shirley Williams (education) and David Ennals (health) were more interested in preserving their departmental budgets. As we have already seen, Bill Rodgers soon switched sides, supporting Healey's tough line, leaving just the triumvirate of Crosland, Lever and Hattersley lined up against Healey's plans. Secondly, the Bennite grouping was so wedded to its Alternative Economic Strategy that it was unwilling to engage in serious talks with the Croslandites in order to defeat Healey.

Standing back from the fray, Callaghan initially allowed each of the three Cabinet groupings – the supporters of Benn, Crosland and Healey – to put their respective cases, often exhaustively, in Cabinet, all the while emphasising the importance of maintaining party unity.

In fact, there existed a numerically superior fourth grouping in Cabinet which would prove decisive in determining the final outcome. These ministers were what Hennessy aptly calls 'the Prime Minister's men',[12] again illustrating Callaghan's strong leadership position among senior ministers. Most of these Cabinet ministers, including Fred Mulley (defence), Merlyn Rees (Home Office), Bruce

Millan (Scottish office), Eric Varley (industry), John Morris (Wales), Roy Mason (Northern Ireland) and Fred Peart (Lord Privy Seal), to varying degrees owed their positions to the Prime Minister, and could be almost guaranteed to weigh in behind Callaghan once his position became clear, provided their own departmental budgets were not unduly affected by the proposed cuts.[13]

The reason behind Callaghan's initial decision to sit on the fence has already been outlined in great detail by Kenneth O. Morgan, the elegant court painter of Labour figures, in his excellent portrait of Callaghan in 1997. Morgan revealed that Callaghan was engaged in high-level presidential-style diplomacy with both President Ford of the United States and Helmut Schmidt, Chancellor of Germany, to see if an unconditional loan (one with no strings attached) could be agreed with the IMF, sending Harold Lever as an emissary to Washington DC.[14] The problem was that neither the Americans nor the Germans were willing to budge. Across the Atlantic, Gerald Ford was a lame duck President about to be replaced by Jimmy Carter,[15] while the German government was culturally and institutionally against high government borrowing. This was understandable, given Germany's record of hyperinflation in the 1930s. The German Bundesbank, in particular, had the constitutional power to block extra borrowing. The Germans therefore took the view that the UK should put its house in order, introducing financial discipline. Little has changed in this regard: the Germans took a similar unyielding stance in their attitude towards the Greeks during the sovereign debt crisis in 2010.

Unfortunately, the IMF, headed by Johan Witteveen, was equally unyielding during acrimonious face-to-face discussions with Callaghan. Unbeknown to the likes of Tony Benn, the Prime Minister stoutly defended the UK government against even more stringent cuts, eventually meeting Witteveen halfway between their respective positions of £2 billion and £3 billion.[16]

Only when it was clear that he could squeeze no more concessions from the IMF did Callaghan decisively back Denis Healey's position near the end of the two-day Cabinet which ended on Thursday 2 December 1976.[17]

While the Benn diaries provide us with an unrivalled account of what was said in Cabinet between September and December 1976, they do not show how Callaghan was able to win over Crosland in private through a series of bilaterals. The Prime Minister had spoken with his Foreign Secretary on a plane journey back from a European finance ministers' meeting at The Hague. Callaghan revealed to Crosland that he intended to back Healey.[18] Crosland now faced the prospect of both the Chancellor and the Prime Minister resigning if a modified version of the IMF loan conditions was not accepted in Cabinet. As Crosland told his wife (and later his biographer), Susan, '…when the Prime Minister joins with the Chancellor, usually they are unbeatable and in this case shouldn't be beaten'. Crosland then privately approached his most loyal supporter, Roy Hattersley, persuading him to change his mind.[19] The following day, Hattersley grudgingly fell into line, arguing bleakly in Cabinet, 'If we have a choice of seeing the government destroyed by the markets or by ourselves, I think it is better that we should not allow it to be destroyed by the markets.'[20]

So, although the IMF Cabinet meetings were the exemplar of collective decision-making in the post-war period, the final policy outcome had been determined by Callaghan via the shrewd use of bilaterals in advance of full Cabinet meetings. The Prime Minister had watched first Attlee and then Wilson operate in this style and had emulated them to great effect. Had the meetings of Cabinet been less expertly handled, and had the Bennites and the Croslandites combined forces, it is arguable whether Callaghan's government would have suffered a repeat of 1931, when Ramsay MacDonald failed to get a package of cuts through his Labour Cabinet, and chose to form a National Government with the Conservatives and some of the Liberals, splitting the Labour Party for a generation.

Whether this is true is a moot point. It is more likely that the Callaghan government would simply have fallen in a vote of confidence in the House of Commons, leaving the path clear for the Conservatives. Callaghan was too steeped in the Labour movement to go into a coalition with the hated Tories.

And yet in later life, Callaghan claimed it 'could have been another 1931'.[21] More accurately, Callaghan spent a great deal of his time effectively squashing Tony Benn's deliberate attempt to make it *appear* that it was 1931 all over again. Benn had gone to the extent of calling up the Cabinet papers from 1931 in order to convince himself that it was 'a complete repeat of what is happening now'.[22] Benn wanted to use the memories of what had happened in 1931 to ramp up accusations of betrayal, arguing in one Cabinet his 'real objection' to what Healey was proposing was that 'it betrays our national interest in terms of growth and jobs and introduces deflation and a slump'.[23] However, when Benn again claimed there was 'an eerie parallel with 1931', Callaghan interrupted angrily, claiming, 'There is no such parallel. I don't accept it. I have been reading the minutes you have been circulating, every one of them, and I don't accept it.' When Benn retorted that there was a parallel because the loan on both occasions hinged on cutting benefits, Callaghan again slapped Benn down, saying, 'Well, I lived through it. You didn't.' In fact, Benn's father, Viscount Stansgate, had been a member of the Cabinet in 1931, and had supported the cuts in unemployment benefit.[24]

As it was, although perpetual accusations of betrayal were bandied about by the left, no Cabinet minister resigned, and this fact was almost entirely down to Callaghan's deft handling of the IMF crisis in Cabinet. By allowing such an exhaustive discussion, everyone felt that they had been allowed to have their say. Even Tony Benn praised Callaghan, 'because he had permitted a more candid talk in the Cabinet than I had ever known in twelve years'.[25]

The fact that Callaghan was able to emerge from the IMF crisis without a single ministerial resignation compares very favourably to the raft of extensive resignations that the subsequent premierships of John Major (1992–97) and Theresa May (2016–19) suffered over Europe. In their defence, Major and May would argue that Callaghan did not have to contend with a 24-hour media. Writing in 1996, Edmund Dell claims that prolonged Cabinet divisions on sensitive economic matters of this kind would not have been tolerated by the money markets in the modern era.[26]

As a result, Dell is one of the few participants of the period who views Callaghan's handling of the IMF crisis negatively, seeing it as 'a farce and a dangerous farce at that'.[27] But Dell never had any feel for the importance of the Labour movement, later defecting to the Social Democratic Party (SDP). As Morgan rightly points out, '…it was not only a matter of satisfying the IMF. It was a matter of keeping government and party together. This Callaghan did supremely well.'[28] Even Shirley Williams, another SDP defector, believes it was 'a brilliant operation'.[29] One would expect Denis Healey to argue in his memoirs that 'the consummate skill with which [Callaghan] handled the Cabinet was an object lesson for all prime ministers'.[30] More impartial is Peter Hennessy's judgement that Callaghan's handling of his colleagues during the IMF crisis was 'the finest display of collective Cabinet government under stress during the post-war period'.[31]

And yet, as Hennessy rightly points out, the ultimate irony about the way in which Callaghan dealt with the IMF crisis is that it did not typify his general attitude to Cabinet government. The Prime Minister was never a natural fan of open government. This was especially the case when dealing with matters relating to official secrets. In June 1976, he was furious when Frank Field, the director of the Child Poverty Action Group, and later a Labour MP, leaked confidential Cabinet documents discussing the possibility of dropping its plans to introduce child benefit. Callaghan later established GEN 29, a special Cabinet committee, with which he intended to tighten Section 2 of the 1911 Official Secrets Act.[32] However, he faced both a liberal Home Secretary in Roy Jenkins and no majority in the House of Commons, and so the plans were dropped.[33]

Even with the Home Office changing hands from Roy Jenkins to Merlyn Rees, Callaghan remained thoroughly set against opening up the inner workings of Cabinet to the public. By February 1978, the Prime Minister had issued a personal minute on the 'Disclosure of Cabinet Committees' in which he refused even to acknowledge their existence, ruling out any disclosure of information about how they worked.[34] Indeed, during the IMF crisis, he had spoken out in no uncertain terms about the damaging effect Cabinet leaks were having – particularly Benn's decision to leak the Cabinet minutes of 1931 to *Tribune* magazine.[35] So, while Callaghan may have favoured open discussion inside Cabinet in certain circumstances, he was a closed book when it came to the disclosure of how these decisions were arrived at.

Moreover, with regards to other sensitive policy matters, particularly regarding defence, Callaghan actively sought to circumvent full Cabinet government. This was especially the case in relation to the consideration of a replacement for the Polaris missile system, when Callaghan established the Nuclear Defence Policy Group outside the Cabinet committee structure, comprising himself, David Owen, the new Foreign Secretary, Denis Healey, the Chancellor, and Fred Mulley, the Defence Secretary.[36] In this regard, he was very close in inclination to Clement Attlee, who had created a secret committee, unknown to the full Cabinet, in order to lay plans for the building of a hydrogen bomb.[37] Callaghan's steering group commissioned Sir Anthony Duff, a senior diplomat, and Professor Sir Ronald Mason, the chief scientific advisor to the Ministry of Defence, to produce a report, which recommended that Polaris be replaced by Trident. In the end, the general election intervened in 1979, and Callaghan's full Cabinet never discussed the issue. Tellingly, before leaving No. 10,

Callaghan left instructions that the Duff–Mason Report be made available to Margaret Thatcher, leaving her government to press ahead with Trident as the replacement for Polaris.[38]

Further evidence of Callaghan's strong leadership approach was shown by the fact that when the IMF crisis was over, he exercised his newly earned dominance to reinforce his grip over economic policy by creating a secret group of senior ministers and advisors called 'the Seminar' to oversee market-sensitive decisions on the setting of interest rates and exchange rate policy, which was not even granted the status of a Cabinet sub-committee.[39]

NO. 10

On becoming Prime Minister, Callaghan had largely inherited the structure of government that had existed under both Harold Wilson and Edward Heath. At its heart was the Cabinet Office, under its secretary, Sir John Hunt, and the Prime Minister's private office, under Sir Kenneth Stowe. Although its basic function was to serve both full Cabinet and its various sub-committees, the Cabinet Office under Sir John took a considerable interest in policy-making on Callaghan's behalf, as well as in the structure of Cabinet, even suggesting at one point that the Treasury should be split up into a Ministry of Finance, and a bureau covering budget matters. Had he won the 1979 general election, Denis Healey might have been moved to the Foreign Office in order to accommodate this change, though a final decision was never made.[40]

Callaghan's more presidential style of government was reflected in the way in which he ran No. 10. As a former Royal Navy officer, Callaghan placed considerable importance on intelligence gathering. He therefore used the Central Policy Review Staff (CPRS) – a unit established under Edward Heath to plan ahead for the long term – to engage in calm reflection, becoming one of the very few post-war Prime Ministers to be able to do so. Only really during the 1978–79 Winter of Discontent did this ability to stand back from the fray desert him. Meanwhile, Callaghan used the Downing Street Policy Unit under Dr Bernard Donoughue and Sir John Hunt in the Cabinet Office to advise him on the day-to-day direction of government policy. Sir John and Callaghan briefly considered creating a Prime Minister's department, but they decided against it.[41]

On the suggestion of Sir Kenneth Stowe in his private office,[42] the Prime Minister kept himself abreast with what his Cabinet ministers were doing by holding regular one-to-one meetings, at which he asked them about their departmental aims, and what factors were standing in the way of achieving them. Callaghan was well briefed by both Bernard Donoughue and Sir John Hunt beforehand, and his natural bonhomie and avuncular style ensured that these sessions worked well.[43]

One of Callaghan's first one-to-one ministerial chats was with Fred Mulley, the education secretary. This was done at the instigation of Bernard Donoughue in the spring of 1976, who suggested education as an area in which Callaghan might want to personally intervene.[44] The end result was Callaghan's famous Ruskin College speech (covered in more detail in Chapter 10), delivered in October 1976. In it, Callaghan called for more rigorous educational standards, the creation of a national curriculum and a greater focus on technical and vocational education. When the Department for Education and Science (DES) moved slowly on a Green Paper on the subject, Callaghan demonstrated his strong leadership skills by asking Mulley's successor, Shirley Williams, to adopt a more radical approach. Little emerged in terms of substance in the short term, but Callaghan's far-sighted ideas were later picked up in a more controversial setting by the Thatcher governments. Nevertheless, the episode demonstrated the willingness of Callaghan and the No. 10 Policy Unit under

Donoughue to make selective interventions, thereby making his own personal stamp on government policy.[45] Indeed, up until the last three months of his premiership (when Callaghan became dispirited by the Winter of Discontent), Donoughue and his team drafted up policy papers on issues as diverse as the role of women in society, law and order, and citizens' rights, which were actively encouraged by the Prime Minister.[46]

In other respects, too, both Callaghan's political office and press office at No. 10 reflected a more presidential approach. Tom Mc-Nally, who had proved his worth to Callaghan as an advisor while the latter was Foreign Secretary, now took a very close interest in all policy issues, domestically as well as internationally. McNally helped to smooth any potential frictions with the civil service and the Policy Unit, allowing political advice to flow to Callaghan un-hindered. Meanwhile, Callaghan's press secretary, Tom McCaffrey, though lower profile than his predecessor, Joe Haines, nevertheless worked seamlessly in tandem with McNally to provide sage advice to Callaghan. Indeed, it is telling that when Callaghan failed to call the general election in the autumn of 1978 when he should have done, neither McNally nor McCaffrey was consulted.[47]

Callaghan's presidential approach carried right on into the 1979 general election campaign, as he projected himself as a 'father of the nation' figure, espousing a message of moderation. Callaghan's 'One Nation', avuncular approach saw him dominate most of the press conferences during the campaign. This was no surprise. The opinion polls showed that Callaghan was far more popular than his party.[48]

In conclusion, while there is little doubt that Callaghan proved 'a superb manager of Cabinet'[49] over the IMF crisis, the ultimate irony of his success was that it led to an increase in his own authority over the running of economic and domestic policy, and a diminution of the very principle of Cabinet government which had oh-so-briefly been on display in those troubled six months from July to December

1976. Thus, Callaghan could be seen as an early example of a more presidential form of Prime Minister. Hitherto, such descriptions have been laid at the door of both Margaret Thatcher and Tony Blair,[50] but in truth, Callaghan had established a more presidential approach to running Cabinet long before either of these Prime Ministers.

NOTES
1   P. Hennessy, *The Prime Minister: The Office and Its Holders Since 1945* (London: Allen Lane, 2000), p. 386.
2   B. Donoughue, *Prime Minister: The Conduct of Policy Under Harold Wilson and James Callaghan* (London: Jonathan Cape, 1987), pp. 95–6.
3   Hansard, HC Deb, 11 March 1976, 5th series, vol. 907, cols 752–7.
4   Quoted in Hennessy, *The Prime Minister*, p. 377.
5   T. Benn, *Against the Tide: Diaries 1973–76* (London: Arrow, 2000), p. 663 – entry for 1 December 1976.
6   P. Hennessy, *Cabinet* (Oxford: Basil Blackwell, 1986), p. 91.
7   Donoughue, *Prime Minister*, p. 91.
8   Cited in *ibid.*, pp. 83–4.
9   Cited in *ibid.*, p. 92; Benn, *Against the Tide*, pp. 596–7 – entry for 15 July 1976.
10 Benn, *Against the Tide*, pp. 724–7.
11 *Ibid.*, p. 667 – entry for 1 December 1976.
12 Hennessy, *The Prime Minister*, p. 386.
13 Donoughue, *Prime Minister*, p. 90.
14 K. Morgan, *Callaghan: A Life* (Oxford: Oxford University Press, 1997), pp. 538, 542–3, 544–5. See also K. Burk and A. Cairncross, *'Goodbye Great Britain': The 1976 IMF Crisis* (New Haven: Yale University Press, 1992).
15 D. Healey, *The Time of My Life* (London: Michael Joseph, 1989), p. 430.
16 Morgan, *Callaghan*, p. 547.
17 Benn, *Against the Tide*, pp. 671–3.
18 Morgan, *Callaghan*, p. 548.
19 S. Crosland, *Tony Crosland* (London: Jonathan Cape, 1982), p. 381.
20 Benn, *Against the Tide*, p. 676 – entry for 2 December 1976.
21 Hennessy, *Cabinet*, p. 285, cited in Hennessy, *The Prime Minister*, p. 385.
22 Benn, *Against the Tide*, p. 649 – entry for 18 November 1976.
23 *Ibid.*, p. 649 – entry for 23 November 1976.
24 Morgan, *Callaghan*, p. 549.
25 Benn, *Against the Tide*, p. 680 – entry for 6 December 1976.
26 E. Dell and J. Hunt, 'The Failings of Cabinet Government in Mid to Late 1970s', *Contemporary Record* (1994), vol. 8, no. 3, pp. 453–72; cited in Hennessy, *The Prime Minister*, p. 389.
27 *Ibid.*, pp. 453–72.
28 Morgan, *Callaghan*, p. 551.
29 Cited in Hennessy, *The Prime Minister*, p. 388.
30 Healey, *The Time of My Life*, p. 431.
31 Hennessy, *The Prime Minister*, p. 385.
32 B. Donoughue, *Downing Street Diary: Volume Two – With James Callaghan in No. 10* (London: Jonathan Cape, 2008), p. 61.

33 P. Hennessy, *Distilling the Frenzy: Writing the History of One's Own Times* (London: Biteback, 2013), pp. 241-2.

34 Hennessy, *Cabinet*, p. 90.

35 Benn, *Against the Tide*, p. 662 – entry for 1 December 1976.

36 Hennessy, *Distilling the Frenzy*, p. 56.

37 Hennessy, *The Prime Minister*, p. 389.

38 Hennessy, *Distilling the Frenzy*, pp. 56-7.

39 Hennessy, *Cabinet*, p. 92; Donoughue, *Prime Minister*, pp. 101-2.

40 Morgan, *Callaghan*, pp. 488-9.

41 *Ibid.*, p. 489.

42 *Ibid.*, p. 490.

43 Hennessy, *The Prime Minister*, p. 391.

44 Donoughue, *Prime Minister*, p. 111.

45 Cited in Hennessy, *The Prime Minister*, p. 381.

46 Morgan, *Callaghan*, pp. 496-7.

47 *Ibid.*, pp. 496-7.

48 *Ibid.*, pp. 692-3.

49 Hennessy, *Cabinet*, p. 88.

50 See, for example, M. Foley, *The British Presidency* (Manchester: Manchester University Press, 2000).

4

STAYING IN THE SADDLE: JAMES CALLAGHAN AND PARLIAMENT[1]

Philip Norton

D URING THE PREMIERSHIP OF James Callaghan, Parliament assumed a role it had not fulfilled since 1931. Callaghan was the first post-war premier to govern without an overall majority in the House of Commons. Clement Attlee (1950–51) and Harold Wilson (1964–66) had survived with single-figure majorities each for a short period. Callaghan's achievement was to govern for longer than either of their two short parliaments. As Kenneth O. Morgan pithily put it, 'His premiership seemed more an essay in survival than anything else, though it was not without achievement in difficult circumstances.'[2]

Julian Amery once observed that a good jockey rides a difficult horse. Callaghan inherited from his predecessor, Harold Wilson, an unsteady steed in the form of the House of Commons. He entered No. 10 just as the government was slipping into minority status in the House and at a time when the Parliamentary Labour Party (PLP)

was notably divided on a range of issues, with a vociferous and organised body of left-wing MPs gathered in the Tribune Group. The
government was thus vulnerable as a result of opposition parties
combining against it and some of its own backbenchers voting with
the opposition.

For the government, there was always the threat of defeat. The
government needed to mobilise a majority for two purposes. One
was to get its specific measures on to the statute book and its budget
approved, and the other was to stay in office. There was an overlap in
that frequent defeats may render the government unable to continue,
but defeats on particular legislative proposals did not raise issues of
confidence.[3] The biggest threat to the government was the carrying
of a motion of no confidence, or the loss of any confidence motion it
moved following defeat on a major policy.

In the event, the government suffered dissent from its own backbenchers on an unprecedented scale as well as a number of defeats
not witnessed before in the era of modern (that is, post-1867) British
politics.[4] Although opposition parties variously combined to defeat
the government, most of the defeats were the result of government
backbenchers voting with the opposition. Given government policy
and Callaghan's pragmatic stance, it is not surprising that the most
frequent dissent came from MPs on the party's left wing. However, the
most significant threat came from MPs on different wings of the party.

CALLAGHAN'S LEADERSHIP

Although Callaghan entered No. 10 at a time that was not propitious for
achieving significant policy goals, he was arguably well placed to cope
with a difficult House of Commons. He had two advantages. The first
was that he knew the House of Commons and he had decades of front-
bench experience. The second was that throughout his premiership,

he was to face a Leader of the Opposition who had limited ministerial experience and who was not particularly sure-footed in leadership.

An effective team

Callaghan was well qualified to be Prime Minister by virtue of his ministerial and parliamentary longevity. By the time he entered Downing Street, he had sat in the House for three decades. When he gave up the party leadership in 1980, he had spent thirty-five years as an MP. He ended his time in the House of Commons as Father of the House (1983–87).

Key to his success as a minister, and to him becoming leader, was his standing with Labour MPs. As Morgan observed, Callaghan had always enjoyed a strong base in the parliamentary party.[5] He cultivated that base from the time he was first elected,[6] both in government and in opposition. 'He spent the Tory years distancing himself from factions within the Labour party and establishing himself as a man of the party.'[7] He also got to know new members. After the October 1974 election, he invited newly elected Labour MPs to meet him at his palatial room at the Foreign Office.

This party base explains his ultimate success in defeating Michael Foot to become Labour leader in 1976. 'More than any other candidate, he had cultivated friends, allies and supporters *where they were needed* – among MPs, within Transport House, and among the unions which consistently voted him as Party Treasurer.'[8] At his first meeting with the PLP as leader, he told MPs that no one person or group held the ark of the covenant. 'Their first loyalty, like his, was to the party.'[9]

He also benefited from the time he devoted to the House of Commons. In part, this may have been a consequence of his principal home not being in London, so – like other MPs in a similar situation – when Parliament was sitting, he spent much of his time in the Palace of Westminster. As Prime Minister, doing so was also instrumental. He devoted time to being in the tearoom and members' dining room so as not to give the impression – as a rare attendance would – of there being a problem. He made a point of regularly attending the weekly Thursday evening meetings of the PLP. He was adept at soothing difficult situations.

He also made a virtue of a necessity, in that the whips frequently required the presence of all Labour MPs to maintain a majority in the division lobbies. That included the Prime Minister, who could sometimes be seen waiting around for a vote in the early hours of a morning. There was an embarrassment when in February 1977 the government lost the Second Reading of the Reduction of Redundancy Rebates Bill by one vote. The Prime Minister was absent unpaired. That was exceptional. Given the demands made of government, what was remarkable was the amount of time that the Prime Minister was seen by other Labour MPs to spend in the House.

Callaghan was adept not only in keeping Labour MPs on side. He was prepared to spend time in the social spaces to lobby MPs of minor parties[10] as well as utilising more structured contact through ministers. He had no compunction in striking deals with nationalist parties and the Ulster Unionists.[11]

He was aided by his choice of ministers, not least those responsible for getting the government's business through the House of Commons. Michael Foot, at one time the leading rebel on the Labour benches, was appointed Leader of the House. Foot was chaotic in organisation, but he was highly respected as a parliamentarian and one who got on well with members of other parties. As Leader of the House, he was both sociable and flexible.[12] His capacity to deal with other parties was to prove crucial to the government's survival.

There was also a strong Whips' Office, one that later acquired iconic status when their activities became the focus of a hit West End play (*This House*). Callaghan recognised the impact of the whips, acknowledging that 'they performed heroically'.[13] He held regular meetings with them. He appointed Bristol South MP Michael Cocks as Chief Whip and kept as Deputy Chief Whip Walter Harrison. Harrison achieved legendary status for his capacity to cajole and manufacture a majority for the government. His skills were summarised by Labour MP Tam Dalyell: 'No subterfuge was beneath him. Some parliamentary colleagues had their arms twisted, often severely. Others were involved in ferocious rows, which Harrison usually won. Others again, like me, succumbed to his charm in asking for party loyalty.'[14]

That, though, is to focus on how Harrison sought to keep potential Labour rebels in line. His success in delivering the government's programme is just as much to be found in Dalyell's next comment: 'His exploits in making arrangements for Irish MPs of Republican tendencies ... to be transported to Westminster for vital votes were the stuff of legend.'[15] Key to understanding how the government survived was, as we shall see, the configuration of parties in the House of Commons.

Foot, Cocks and Harrison were at the forefront of mobilising a majority for the government, but they were aided by another legendary figure, Freddie Warren, the long-serving principal private secretary to the government Chief Whip, housed in 12 Downing Street. He constituted the official oil in the machinery of the 'usual channels', that is, the contact between government and opposition whips to facilitate parliamentary business; he had extensive experience, was an expert on procedure, and had served successive governments. He retired in 1978 and was succeeded by another effective operator, Murdo Maclean.

There was thus an effective team serving Callaghan in the delivery of the government's business. They faced a task unprecedented in post-war British history.

An inexperienced opposition
Callaghan was also helped by the fact that he faced a new and untested Leader of the Opposition. Margaret Thatcher replaced Edward

Heath as Conservative leader a year before Callaghan entered Downing Street. She had fought against the established leadership and took
time both finding her feet in the House of Commons and in surround-
ing herself with like-minded supporters. Although the Conservative
Party was able to do well in the battle of ideas, it faced problems in
the House of Commons. Thatcher was to develop an eponymous
philosophy, but Thatcherism was a consequence of electoral victory
in 1979 and not the other way round.[16] Thatcher had difficulty establishing her authority within her party. In the Commons, she never
seemed comfortable.[17] It was a problem she recognised herself. She
was not a former Prime Minister. She did not feel comfortable speaking from a prepared text. She often came across as over-prepared
and hectoring.[18] She conceded that she never managed to score more
than a draw against Wilson and Callaghan.[19] A consequence, according to John Campbell, was that she spoke less frequently than before
in the House.[20]

According to Callaghan's senior policy advisor, Bernard Donoughue, 'nobody in No. 10 ever worried about the attacks from the
Conservative Party opposite. Mr Callaghan certainly always dominated Mrs Thatcher in the Commons.'[21] Although the Prime Minister
conceded that he disliked Prime Minister's Questions, he gave the
impression of being at his ease in facing the Conservative leader.
Indeed, he came across as being in quiet command. 'He leant on the
despatch box, said one backbencher, like a farmer on a gate. He was
like a man in his own parlour, said another.'[22] As we shall see, he also
outmanoeuvred the opposition in 1977 in negotiating the Lib–Lab
Pact when the Conservatives thought they looked likely to defeat the
government in a vote of no confidence.

Although Callaghan led a divided party, he faced an opposition that
was also divided on a range of issues,[23] including European integration and devolution. When the Scotland and Wales Bill came before

the House of Commons in 1976, the shadow Scottish Secretary, Alick Buchanan-Smith, and his deputy, Malcolm Rifkind, resigned in opposition to the party line. Dissenting votes by Tory MPs on occasion offset votes by dissenting Labour Members.

However, the dissent by Tory backbenchers, although significant – during the parliament, there were 240 divisions in which one or more Conservatives voted against the party whip[24] – was less pronounced than on the government benches. There were more divisions in which Labour MPs dissented. Labour MPs, as we shall see, also divided on a more factional basis. Even so, had Callaghan faced a more effective Leader of the Opposition and a united Conservative Party, he would have had greater difficulty than he did in keeping the ship of government afloat.

GETTING ITS MEASURES

The challenge throughout Callaghan's premiership was mobilising a majority to get the government's measures. Callaghan became Prime Minister on 5 April 1976. The previous day, Labour MP John Stonehouse, on trial for insurance fraud, had announced he had joined the English National Party. He formally resigned the Labour whip on 7 April. His defection tipped the government into minority status in the House of Commons. Stonehouse resigned from the Commons on 27 August, following his conviction, and in the by-election that followed his seat was won by the Conservatives. With further by-election losses, and three defections, during the parliament, the government slipped further into minority status.

Labour, though, remained by far the largest party in a House of minorities. At the October 1974 election, it had a 42-seat advantage over the Conservatives. If the Conservatives voted against the government, the outcome depended on the voting behaviour of the thirteen Liberals, eleven Scottish Nationalists, three Plaid Cymru MPs and twelve MPs from Northern Ireland. Only Unionist MPs returned from Northern Ireland (six Ulster Unionists, three Vanguard and one Democratic Unionist) may be seen to have a natural tendency to side with the Conservatives. However, the Ulster Unionists had severed their links with the Conservatives earlier in the decade and, in any · event, were not notably assiduous in turning up in Westminster.[25] They were also not averse to doing deals that favoured the province. As Callaghan noted in his memoirs, 'Whatever the state of United Kingdom politics, the first priority of Northern Ireland's Members is Northern Ireland.'[26] There was thus as much, if not more, of a challenge for the Conservative opposition to garner support from other parties as there was for the government. If anything, nationalist MPs were more likely to vote with Labour than the Conservatives and the government was in a position to offer policies sought by nationalist parties in a way that the opposition was not.

However, for the government, offering something to nationalist parties was not risk free. The PLP was not only split on a factional left–right basis but also on some key policy issues unrelated to the economic issues that divided left and right. They particularly included European integration and devolution. There was a significant minority of Labour MPs opposed to devolution. Devolution was to prove a key stumbling block to government and its failure to deliver it was at the root of its demise in 1979.

There are four key features of Callaghan's premiership in getting the government's measures through parliament. The first was the sheer scale of dissent by backbench MPs. The second was what it failed to deliver because of defeat by a combination of opposition parties. The third was what it failed to achieve because of defeat deriving from dissent by its own backbenchers. And the fourth was what it failed to deliver because of defeat in the House of Lords.

Unprecedented levels of dissent

Until the 1970s, cohesion was a feature of parliamentary parties. There were, as Ozbudun put it, 'occasional deviations',[27] but they hardly dented the perception of parties exercising what Sam Beer described as Prussian discipline in ensuring MPs voted loyally with their parties.[28]

That changed in the House of Commons at the start of the 1970s under the Conservative government of Edward Heath.[29] The period of Labour government that followed witnessed backbench dissent on an unprecedented scale. During the course of the 1974–79 parliament, more than 80 per cent of Labour MPs voted once or more against the party whip. Expressed as a proportion of the parliamentary party, that number on the Conservative side is even higher, but involved fewer MPs voting against on a frequent basis. Whereas just over 18 per cent of Labour MPs voted against the whips on forty or more occasions, the percentage on the Conservative side was only 4 per cent.[30]

Not only were Labour MPs willing to vote against the government frequently and in considerable numbers, but the incidences of doing so increased markedly under Callaghan's premiership. Each session saw the number of divisions in which Labour MPs voted against the government grow substantially. In the first two sessions – that is, principally under Wilson's premiership – Labour MPs voted loyally with the government, with no dissenting votes, in well over 80 per cent of votes. There were dissenting votes cast in fewer than 15 per cent of divisions in the first session and fewer than 18 per cent in the second.[31]

In the first full session of Callaghan's premiership (1976–77), one or more Labour MPs voted against the government in 30 per cent of the votes; in the following session it was 36 per cent of divisions, and in the final 1978–79 session 45 per cent of divisions.[32] In other words, by the end of his premiership, Callaghan was seeing one or more of his MPs vote against the government in almost every other division.

The dissent was remarkable for its scale and for its consequences.

One consequence was essentially reputational, contributing to the perception of a divided government. Although most occasions of dissent involved few MPs and were hardly noticed against the backdrop of the government's attempts to deal with bodies outside Parliament, the occasions when a large number of Labour MPs defied the whips were sufficiently frequent to undermine the government's reputation. The other consequence was the impact on government policy. When Labour MPs voted in large numbers with the opposition, the government went down to defeat. The defeats were few, relative to the sheer number of occasions of dissent, and on occasion the defeats were symbolic rather than substantive, but some defeats were major, effectively negating some of the government's key policies.

Defeat by the opposition parties

The fact of being a minority government meant that Callaghan's administration was always vulnerable to opposition parties combining to defeat it in a vote, but in the event it was more in danger from a combination of dissident Labour MPs and the opposition. During the 1974–79 parliament, the government was defeated nineteen times as a result of opposition parties joining together in the division lobbies. All nineteen occurred under Callaghan's premiership. The number, taken alone, is remarkable, but pales beside the twenty-three resulting from Labour MPs voting with the opposition.

The most important defeat was demonstrably that on a vote of no confidence in March 1979, discussed below, which proved fatal. Prior to that, the most significant defeats were on the Finance Bill in 1978, when an amendment to reduce the basic rate of income tax from 34 per cent to 33 per cent, and another to raise the levels at which higher rates of income tax would apply, were carried.

Defeat by its own backbenchers

The whips had to work hard on Labour MPs in all parts of the party.

The Tribune Group was the organised voice of the left and produced the most vocal and persistent dissenters, though not the most effective. The group met regularly – once or twice a week – and sought to coordinate the activity of its supporters.[33] Of the sixty-nine divisions in the 1974–79 parliament in which forty or more Labour MPs voted against the whips, Tribune MPs formed a majority of the dissenters in all but five of them.[34] The greater the number of dissenting votes cast, the greater the proportion of Tribune MPs.

Tribune Group MPs may have voted against the government, but that does not mean they were voting with the opposition. The opposition was often closer to the government's position and so variously abstained or voted with the government. Few of the government defeats during Callaghan's premiership were attributable to the votes of Tribune Group MPs.[35] The government was also vulnerable to dissent by MPs on the party's right, but they generally were supportive of Callaghan and account for only one defeat (on the Dock Work Regulation Bill) during his premiership.

The most significant threat came from MPs from all parts of the party combining. The threat was realised both in quantitative and qualitative terms, accounting for most of the defeats suffered by the government and on major issues, including the government's constitutional flagship legislation. MPs from all wings of the party combined to defeat its devolution legislation, first through defeating a guillotine motion for the Scotland and Wales Bill in 1977 and then imposing referendum requirements in the Scotland and Wales Bills.[36] The 'Cunningham amendment' – stipulating that 40 per cent of those eligible to vote had to vote yes for devolution to proceed – was carried and sustained by MPs opposed to devolution from all parts of the party – from Eric Heffer and Dennis Skinner through to Tam Dalyell and Leo Abse.

Defeat by the House of Lords

The number of government defeats at the hands of MPs pales into insignificance against the number imposed by the House of Lords. During the parliament, the Labour government lost 347 votes in the Upper House.[37] For the government, there were two problems in seeking to overturn the defeats. One was time. If the Lords insisted on an amendment, the process could be time-consuming, albeit successful if the government could muster a majority in the Commons. The second problem was that it could not always be sure it could muster such a majority. Seven of the government defeats in the Commons during the parliament – six of them under Callaghan – were on motions to disagree with Lords amendments. Baldwin has argued that the conflict was not one, as portrayed by government, of the Lords versus the Commons, but rather one of Parliament versus government,[38] the government constrained by an alliance of members in both Houses. Of the defeats on motions to disagree with the Lords, four were on amendments to the Scotland and Wales Bills. Had the government enjoyed a comfortable majority in the Commons, it would not have had the difficulties it had in seeking to overcome defeats in the Lords.

SURVIVING

A precondition to getting its measures through was remaining in office. That entailed mobilising a majority in the event of a confidence vote. By convention, a government resigned or sought a general election if it lost the confidence of the House of Commons. A loss of confidence was shown by the House passing an explicit motion of no confidence (or defeating a motion of confidence) or by defeating a motion to which the government had attached confidence. If the government lost an important vote, it could subsequently put down a motion of confidence to demonstrate it maintained the confidence of the House (or, if it didn't, the opposition could table a motion of no confidence). Otherwise, no issue of confidence was raised if a government lost a vote in the division lobbies.[39] A government that kept losing votes may decide it could not govern effectively, and opt for an election, but that was a matter for the Prime Minister. It was not required by convention to resign. It was thus possible for the Callaghan government to continue in office, despite the absence of an overall majority, as long as it did not lose a confidence vote.

When a motion of no confidence was tabled by the opposition early in 1977, it looked as if the government may lose. Callaghan negotiated a deal with Liberal leader David Steel.[40] It was a deal that was essentially instrumental: as Edward Pearce put it, an 'alliance of people who didn't want an election'.[41] Callaghan succeeded in keeping the PLP on side over the pact. He reassured the MPs that it was not a coalition. Although many Labour MPs, including four members of the Cabinet, were not happy with the deal, tribal loyalty prevailed. As left-wing Labour MP Eric Heffer recalled, 'I had strong reservations about this but I realised that good friends like Audrey Wise could well lose their seats if we went to the country immediately and I felt it right to play for time irrespective of the risks.'[42] Labour MPs disliked the Liberal Party, but they feared the return of a Conservative government even more. Furthermore, as Peter Shore came to believe, it was successful not only because it kept Labour in power 'but also because it was seen as highlighting the negotiating skills of the Prime Minister as the Liberals secured very little from it'.[43]

The pact did not ensure victory for the government in all votes, but it did ensure Liberal support to sustain the government in office. The no confidence motion was defeated by 322 votes to 298. After the pact came to an end, the government was able to mobilise the support of nationalist MPs who were keen to see the government's devolution legislation reach the statute book.[44]

It was only after the failure of the referendums in Scotland and Wales to deliver the 'Yes' vote required by the Scotland and Wales Acts that nationalist support disappeared and the SNP tabled a motion of no confidence. The result, as Callaghan noted in the debate on 28 March, was a coming together of Conservatives opposed to devolution and the SNP and Liberals who supported it.[45] The skills of the government whips failed to mobilise a majority. One Labour MP, Dr Alfred Broughton, was close to death and Callaghan agreed that he should not be brought to Westminster.[46] But it was to be the actions of MPs from Northern Ireland that sealed the fate of the government. The SDLP MP Gerry Fitt, normally a supporter, voted against the government and the Republican Frank Maguire, who had turned up, abstained from voting. The government lost by one vote. Callaghan immediately conceded a general election: 'We shall take our case to the country.'[47]

CONCLUSION

The relationship between Callaghan and the House of Commons was but one of several crucial relationships in ensuring that the government was able to govern. It was a relationship often overshadowed by the others. In Peter Hennessy's analysis of the Callaghan premiership, it merited only a passing mention.[48] It was, though, core to the government's survival.

Despite the sheer level of backbench dissent, and not infrequent government defeats, the parliament came close to lasting fully five sessions. That it survived is largely due to Callaghan's skill in handling the House of Commons. One Labour MP of the period noted that Callaghan revelled in being Prime Minister, not least because – being older than Wilson – he had not expected to get the keys to No. 10. The pressures would likely have destroyed a lesser man, but Callaghan rose to the challenge. Indeed, he appeared to relish it. As he recalled, other than the last few months of the Winter of Discontent, he enjoyed every minute of it.[49] He knew the House of Commons and dominated it.

NOTES

1 Part of this analysis draws on interviews with those who served in the 1974–79 parliament. I am especially grateful to Bruce Grocott (Lord Grocott), Ann Taylor (Baroness Taylor of Bolton) and, in earlier research, Ted Graham (Lord Graham of Edmonton) for sharing their recollections.

2 K. Morgan, *Labour People*, revised edn (Oxford: Oxford University Press, 1992), p. 275.

3 P. Norton, 'Government Defeats in the House of Commons: Myth and Reality', *Public Law* (Winter 1978), pp. 360–78.

4 P. Norton, *Dissension in the House of Commons 1974–1979* (Oxford: Clarendon Press, 1980), p. 441.

5 Morgan, *Labour People*, p. 266.

6 C. Hitchens and P. Kellner, *Callaghan: The Road to Number 10* (London: Cassell, 1976), pp. 24, 28–38.

7 B. Redhead, 'James Callaghan', in J. P. Macintosh (ed.), *British Prime Ministers in the Twentieth Century, Vol. II: Churchill to Callaghan* (London: Weidenfeld & Nicolson, 1978), p. 219.

8 Kellner and Hitchens, *Callaghan*, p. 176.

9 Redhead, 'James Callaghan', p. 229.

10 J. Hayes, *An Unexpected MP* (London: Biteback, 2014), p. 125.

11 J. Callaghan, *Time and Chance* (London: Fontana, 1988), pp. 453–4.

12 K. Morgan, *Michael Foot: A Life* (London: HarperCollins, 2007), pp. 332–3.

13 Callaghan, *Time and Chance*, p. 442.

14 *The Independent*, 24 October 2012; see also J. Ashton, *Red Rose Blues* (London: Macmillan, 2000), pp. 180–82.

15 *The Independent*, 24 October 2012.

16 D. Kavanagh, 'The Making of Thatcherism, 1974–1979', in S. Ball and A. Seldon (eds), *Recovering Power: The Conservatives in Opposition Since 1867* (Basingstoke: Palgrave Macmillan, 2005), pp. 219–40; P. Norton, 'Margaret Thatcher, 1975–79', in T. Heppell (ed.), *Leaders of the Opposition* (Basingstoke: Palgrave Macmillan, 2012), pp. 97–8.

17 J. Campbell, *Margaret Thatcher, Vol. I: The Grocer's Daughter* (London: Jonathan Cape, 2000), p. 318.

18 Norton, 'Margaret Thatcher', p. 99.

19 M. Thatcher, *The Path to Power* (London: HarperCollins, 1995), p. 313.

20 Campbell, *Margaret Thatcher*, p. 344.

21 B. Donoughue, *Prime Minister: The Conduct of Policy under Harold Wilson and James Callaghan* (London: Jonathan Cape, 1987), p. 187.

22 Redhead, 'James Callaghan', p. 231.

23 Norton, *Dissension in the House of Commons*, pp. 451–7.

24 *Ibid.*, p. 428.

25 P. Norton, 'Conservative Politics and the Abolition of Stormont', in P. Catterall and S. McDougall (eds), *The Northern Ireland Question in British Politics* (Basingstoke: Macmillan Press, 1996), pp. 129–42.

26 Callaghan, *Time and Chance*, p. 454.

27 E. Ozbudun, *Party Cohesion in Western Democracies: A Causal Analysis* (London: Sage Publications, 1970), p. 316.

28 S. H. Beer, *Modern British Politics* (London: Faber, 1969), pp. 350–51.

29 P. Norton, *Dissension in the House of Commons 1945–74* (London: Macmillan, 1975), pp. 610–11; P. Norton, *Conservative Dissidents* (London: Temple Smith, 1978).

30 Norton, *Dissension in the House of Commons*, p. 435.

31 *Ibid.*, p. 437.

32 *Ibid.*, p. 437.

33 *Ibid.*, p. 434.

34 *Ibid.*, p. 434.

35 *Ibid.*, pp. 442–3.

36 *Ibid.*, pp. 443–4.

37 P. Norton, 'Introduction: Parliament in Perspective', in P. Norton (ed.), *Parliament in the 1980s* (Oxford: Basil Blackwell, 1985), p. 14.

38 N. D. J. Baldwin, 'The House of Lords and the Labour Government 1974–79', *The Journal of Legislative Studies* (1995), vol. 1, no. 2, pp. 218–42.

39 Norton, 'Government Defeats in the House of Commons: Myth and Reality', pp. 360–78.

40 S. Hoggart and A. Michie, *The Pact* (London: Quartet, 1978).

41 E. Pearce, *Denis Healey: A Life in Our Times* (London: Little, Brown, 2002), p. 506.

42 E. Heffer, *Never a Yes Man* (London: Verso, 1991), p. 163.

43 K. Hickson, J. Miles and H. Taylor, *Peter Shore: Labour's Forgotten Patriot* (London: Biteback, 2020), p. 103.

44 P. G. Richards, *Mackintosh's The Government and Politics of Britain*, 6th edn (London: Hutchinson, 1984), p. 85.

45 Hansard, HC Deb, 28 March 1979, vol. 965, col. 471.

46 P. Norton, 'Parliament', in A. Seldon and K. Hickson (eds), *New Labour, Old Labour* (London: Routledge, 2004), p. 201.

47 Hansard, HC Deb, 28 March 1979, vol. 965, col. 589.

48 P. Hennessy, *The Prime Minister: The Office and Its Holders Since 1945* (London: Allen Lane, 2000), pp. 392–3.

49 P. Hennessy, *Muddling Through* (London: Gollancz, 1996), p. 44.

5

CALLAGHAN AND THE EXTRA-PARLIAMENTARY LABOUR PARTY

Eric Shaw

J AMES CALLAGHAN'S RELATIONS WITH the extra-parliamentary Labour Party were fraught throughout his years as leader. At first glance, this seems odd, since no politician seemed better equipped to manage the party. With his long experience, he had an intimate knowledge and instinctive feel for Labour's traditions, customs and ethos. With deep roots in the labour movement, he had long-standing and close relations with the trade unions, then at the height of their power. The role he had adopted through his many years as a senior figure in the party was as a unifier and consensus-builder, and to this end he had carefully fostered an image as a bluff, genial and avuncular elder statesman: 'Sunny Jim'. He was described by the man who was to be his nemesis, Tony Benn, in September 1973 as 'very charming ... an agreeable and skilful politician, marvellous at getting his own way ... a shrewd political figure'.[1] He was a powerful and impressive conference speaker who 'never neglected a detail, never miscalculated the votes, never forgot a face'.[2] But he was, as any effective party manager needs to be, a tough, no-nonsense operator who could be brusque and ruthless.[3] As his biographer observed, 'he could be a terrifyingly hard man; he could threaten with a barely concealed hint of menace. Critics would be threatened with total oblivion.'[4] Callaghan seemed well qualified to steer Labour through what was bound to be a stormy and turbulent period.

Yet, under his leadership, the party became more fractious, more truculent and more divided than at any time since the war. For all his talents as party manager, Callaghan was unable to hold Labour together and avert a dangerous split between the government and the extra-parliamentary party. To understand why, we must explore two factors, institutional and environmental, that constrained and shaped the way he managed the party. How Labour leaders discharge their functions is affected by party rules and institutional arrangements which influence how power is distributed between its various component bodies, and how decisions are reached. Secondly, how they enact their role is also and inevitably affected by external circumstances, the problems they confront and the economic, social and political pressures to which they are exposed. Callaghan's misfortune was, in April 1976, to inherit from his predecessor as Prime Minister, Harold Wilson, a polarised party riven by disputes and an economy in turmoil – and both without an effective parliamentary majority. In what follows, we discuss these two sets of constraints in turn.

Within the Labour Party there have always been ambiguities and disagreements about the precise role of the party leader, the relations between the PLP (Parliamentary Labour Party) and the wider party and the location of decision-making rights. This reflects the fact that there is an inbuilt tension between Labour's doctrine of internal party democracy and the prerogatives conferred upon the Cabinet by the conventions of parliamentary government.[5] For the exponents of Labour's traditional doctrine of party democracy on the party's left, the annual conference was the sovereign body, the 'fundamental expression' of intra-party democracy with the right to formulate the party programme and, ultimately, the manifesto.[6] From this perspective, what Katz has called 'the party in public office' was 'the agent of the party on the ground'.[7]

The impact of this tension was mitigated until the 1960s by a broad consensus which accepted that the party conference should set the programmatic direction of the party, though the PLP should exercise discretion over matters of timing and priority. This consensus was underpinned by a high level of institutional integration facilitated by right-wing control over all key institutions, conference, the PLP and the National Executive Committee (NEC). There was never complete agreement over the precise delimitation of powers between conference, the NEC and the PLP, but a broad community of interest and outlook among the major centres of power in effect bolstered the strength of the parliamentary leadership.

Institutional integration began to disintegrate in the late 1960s as a result of a major leftwards tilt in the unions – especially in the two largest, the Transport and General Workers' Union (TGWU) and the Amalgamated Union of Engineering Workers (AUEW). The net result was that by 1974, the left had more or less secured a majority both in conference and on the NEC. The effect was mounting strain between the leadership and the wider party. Indeed, as the party slid to the left and the solid conference majority which used to sustain the parliamentary leadership disappeared, so too did the party right's allegiance to the concept of conference sovereignty. They came to endorse the view propounded by Robert McKenzie in his classic analysis that the attempt to subject the PLP to extra-parliamentary direction breached 'the conventions of the parliamentary system'.[8] This was the view taken by Labour Prime Minister Harold Wilson in the late 1960s when critical resolutions were passed by conference with increasing frequency. He shrugged these off, observing cynically but candidly, 'We only take notice of Conference resolutions when it suits us, everyone knows that.'[9]

By the time Labour returned to power in 1974, most of the leadership had discarded 'the party's traditional views on mandates, Conference sovereignty and intra-party democracy'.[10] The left played a major part in the framing of the manifestos for the two 1974 elections, which contained radical proposals, especially over industrial and economic policy, capped by the pledge to bring about 'a fundamental and irreversible shift in the balance of power and wealth in favour of the working people and their families'. Once in power, Wilson made clear that he had no intention of implementing any manifesto commitments to which he objected.[11] As Callaghan, appointed Foreign Secretary, baldly stated, 'You can't write a manifesto for the Party in opposition and expect it to have any relationship to what the Party does in Government. We're now entirely free to do what we like.'[12] Inevitably, relations between the government and the NEC, in its role as the custodian of conference decisions, deteriorated.

Callaghan inherited not only a fractured party but an economy in crisis. Inflation was surging, unemployment mounting, the balance of payments deteriorating, the budget deficit widening rapidly and speculative pressure against sterling was relentless. 1975 'was the year in which the wheels fell off the Government's policies'.[13] The traditional levers of demand management seemed helpless to combat the new phenomenon of stagflation – an unprecedented combination of rapid price increases, swelling unemployment and minimal growth. All this very sharply curtailed the government's margin of manoeuvre, and after implementing a batch of expensive spending pledges, the government, under relentless pressure from the money markets, began to row back. The party's own solutions to economic decline as prescribed by the 1974 manifestos – a major increase in economic regulation, industrial intervention and public ownership – were dismissed by the government as irrelevant, damaging and hopelessly unrealistic. Rather than tacking to the left, as anticipated by the 1974 manifestos, the government, in response to the intensifying economic crisis, moved to the right – in particular by pruning the public sector – and relations with the NEC, for which Wilson barely concealed his contempt, worsened. As a result, the party inherited by Callaghan was one where the relationship between the government and the NEC (backed by conference) became increasingly acrimonious.

POWER AND POLICY-MAKING

Relations between Wilson and the NEC, then, were icy when he left office. Callaghan initially sought to improve them by establishing mechanisms for smoothing out differences. 'I was only too aware', he recalled in his memoirs, 'of the need to keep Ministers and members of the NEC in tandem if possible … And I not only enjoined on Ministers the need to consult but established a machinery for regular consultation.'[14] It was agreed that quarterly meetings would be held between the NEC and the Cabinet to give the former the opportunity to articulate grievances, to improve consultation and to find as much common ground as possible. The head of the PM's political office, Tom McNally, was charged with keeping him informed about party developments, alerting him to problems likely to arise and performing 'an indispensable liaison role'.[15] Unlike his predecessor, Callaghan attended NEC meetings regularly, though he found the experience 'complete purgatory'.[16] Callaghan also sought to shore up his support on the executive, charging his political advisor, David Lipsey, to work with John Golding MP, a right-wing trade union official and a tough and wily political operator,[17] to strengthen the right-wing bloc on the NEC; but attempts to arrest its continued drift to the left failed.

There was no improvement in relations between the government

and the NEC. Callaghan and his aides blamed the executive's ob-
duracy and ideological intransigence. As one senior political advisor
later claimed, No. 10 made determined attempts to conciliate the
NEC, but 'the willingness to meet half-way was not there'.[18] In truth,
the obstacles blocking greater cooperation between the government
and the NEC were formidable. The NEC saw itself as discharging its
function as the voice of the wider party and believed that it had a right
not only to be consulted by ministers but for its policy proposals to
be given serious consideration. Callaghan, however, had absolutely
no intention of conceding to the executive any right to influence the
work of his government, and its impact on policy-making was negli-
gible. As Geoff Bish, Labour's research secretary, reflected, its status
'vis à vis the Labour Government was, in practice, that of a mere pressure group, just one among many'.[19]

However, if the NEC had little input over government policy, the
government had equally modest influence over party organisation.
Under Labour's constitution, responsibility for internal organisation, staffing and discipline lay with the NEC, subject to approval
by conference. Until the late 1960s the executive effectively placed
its command of the party machine at the disposal of the party leader,
who, therefore, could usually rely upon the party machine to afford
protection against political dangers. By the mid-1970s this had ceased
to be the case. The alarm bells were first rung by the high-profile
deselection of Reg Prentice, then a government minister, by his left-
wing constituency party. In the past, the NEC would have rallied
behind the MP and blocked this deselection but, now run by the left,
it refused to do so.

The issue was eventually overshadowed by mounting anxieties
over the activities of the Militant Tendency, the visible arm of the
secretive Trotskyist Revolutionary Socialist League. Unlike other
Trotskyist organisations in the 1960s and 1970s, Militant had decided to work within the Labour Party by adopting the tactic of what

came to be known as 'entryism'. The tactic involved an organised, centrally directed, disciplined but anonymous drive to infiltrate the party, with the object both of gaining adherents and taking control of constituency parties. Militant was, in effect, a 'party within a party'. It gained an early success in 1967 in capturing the party's youth wing, the Labour Party Young Socialists. By the late 1970s it was focusing its efforts on constituency organisation, 'many of which', it claimed, were 'shells dominated by politically dead old men and women ... ossified little cliques'.[20] By the mid-1970s Militant remained a small organisation, but its influence was expanding, giving rise to some apprehension among MPs and party organisers. In September 1976, the NEC agreed to allow the National Agent (head of Labour's Organisation Department), Reg Underhill, to prepare a report on 'entryist activities'. Underhill, a highly regarded party official, compiled a substantial report concluding 'beyond any doubt whatever that there is a central organisation associated with Militant with its own membership and full-time organisers'.[21] However, the NEC's left majority declined to take any action, dismissing Militant as a mere political nuisance which posed no threat to the party. Then, in the autumn of 1976, the executive, in an extraordinary decision, appointed a leading Militant activist, Andy Bevan, as its Youth Officer.

Pressure was growing within the PLP to take firm measures against the Trotskyist organisation. In his speech at the 1976 conference Callaghan warned against 'a new factor creeping into the party', political elements 'who seek to infiltrate our party and to use it for their own end'.[22] In 1977, the NEC was persuaded to act, establishing a subcommittee to consider the issue anew. But it had a left-wing majority and predictably refused to move against Militant.[23] The NEC left chose to represent demands for tough action against the Trotskyists as a concealed threat to themselves. Some senior left-wingers, such as Tony Benn and Eric Heffer, regarded Trotskyists as perhaps somewhat misguided and overly exuberant, but comrades notwithstanding. Others, such as Ian Mikardo, had fewer illusions but objected to any resort to discipline on principle.

After Labour's eviction from office, and in the final year of Callaghan's leadership, Underhill's successor as National Agent, David Hughes, again urged action but his advice was disregarded. To an irate Callaghan, the NEC's stance smacked both of complacency and short-sighted factionalism, but during his years as PM he had much weightier problems on his mind. In normal circumstances, the whole matter would have been delegated to prime ministerial aides working in conjunction with party officials. But with the NEC in no mood to cooperate, this option was not available. Yet what the whole incident demonstrated was that without NEC collaboration, there was little Callaghan could do to combat the growing peril posed by Militant. By the time the party confronted the problem, cautiously under Michael Foot and then more decisively under Kinnock, its scale had swollen dangerously, and it took much time, effort and energy to resolve, to the party's cost.

The NEC's behaviour over Militant was an illustration of the oppositional role it had adopted by the mid-1970s. As Peter Shore, a centre-left Cabinet minister under Callaghan, wrote, 'Contrary to the experience of all previous Labour Governments which had enjoyed the general support of the NEC and of its Head Office, the NEC became in these years a principal, if not the principal, source of criticism of the Labour Government.'[24] NEC committees and sub-committees, which proliferated in the 1970s, released a continuous flow of reports and statements, almost always sharply interrogating and attacking the government's record. To Callaghan, this not only betrayed a dismal ignorance of economic realities but amounted to disloyalty to their government. As his political aide David Lipsey recollected, 'Here he was, as he saw it, trying to save the country, never mind the party, and the left on the national Executive were trying to destroy both.'[25]

In 1978 Minkin noted the 'increasing institutional independence and ... growing policy differentiation between the Labour Party and the Labour Government'.[26] What this meant in practical terms was that while the NEC had minimal influence over the government, the government had little control over the executive. Senior left-wing members of the NEC (including Tony Benn) were determined to transform it into what Richard Crossman had called the 'battering ram of change'. Crossman distinguished between current policy, which was the jurisdiction (when Labour was in office) of the government, and future policy, for which the NEC should be responsible; this would ensure that the party would not lose its radical cutting edge. Such a view was quite consistent with Labour's constitutional conventions, which empowered the executive to draft policy statements to be submitted to conference for approval. Those items endorsed by conference by a two-thirds majority were included in the party's programme from which the manifesto was supposed to be drawn.[27]

In the late 1970s the NEC embarked on its role as 'battering ram of change' with enthusiasm. These years witnessed a major expansion of the NEC's policy-making apparatus with the establishment of an extensive network of sub-committees and study groups containing representatives from MPs, trade unionists, academic experts and pressure group representatives, many of them from the left. Their work culminated in the publication of the policy statement, 'Labour's Programme for Britain 1976', endorsed by conference that year. This lengthy and detailed document called for an ambitious programme of nationalisations, schemes for enhancing industrial democracy, a highly interventionist industrial policy and expanded social spending, as well as an end to the UK's nuclear role and the abolition of the House of Lords.

The next step was to incorporate these policies into Labour's next manifesto. Under party rules, the NEC and the Cabinet were charged with deciding jointly 'which items from the Party programme shall be included in the manifesto'. Initially there seemed to be some willingness on both sides to seek compromise over the shape of the manifesto. Between January and March 1979, a Manifesto Working

Group comprising members of the NEC and the Cabinet met regularly and managed to reach some measure of agreement.[28] However, the NEC's priority was to avoid vague and ambiguous formulations and ensure that 'the views and priorities of the Party' were expressed in precise and binding pledges.[29] This was precisely what Callaghan was determined to avoid. He insisted that the manifesto should be designed to appeal to the public and reflect government policies and priorities: it must not be saddled with unpopular commitments simply because conference had endorsed them.[30] The consultation between the government and the executive was probably little more than window-dressing for, behind the scenes, Callaghan instructed his staff to prepare a separate No. 10 draft manifesto. It was this draft, prepared without any input from the NEC, that was presented to the Clause V meeting. Faced with a *fait accompli* and with an election imminent, the executive felt it had no option but to endorse a text which Bish judged to be 'remarkably weak in terms of Party policy'.[31]

Callaghan's démarche was deeply resented by the NEC and conference and it set the stage for the outbreak of hostilities that engulfed the party in the months following the 1979 election defeat. But to a large degree, the breakdown over the manifesto was inevitable. Whatever the procedure specified by Labour's constitution, hard-headed political realities dictated that the manifesto must reflect government policy. As Bish acknowledged, 'it was almost impossible for it to change tack just for the Manifesto'.[32] By 1979 a compromise manifesto was not feasible because the programmatic gulf between government and party was unbridgeable. What follows seeks to explain why.

THE BREAKDOWN OF CONSENSUS

Differences over power, policy and party democracy were greatly exacerbated by Labour's deepening ideological polarisation. There have always been major divergences within the party over such matters as nationalisation, the balance between state regulation and market forces, taxation and defence policy. However, a shared commitment to the use of Keynesian techniques to sustain full employment and economic growth, and to high levels of public spending to promote equality and alleviate poverty supplied a core of consensus which helped knit the party together. But by the mid-1970s this consensus was breaking down as inflation appeared to spiral out of control, output and productivity fell, and the value of the pound sank, culminating in the IMF crisis of 1976 (see Chapter 7).

From this Callaghan and his critics in the wider party drew fundamentally different lessons. Callaghan, 'instinctively conservative on economic matters' and increasingly influenced by monetarist ideas, became convinced that if the crisis was to be surmounted, price stability must replace full employment as the main priority of economic policy.[33] Crosland understood the wider ideological implications of this decision for his brand of social democracy. Privately he bemoaned 'the breeding of illiterate and reactionary attitudes to public expenditure' among ministerial colleagues[34] and feared that cuts on the scale envisaged would derail the egalitarian project to which he had devoted his political life. From a rather different perspective, the left-controlled NEC Loan Agreement concurred with this analysis. As Benn told the Tribune Group of left-wing MPs in February 1977, 'The dilemma for social democrats was that high public expenditure based on full employment, which could then redistribute wealth, was no longer an option.'[35] The only feasible route to achieving greater equality and social justice was the socialist approach embodied in the Alternative Economic Strategy, which included greatly expanded public ownership, much tighter regulation of the economy and import and capital controls. This, of course, was utterly unacceptable to the right of the party. With the left moving further to the left and the government to the right, the common ground which had

imparted a degree of ideological coherence to the party was shriv-
elling. As Healey commented, 'To move halfway towards each other
from opposite sides of the Grand Canyon would be a disaster.'[36] Benn
agreed: 'The centre had fallen away.'[37]

For many commentators (though not all), the IMF Loan Agreement did indeed represent 'a turning point in the philosophical basis
of economic policy, shattering the consensus that full employment
should be the principal object of economic policy'.[38] For the left in
the wider party it was a betrayal, a traducing of party policy and a
shameful abandonment of Labour's core values. But Callaghan, from
his cautiously pragmatic standpoint, saw matters in a radically different way. He believed that, in the least propitious of circumstances and
faced by unrelenting political and market pressures, he had negotiated a fair and reasonable agreement – far less punitive than the IMF
initially wanted. In consequence he reacted with fury to what he saw
as wholly unreasonable, dogma-driven and politically inspired NEC
attacks.[39] 'Here we were running a government which was fast losing
its majority,' his aide David Lipsey recalled, 'amidst a grave economic
and political situation to be stabbed in the back, month after month,
by those with no interest in winning the next election.'[40] There was
no meeting of minds.

Yet the civil war that was to envelop the party was not, as yet, inevitable. From 1977 the economy steadily recovered as exports grew,
the value of sterling rose, and interest rates, public borrowing, unemployment and inflation all fell.[41] As the economy recuperated, so
did Labour's standing in the polls, and there was a widespread ex-
pectation that Callaghan would call an election in the autumn of 1978.
That autumn he announced a tighter and wholly unrealistic 5 per
cent norm for the next phase of incomes policy, which most trade
union leaders swallowed as an electioneering ploy. But he decided
not to call an election, thereby saddling the government with an un-
deliverable pay policy. Sympathetic trade union leaders warned they

were losing authority over their rank and file. Three years of rigorous wage restraint were provoking increasing restiveness on the shop floor, especially among public sector employees already suffering from the IMF-prescribed public expenditure squeeze. Furthermore, in 1978 the two union architects of incomes policy, Jack Jones and Hugh Scanlon (leaders of the TGWU and the AEUW), retired, and without their authority, prestige and political weight the prospects of the unions agreeing to a third phase of incomes policy vanished. Callaghan's political skills seem to have deserted him and his dogged determination to proceed with the new pay limit proved to be a fatal blunder.[42] It was, Healey later recollected, a case of 'hubris'. If the government had been content with a formula like 'single figures', the Winter of Discontent and all its disastrous consequences might well have been avoided.[43]

The rest was, so to speak, history. The strike wave unleashed by the breakdown of pay restraint had disastrous political repercussions. The Winter of Discontent demolished Labour's reputation for economic competence and, for many voters, transformed its traditional close relationship with the trade unions from an advantage to a major liability.[44] This calamitous period not only buried Labour's hopes for the next election (and for subsequent ones) but acted as the seedbed for a fratricidal struggle for power in the party which was unprecedented in its length, severity and destructive consequences.

CALLAGHAN AS OPPOSITION LEADER

Callaghan's final year as Labour leader proved to be his most dismal. Left to his own volition, he probably would have resigned after the 1979 election, but he came under strong pressure from the PLP to remain and help staunch the left-wing wave crested by the charismatic Tony Benn.[45] Though his prestige had suffered he was still widely admired, and his powers of persuasion remained formidable. But the circumstances he faced were daunting and his task almost hopeless.

The left's analysis of the defeat was simple: by its stubborn refusal to implement party policy and its endless spending cuts, the government had alienated Labour voters. The NEC had found itself powerless to prevent this, lacking any effective mechanisms by which it could induce the Cabinet to respect the will of the party. The only way to resolve this problem, the left concluded, was through constitutional reform, which could shift the balance of power decisively away from the party in office and in favour of the party on the ground. The campaign for constitutional reform, launched immediately after Labour's loss of power, was orchestrated by the Campaign for Labour Party Democracy (CLPD), an organisation of grassroots activists set up in 1973. It advocated three main measures. The first, and most contentious, was the introduction of mandatory reselection: that is, a system by which each sitting MP would be required to face an election before being readopted as a Labour candidate. This, it was anticipated, would render them much more sensitive to rank-and-file opinion. The second reform was to transfer the right to select the party leader from the PLP to an electoral college comprising MPs, the affiliated unions and the constituency parties. The third was the placing of the right to frame the manifesto solely in the hands of the NEC.

For Callaghan, what he saw as the drive to transform MPs into creatures of constituency activists was profoundly undemocratic and a breach of the conventions of British parliamentary government.[46] Callaghan's problem was that, under Labour's constitution, the NEC and not the parliamentary leadership possessed the right to initiate rule changes and, in contrast with past practice, to choose to spearhead the campaign for the three reforms. This immediately placed the leader on the defensive. Furthermore, there were serious divisions within the PLP about how best to resist the drive for constitutional change. There were those who favoured a confrontational strategy: an all-out assault on the left's hold on the party. But Callaghan, fearful this would precipitate a civil war, rejected this advice and agreed to the proposal of the GMB, the municipal workers' union, to set up a commission of inquiry into party organisation. Unfortunately for Callaghan, the left managed to secure a majority on the commission and he was unable to dissuade it from agreeing to mandatory reselection and the establishment of an electoral college to elect the leader, reforms that were subsequently approved by conference. Shortly after, a section of the right, including Roy Jenkins, David Owen and Shirley Williams, defected to form the Social Democratic Party.

It was the first major party split since 1931 and testified to Callaghan's loss of authority. Indeed, during this last phase of his leadership he 'seemed old, lonely, the target of an embittered and determined left on every issue' and the butt of 'many wounding personal attacks'.[47] He resigned the leadership in autumn 1980 before a new leadership election procedure was installed in the hope that, with the franchise still precariously in the PLP's hands, Healey would enter into the inheritance for which, by experience and talent, he seemed eminently well-qualified. But it was not to be.

CONCLUSION

Conflict between party and government is inherent in a party of the left. 'It is in the nature of a democratic party of the Left', Peter Shore observed, 'that a majority of its most enthusiastic and active members will be anti-authoritarian, restless for change, distrustful of assertive leadership.'[48] Ministers will always be the object of mistrust to those who suspect them of subordinating party programmes and principles to the allures of office, prestige and power. Equally, government leaders are bound to become impatient with those in the wider party who, not having to shoulder the responsibilities of government nor grapple with the practicalities of decision-making, feel free to agitate for policies which, to the leaders, are unrealistic and unpopular.

But such conflicts can be managed, and Callaghan, by background, experience and personality, seemed well-suited to balancing and reconciling the desires and priorities of government and party. His combination of joviality, astuteness and iron-fistedness seemed to equip him with the ideal qualities of a party manager. But it was his misfortune both to preside over a bitterly divided and fractious party and to inherit the premiership at a time of economic crisis whose effect was to unleash within the Labour Party a profoundly disruptive process of ideological polarisation. Callaghan 'regarded Attlee's consensus as his abiding point of reference and always took it as his ideological starting point'.[49] But this consensus was palpably disintegrating – challenged from both left and right, not least by Callaghan himself. By the late 1970s the ideological fissure between government and party was too wide to straddle: Labour, the former minister Joel Barnett recorded in his memoirs, was 'so divided that it is difficult even to regard it as a coalition'.[50] It was Callaghan's final tragedy that in his last year as leader, he witnessed, as little more than a helpless bystander, a party in a fratricidal struggle for power.

NOTES
1   T. Benn, *Against the Tide: Diaries 1973–76* (London: Hutchinson, 1989), p. 62.
2   K. Morgan, *Callaghan: A Life* (Oxford: Oxford University Press, 1997), p. 756.
3   K. Theakston, 'Political Skills and Context in Prime Ministerial Leadership in Britain', *Politics and Policy* (2008), vol. 30, no. 2, pp. 288–9.
4   Morgan, *Callaghan*, p. 751.
5   M. Foley, *John Major, Tony Blair and a Conflict of Leadership* (Manchester: Manchester University Press, 2002), p. 68.
6   L. Minkin, *The Labour Party Conference* (Manchester: Manchester University Press, 1978), p. 5.
7   R. Katz, 'No man can serve two masters: Party politicians, party members, citizens and principal-agent models of democracy', *Party Politics* (2014), vol. 20, no. 2, p. 185.
8   R. McKenzie, *British Political Parties* (London: Heinemann, 1964), p. 645.

9   Benn, *Against the Tide*, p. 38.

10 Minkin, *The Labour Party Conference*, p. 11.

11 *Ibid.*, p. 316.

12 Benn, *Against the Tide*, p. 194.

13 V. Bogdanor, 'The IMF Crisis of 1976', 19 January 2016: https://www.gresham.ac.uk/lectures-and-events/the-imf-crisis-1976

14 J. Callaghan, *Time and Chance* (London: Collins, 1987), p. 459.

15 *Ibid.*, p. 406.

16 Interview, Lord Lipsey.

17 *Ibid.*

18 *Ibid.*; see also B. Donoughue, *The Heat of the Kitchen: An Autobiography* (London: Politico, 2003), p. 127.

19 G. Bish, 'The Programme of Work', Home Policy Committee of the NEC RD, 6 June 1979.

20 E. Shaw, *The Labour Party Since 1945* (Oxford: Blackwell, 1996), p. 219.

21 E. Shaw, *Discipline and Discord in the Labour Party: The politics of managerial control in the Labour Party, 1951–87* (Manchester: Manchester University Press, 1988), p. 219.

22 J. Callaghan, Leader's Speech, Labour Party Conference, 1976: http://www.britishpoliticalspeech.org/speech-archive.htm?speech=174

23 Shaw, *Discipline and Discord in the Labour Party*, p. 221.

24 P. Shore, *Leading the Left* (London: Weidenfeld & Nicolson, 1993), p. 120.

25 D. Lipsey, *In the Corridors of Power* (London: Biteback, 2012), p. 115.

26 Minkin, *The Labour Party Conference*, p. 317.

27 *Ibid.*, p. 331.

28 Bish, *The Programme of Work*.

29 *Ibid.*

30 T. Benn, *Conflicts of Interest: Diaries 1977–80* (London: Arrow, 1990), p. 479; D. Butler and D. Kavanagh, *The British General Election of 1979* (London: Macmillan, 1980), p. 52.

31 G. Bish, *Drafting the Manifesto: The Record and the Lessons*, Home Policy Committee of the NEC RD, 23 July 1979.

32 *Ibid.*

33 B. Donoughue, *Prime Minister: The Conduct of Policy under Harold Wilson and James Callaghan* (London: Jonathan Cape, 1987), p. 82.

34 Quoted in D. Reisman, *Anthony Crosland: The Mixed Economy* (Basingstoke: Macmillan, 1997), p. 40.

35 Benn, *Conflicts of Interest*, p. 43.

36 *Ibid.*, p. 38.

37 *Ibid.*, p. 43.

38 K. Burk and A. Cairncross, *'Goodbye, Great Britain': The 1976 IMF Crisis* (New Haven: Yale University Press, 1992), p. 129; M. Crook, 'The Labour Governments 1974–1979: social democracy abandoned?', *British Politics* (2018), vol. 14, pp. 86–105.

39 Donoughue, *Prime Minister*, p. 98.

40 Interview, Lord Lipsey.

41 Morgan, *Callaghan*, pp. 558–9; Crook, 'The Labour Governments 1974–1979', pp. 86–105.

42 Theakston, 'Political Skills and Context in Prime Ministerial Leadership in Britain', p. 291.

43 D. Healey, *The Time of My Life* (London: Penguin, 1990), pp. 462–3.

44 Donoughue, *Prime Minister*, pp. 185–6.

45 Morgan, *Callaghan*, p. 703.

46 *Ibid.*, p. 710.

47 *Ibid.*, pp. 712, 714.

48 Shore, *Leading the Left*, p. 191.

49 Morgan, *Callaghan*, p. 749.

50 Quoted in Bogdanor, *The IMF Crisis of 1976*.

6

THE 1979 GENERAL ELECTION[1]

Mark Garnett

O N 25 J U LY 1978 James Callaghan defended his government's record in a House of Commons debate on the economy. Earlier that day he had told the head of his policy unit, Bernard
Donoughue, that he proposed to take personal aim at the opposition
leader, Margaret Thatcher, for the first time. Donoughue left the
Commons in the early stages of Callaghan's speech but, thanks to the
recent introduction of permanent radio broadcasts from the House,
he caught the Prime Minister's closing remarks during his journey
home:

> The right hon. Lady's every speech is a rallying cry to prejudice.
> The Tory Party once aspired to lead one nation and to speak for one
> nation. Now the Tory Party, many of its members reluctant and sullen,
> has to listen to the language of division the whole time. That call to
> division will fall on deaf ears. The British people have come to know
> that they achieve most when they work together, when they work in
> unison, in social justice and in fair play.[2]

Donoughue rejoiced at 'a tremendous triumph for the PM … Mrs Thatcher was clearly wrong-footed'. After her reply to Callaghan, 'she sat down in silence'.[3]

A few days later Parliament rose for its summer recess. Arriving in France for his holiday, Donoughue noted the 'unanimous' verdict of the British press – Callaghan had trounced Thatcher. It was, Donoughue felt, the perfect prelude to the general election campaign which he expected Callaghan to announce soon after parliament reassembled.[4]

Yet Callaghan had not made up his mind, and eventually decided to delay the election. When it finally came, the timing was forced upon him. In the confidence debate held on 28 March 1979 Callaghan delivered a speech which Donoughue judged to be 'superb'; but the Prime Minister told him that 'speeches don't make any difference. We won't get the votes and that's what matters.' The government was duly defeated, by a single vote, and Parliament was dissolved. It was during another car journey, two weeks later and with the campaign in full swing, that Callaghan reflected, 'If people have really decided they want a change of government, there is nothing you can do.' Although Donoughue's published accounts differ slightly, his testimony has been taken as evidence that Callaghan had detected a 'sea change' in the public mood, which was in favour of Thatcher and the Conservatives.[5]

The 1979 general election was the most significant since 1945, starting a run of four consecutive Conservative victories and an eighteen-year spell of soul-searching for Labour. Understandably, the 1979 contest featured prominently in Labour's internal wrangling. Would the party have fared better if it had presented the public with a more radical policy programme? Or was it doomed by association with the radical left and the trade unions?

This chapter is not a resumption of that inquest, focusing rather on Callaghan's personal role in the defeat. It examines his reasons for rejecting an early election, and his part in the campaign which ended in defeat on 3 May 1979. Apart from asking whether Callaghan could have played his cards more effectively, it differs from previous accounts by examining his use of his position as Prime Minister in the context of developments affecting the British electorate at the time.

AUTUMN 1978 - THE ELECTION THAT NEVER WAS

Although Bernard Donoughue departed for France in good spirits after the summer recess, Callaghan had much to ponder as he retreated to his Sussex farm, where he spent almost the whole of August. Discussions with senior colleagues in the weeks before the recess had increased Callaghan's confidence that the government, which could no longer rely on the support of the Liberals, might nevertheless cobble together Commons majorities thanks to the votes of the nationalist parties of Scotland and Wales, along with at least some of the Ulster Unionists and the Social and Democratic Labour Party (SDLP). This assurance, which was provided with considerable enthusiasm by Leader of the House Michael Foot, encouraged Callaghan to think more seriously about playing a longer electoral game.

Callaghan's priority, whenever the election came, was to liberate his government from the hand-to-mouth existence which he and his predecessor Harold Wilson had endured since 1974. Reflecting on the polling evidence available to him in August 1978, the Prime Minister could not be certain that his party would secure an overall majority if he called an autumn election. Although Labour enjoyed an overall lead in the polls, Callaghan was troubled by regional variations, particularly in the West Midlands seats which had helped to thwart Harold Wilson's 1970 re-election campaign. In addition, Labour had performed poorly in two by-elections held on 13 July (Penistone and Manchester Moss

Side). These data seem to have convinced Callaghan – like Gordon Brown in 2007 – that an early poll would not produce the result he wanted; at best, there was likely to be another hung parliament and a further period of bargaining with minor parties. On Callaghan's private calculations, indeed, the Conservatives would win the most seats (albeit by the slenderest of margins – 305 to 304). These predictions seemed to be verified by polling evidence produced by Robert Worcester of MORI in early September.[6] But by then Callaghan had already reached a decision – there would be no early election.

In opting for delay, Callaghan was preferring the polling data to more substantive considerations, particularly economic indicators. Compared to the ruinous situation of 1976, which had forced the government to apply for support from the International Monetary Fund (IMF), the position seemed to have stabilised. By July 1978 price inflation had fallen to about 8 per cent, while average wages increases were around 15 per cent. Living standards were thus rising for many voters when Callaghan made his decision, and Britain's balance of payments was in surplus. Economists such as David Blake of *The Times* saw this 'feel-good' moment – which was likely to have an exaggerated effect because of the preceding period of gloom – as a window of electoral opportunity which would soon slam shut due largely to pent-up inflationary forces.[7]

The other factor which pointed to an early election was Labour's trump card in the 1974 contests – its relationship with the trade unions. In July 1978 Callaghan had prescribed a 5 per cent 'norm' for pay settlements – a more rigid and ambitious formula than most Cabinet colleagues would have adopted. Since price inflation was still appreciably higher than 5 per cent, this in effect was a request for union leaders to acquiesce in a cut in living standards for their members. It was natural to regard this 'unrealistic' policy as an electoral gambit – a statement of intent designed to give the impression of economic rigour in advance of an early election.[8] Once the government had secured a workable Commons majority, it could negotiate a more flexible formula with the unions.

Last, but by no means least, Callaghan could expect that an autumn 1978 election would mark a return to two-party politics, rather than being complicated by rising support for the Liberals and 'others', as had been the case in the two 1974 contests. The government's promise of devolution to Scotland and Wales looked likely to impede the electoral progress of the Scottish National Party (SNP) and Plaid Cymru. The Liberals, who had benefited from 'protest votes' in 1974, had already been damaged by their unproductive parliamentary pact with Labour before the arrest of their leader, Jeremy Thorpe, on a charge of conspiracy to murder, in early August 1978 (that is, *before* Callaghan decided against an early election).

Thus, Callaghan's decision to delay the election – which, by his own account, he took on 17 August – reflected a feeling that 'things could only get better' for his government, in defiance of compelling evidence that they were likely to deteriorate. There were other factors which supported delay until 1979 – a more up-to-date electoral register was expected to be helpful to Labour, and memories of the Conservatives' expensive pre-election publicity campaign (featuring the notorious 'Labour isn't working' poster) would have faded.[9] Yet these were marginal considerations compared to the weighty indicators suggesting that, for Callaghan, it was either now or never. The truth was that Callaghan did not assess the evidence impartially: he had never liked the idea of an early election. Since he kept his decision entirely to himself for more than two weeks, he could have changed his mind before announcing his intentions. His refusal to think again is suggested in his reported remark to the West German Chancellor Helmut Schmidt, when a survey published at the end of August gave Labour a four-point lead over the Conservatives: 'I don't believe in [opinion polls]. I don't trust them.'[10] More likely, he did not *want* to believe in any evidence that suggested he was about to make a serious miscalculation.

Although he had made up his own mind, Callaghan went through the formalities of a consultation exercise. Almost all of his Cabinet colleagues submitted their thoughts in writing. A small majority (10 to 8) favoured going early, but in Callaghan's mind the minority carried more weight: the 'delayers' included the Chancellor, Foreign Secretary and Home Secretary (Denis Healey, David Owen and Merlyn Rees) as well as Foot. On 1 September he was visited at his home by six key union figures, all of whom were well-disposed towards Callaghan. The mood of this informal gathering was clearly in favour of an early election, but the Prime Minister gave no sign that he had decided either way. Four days later Callaghan delivered a speech to the Trades Union Congress in which he cherry-picked the positive elements of the government's record, in typical pre-election mode, but refused to divulge his thinking on an election. Instead, he sang a verse from a musical-hall song – 'Waiting at the Church' – about a would-be bride who set the date for her wedding only to discover that the groom had left her 'in the lurch'. The only rational interpretation of this surreal vocal exhibition was that Callaghan was still set on an early election but was saving the announcement for another occasion. In the context of his real thinking on the subject it becomes even more mystifying, not least because he knowingly misattributed the song to the well-known Marie Lloyd rather than the real artist, the relatively obscure Vesta Victoria.[11] One can only surmise that he was overcome by the sheer enjoyment of holding a secret.

On 7 September Callaghan stunned his Cabinet colleagues by announcing that he had notified the Queen in writing that he would not be seeking an early dissolution. He informed them that further discussion would be fruitless since he had no intention of bothering the monarch with another letter which contradicted the first one. Tony Benn (an advocate of an early poll) was 'most surprised, and indeed angry that the Cabinet had not discussed a decision of this magnitude'. Benn's diary record probably understates his reaction at the time. Callaghan referred to consultations with senior colleagues and followed the orthodox constitutional line by stressing that he was wholly responsible for the decision. Yet on this critical occasion Benn was justified in thinking that the Prime Minister had made a mockery of Cabinet government by canvassing ministerial opinions after the decision had been taken, and then presenting colleagues with 'a *fait accompli*'.[12] In July 1974 Harold Wilson had decided on an October election, apparently without consulting anyone, following his own precedent in February 1966. However, on these occasions nobody was surprised or angered because the rationale had been clear. Callaghan might have thought proper consultation in 1978 would merely have confirmed what he already knew – namely, that senior colleagues disagreed. However, since he was always minded to delay the election, it is significant that he denied colleagues on the opposite side of the argument the chance to present their case at an appropriate time.

As it was, Callaghan had managed to fool everyone, including his own special advisors, who had continued to brief the press, with considerable confidence, that there would be an October election.[13] Joan Lestor, a former minister who until recently had served as the Labour Party's chair, had to cancel the party she had arranged for retiring MPs. Donoughue's immediate reaction on hearing the news on 7 September was that 'the PM was mad and badly wrong'.[14] The Prime Minister had decided to stick to his decision, even though the votes and speeches at the TUC in the first week of September indicated clearly that the 5 per cent pay norm would not be respected by the trade unions. While Callaghan was singing to delegates, he would have done better to assess a new mood within the union movement, as seasoned power-brokers like Jack Jones (transport workers) and Hugh Scanlon (engineers) stepped aside in favour of less dynamic leaders.

After the Cabinet meeting Callaghan explained his decision in a televised broadcast. This long-forgotten performance is probably the best clue to his real thinking. He presented himself as the embodiment of the national interest, concluding with the exhortation, 'Let us pull through together.'[15] This was entirely in keeping with his conduct since the confidence debate of 25 July. Callaghan had convinced himself that he could appeal to voters over the heads of union leaders and Labour Party members (who were strongly in favour of an early poll and deeply sceptical about the 5 per cent norm). The Prime Minister believed that under his unifying leadership – such a marked contrast to the divisive Thatcher – the common sense of the British people would assert itself; and even if the new pay guidelines proved unrealistic, the spirit of Callaghan's proposal would be followed closely enough to prevent an explosion of pay and price inflation in 1979. Callaghan's broadcast, in short, was a 'presidential' performance – an example of what Michael Foley termed 'leadership stretch' – to match anything that Thatcher ever managed.[16]

In the British context, the adoption of a 'presidential' role for electoral purposes invited (even demanded) a 'populist' turn. On 3 October Callaghan addressed the Labour conference, encouraging his party and the country to look back on recent problems as unpleasant and irrelevant memories. The idea that Britain was facing 'its most dangerous crisis since the war' when he became Prime Minister was well founded, but that was 'the pit from which we have escaped and to which we do not intend to return. Today, nobody denies that the Labour government and the people, working together in partnership, have confounded the pessimists.'[17] Tony Benn – a well-qualified judge of populist performances – judged it 'the best speech I had ever heard from a Party Leader at Conference', despite the fact that on the previous day he had exulted over votes which undermined the 5 per cent norm and discredited the ministerial loyalists who had spoken up in Callaghan's favour.[18] The press reaction to Callaghan's performance was almost equally positive; but as the pre-August Callaghan would have put it, 'speeches don't make any difference'.[19]

MAY 1979 – THE ELECTION THAT WAS

It seems that in the weeks before his 7 September broadcast Callaghan took particular pleasure in wrong-footing the press – both the broadsheets and the tabloids. Whether or not he damaged his reputation among trade unionists with his Marie Lloyd impersonation, he certainly did not endear himself to Fleet Street's finest by allowing his advisors to mislead them. The tabloids had the last laugh, starting with the Guadeloupe Conference of January 1979. During the meeting itself, various media outlets exerted themselves to secure photographs of the Prime Minister (with and without his wife Audrey) relaxing in the sunshine while voters back home were enduring the combined impact of sub-zero temperatures and industrial anarchy.

The tactics of the press pack and their paparazzi hirelings turned out to be more inspired than they could possibly have known. At Guadeloupe, Callaghan found confirmation of the pseudo-presidential guise which he had adopted during the saga of the election that never was. Whatever Cabinet colleagues, union leaders or newspaper editors might think of him, on the international stage he was a respected figure who could maximise Britain's influence despite the industrial disorder back home. If his fellow leaders spoke of his government's domestic problems, they tended to do so in a spirit of commiseration. On his return there was some discussion about the advisability of a press conference. Callaghan decided to go ahead, rather than giving himself time to overcome his jet lag and to accommodate himself to the disorientating difference between the deferential atmosphere at the summit and the feeding frenzy of the British press. His understandable inability to find the right tone furnished *The Sun* with the immortal headline 'Crisis? What Crisis?'.[20]

By the time Callaghan was forced to face the voters on 3 May 1979, the rationale for his decision of the previous August had collapsed.

Whatever his private delusions, there had never been a chance that he could lead Labour to a comfortable overall majority. However, he continued to hope that something could be snatched from the turmoil which began almost as soon as his melodious notes at the TUC had faded away. By May 1979 he could be regarded both as the chief architect of his party's impending defeat and its only chance of clinging on to power.

Having taken personal responsibility for the election that never was, Callaghan had no alternative but to adopt the same 'presidential' approach to the contest which eventually took place. This meant he would have to control Labour's campaign, even if this risked further displeasure from more radical colleagues and their grassroots supporters. On 2 April 1979, the party's National Executive Committee (NEC) met to discuss the manifesto. At that time, there were two contrasting drafts – a radical document, reflecting the ideas of the NEC, and an alternative version composed by Callaghan's special advisors, Tom McNally and David Lipsey. Mainly by stressing his 'heavy burden of responsibility', Callaghan ensured that his preferred version was adopted, with some cosmetic changes. The outmanoeuvred Tony Benn noted in his diary that 'I shall have to think very carefully about future manifestos'. In particular, he should have thought twice before revealing, near the end of the meeting, that it would be his birthday at midnight, which allowed Callaghan to dissipate any remaining tensions by leading his colleagues in another song. The defeat of the left was confirmed at a further meeting, where (for example) the party's class warriors found themselves having to give up a proposed ban on foxhunting in return for a commitment to prohibit the gratuitous slaughter of deer.[21] Since the Conservative manifesto disguised Thatcher's true intentions, the election which ended any notion of a post-war 'consensus' was thus fought between two parties with misleadingly moderate programmes.

Having imposed his will over the contents of the manifesto,

Callaghan seized total control over the conduct of the Labour campaign. All the key decisions were taken at early-morning meetings at No. 10 between the Prime Minister, special advisors and PR consultants, leaving the official campaign committee with no effective role. After a press conference at 9.30 a.m. the Prime Minister would leave London for a series of forays into marginal constituencies, as well as his own constituency base in Cardiff. If anything, Callaghan's campaign was 'more truly presidential' than Thatcher's; it eschewed the superficial aspects of US politics which Thatcher accepted (advice on appearance, tone of voice and so on) while embracing its *substance* (creating the impression that the contest was between the reckless and inexperienced Thatcher and the tried-and-trusted 'Uncle Jim', rather than being fought out between candidates in sub-national constituencies).[22]

For Callaghan's team, the only missing ingredient from the US presidential formula was a televised debate between the two main party's leaders. Before 1979, it had become routine for opposition leaders to demand a face-to-face confrontation, and for disdainful Prime Ministers to reject the idea. This time the challenge for a debate came from Downing Street. Mrs Thatcher was more than willing to rise to the bait but was dissuaded by her advisors.[23]

Callaghan was delighted when he learned that Thatcher had shirked his challenge.[24] His immediate reaction was understandable, since effectively he had scored a victory over his opponent without having to exert himself. However, in those days when television viewers were restricted to just three channels, a debate between the party leaders during an election campaign would have attracted a mammoth audience, including almost every uncommitted voter who took politics seriously. In short, a debate between the two major party leaders might have been a game-changer in 1979. Callaghan should not have been surprised that the Conservatives declined the invitation, but it is surely significant that his reaction was not tinged by disappointment.

Callaghan's attitude to Thatcher is one of the most intriguing elements of the 1979 campaign, betraying his new understanding of electoral politics as essentially 'presidential' in nature. He regarded her as a right-wing extremist who was likely at some point to alienate floating voters by revealing her true colours – hence, at least in part, his preference for a protracted five-week campaign which would maximise the chances that she would break free of her media-minders. Yet he was anxious not to draw attention to his leading opponent, as if afraid that she would prove an electoral asset for the Conservatives after all. As a result, although Callaghan was well aware of the importance of the election, he never followed through on hints that he would personalise the battle for votes. Indeed, compared to the two contests of 1974, there was less negative campaigning from the party leaders in 1979;[25] despite the underlying polarisation of political debate, there was a prevailing spirit of politeness.

Rather than attacking Thatcher directly, Callaghan used a tactic commonly employed by the opposition leader's 'wet' Conservative critics, following up the rhetoric of his July 1978 speech by using the language of 'One Nation' as an implicit contrast to her divisive approach. Callaghan was no more successful than the wets, not least because Thatcher's PR advisors were aware of the danger and took steps to make her look and sound non-threatening. A more important problem for Callaghan was that even if the protagonists were keen to avoid confrontation, their media allies had no such inhibitions. In this respect, the situation had changed since 1974 even though the line-up of newspapers on each side was roughly the same. The proprietor of *The Sun*, Rupert Murdoch, was not at this stage a wholehearted admirer of Mrs Thatcher. However, he thought that Callaghan's government was a disaster and was prepared to risk upsetting the tabloid's working-class readers by making a determined effort to promote a change of government. Thus, apart from the wounding 'Crisis? What Crisis?' headline, it was *The Sun* that distilled the industrial anarchy of 1978–79 into the Shakespearian phrase 'Winter of Discontent'. On the morning of the election, Murdoch showed his ability to find the *mot juste* by changing the paper's original headline from 'Vote Tory Today' to 'Vote Tory This Time'. Readers were being asked to lend their votes to the Conservatives on this single occasion, rather than being told to renounce their traditional allegiance to Labour.[26]

Although *The Sun*'s impact on voting behaviour could not be measured, it had overtaken the Labour-supporting *Daily Mirror* as Britain's best-selling newspaper in 1978. The *Daily Mail* had no need for nuance, given its long-established Tory leanings; but its ingrained anti-Labour sentiments were expressed with fewer inhibitions compared to 1974 or 1970. Early in the campaign Donoughue reflected that 'most of the papers have become total propaganda sheets. The *Daily Mail* might as well be published in Tory Central Office – except that even they, employing some decent people, might find its malicious lies embarrassing.' He predicted (correctly) that the *Mail*'s editor David English would be rewarded with a knighthood for disclaiming any pretence to political balance.[27]

While the government's record provided the Tory press with ample material for negative campaigning, there was plenty to say for it on the positive side. When voters were asked to name the key issues of the campaign, their most popular choices were prices and unemployment. Labour was the preferred party in both of these areas. However, the next three issues on the list – taxation, strikes and law and order – were 'owned' by the Conservatives (by very considerable margins in the cases of tax and law and order). On those issues where Labour was favoured, voters were sceptical that *either* party could be successful. By contrast, in specific areas (such as the proposal to allow long-term council tenants to purchase their properties), voters tended both to approve the policy and to think that it could be delivered – by the Conservatives.[28]

Callaghan's party was fighting an election forced upon it by defeat

in a parliamentary vote of confidence, after a virtually unbroken series
of policy reversals since the Prime Minister decided against an early
election. The policy failure which precipitated the government's
defeat in the Commons – its inability to deliver devolution to Scotland and Wales – was all the more damaging since it had never enjoyed much support among English voters in the first place. Against
this background it is remarkable that anyone thought Labour could
win the 1979 general election – and that one opinion poll in the last
few days (taken by NOP on 29–30 April) actually gave the party a
slender lead.[29]

The result of the election itself was much more decisive – an overall majority of forty-four seats for the Conservatives, who achieved
the largest winning margin in terms of votes since 1935. The overall
national swing (5.2 per cent) was the most significant since 1945. The
main reason for Labour's defeat was a mass desertion among working-
class voters, whether or not they were members of a trade union.
Compared to the last election (October 1974) there was a fifteen-point
increase in the Conservative vote among the skilled working class; in
this crucial demographic cohort, levels of support for Labour and the
Conservatives were equal in 1979 (at 41 per cent), compared to a 23-
point lead for Labour in 1974. Among semi- and unskilled workers,
a 35-point advantage for Labour in 1974 dwindled to one of fifteen
points (49–34, compared to 57–22).[30]

Another marked feature of the voting was the increased support
for the Conservatives – compared to the contests of 1974 – from the
youngest (eighteen- to 22-year-old) voters, and the cohort aged between forty-five and sixty-four, who were nearing retirement but still
youthful enough to vote in large numbers in the next few elections.
According to Ipsos MORI, the change from 1974 among the youngest
voters was almost the same as the shift among the skilled working
class – a considerable Labour lead (42–24 points) was wiped out. In
the older age group, a significant Labour lead had been converted

into a comfortable Conservative advantage. In regional terms, the election ushered in another familiar pattern of the Thatcher years – a 'north–south divide', or, more accurately, a 'centre–periphery' split, with the Conservatives advancing in English seats south of the River Trent and Labour holding on in the north of England (while actually increasing its vote share in Scotland).[31] The outcome was symbolised by a swing of 11 per cent in the Essex constituency of Basildon, turning a safe Labour seat into a totem of Tory electoral success from 1979 until it swung back sharply in the 1997 New Labour landslide.

Callaghan himself had remained hopeful to the end. Nevertheless, one explanation for his conduct throughout the campaign is that he always had at least half an eye on his personal reputation. As Ivor Crewe put it in his post-election analysis, 'Had the voters been asked to choose a prime minister, Callaghan would still be in 10 Downing Street.' He was preferred to Mrs Thatcher in all the polls conducted during the campaign, and one survey less than a week before the election put him an 'astonishing' twenty-four points ahead.[32] Although his final lead was much more modest, such findings gave Callaghan the luxury of deciding whether or not to stay on as Labour leader after the defeat. For his party, his decision to persevere was hardly less damaging than his electoral miscalculation; but at least when he relinquished the party leadership in November 1980 – to be replaced, suitably enough, by Michael Foot, who had done most to persuade him against an autumn 1978 election – he could feel that he had salvaged some of his dignity.

CONCLUSION

If James Callaghan had called a general election in the autumn of 1978, he could have taken a leading role in a Labour campaign which would have run along similar lines to that of 1970. Like Harold

Wilson in that election, he could have tried to reassure voters that although the road had sometimes been rocky, Britons had no reason to doubt the competence of the incumbent government. Wilson, of course, had called an early election and had been defeated. The same fate might have befallen Callaghan; but at least he would have fulfilled his duty to the party he led by giving it the best possible chance of success, and even on the most pessimistic prospectus offered by the opinion polls of August 1978 the Conservatives would have lacked the parliamentary cushion that allowed Mrs Thatcher to embark on her economic experiment.

Before calling the 1970 general election, Wilson took extensive soundings within his party.[33] By taking the decision to delay the election on his own authority, after pressing for a 5 per cent pay norm which even his loyal supporters thought over-ambitious, Callaghan had effectively distanced himself from his party and the mainstream labour movement. If things had gone well for his government in subsequent months, he might have been able to effect a reconciliation of sorts and run an orthodox campaign as part of a team. Instead, adverse developments condemned him to bypass the party's policy-making machinery and devise a 'presidential' electoral strategy along with a small team of special advisors and PR operatives.

Callaghan was staking everything on the hope that in an era of electoral volatility, in which voters would be basing their decisions on short-term factors, he could exude an aura of governing competence which would be sufficiently impressive not just to see off Mrs Thatcher's challenge but also to efface memories of proven incompetence, particularly the Winter of Discontent. Previous accounts of voting behaviour had allocated only marginal importance to public perceptions of party leaders, compared to long-term factors such as social class.[34] Evidently Callaghan had perceived that party leaders were far more important than academics supposed; but in effect he was resting his hopes of re-election on the possibility that the popularity of specific individuals could trump all other influences over voting behaviour. This was not entirely fanciful, in that the electorate now seemed ready to base its decisions on short-term factors rather than the old bonds of social class. But in 1979 there were plenty of other transient influences pushing members of Labour's old voting base towards the Tories (or the Liberals, or abstention) – and a more aggressive anti-Labour press, epitomised by *The Sun*, was more than willing to assist this decisive shift in British voting behaviour.

Even when the election campaign seemed to be going well for Callaghan, for understandable reasons he continued to be haunted by the avoidable miscalculation of August 1978. This explains his allusion to the possibility that a 'sea change' had occurred in British politics, favouring Thatcher and her party. He would have known that his interlocutor, Bernard Donoughue, was an acute academic observer of political developments who would remember the remark and record it for posterity. When such seismic shifts occur, Callaghan claimed, 'there is nothing you can do' – that is to say, the individual is impotent when confronted with nameless historic forces.[35] In reality, Callaghan's maladroit personal decisions had helped to ensure a protracted period of political dominance by another individual, while the non-Thatcherite majority split their votes between Labour and the SDP–Liberal alliance which his mistakes had done so much to create. It took Callaghan's party fourteen years after he laid down the leadership to decide that its best chances of returning to office lay in the choice of another centre-right populist.

NOTES

1 The author is grateful to David Denver and Richard Johnson for their comments on this chapter, although any remaining errors of fact or interpretation are his own responsibility.

2 Hansard, HC Deb, 25 July 1978, vol. 954, col. 1393.

3 B. Donoughue, *Downing Street Diary: Volume Two – With James Callaghan in No. 10* (London: Hutchinson, 2008), p. 249.

4 *Ibid.*, p. 250.

5   *Ibid.*, pp. 371, 483–4; B. Donoughue, *The Heat of the Kitchen* (London: Politico, 2003), p. 277, where the quotation does not mention Thatcher.

6   K. Morgan, *Callaghan: A Life* (Oxford: Oxford University Press, 1997), p. 638.

7   D. Leonard, 'The Labour Campaign', in H. R. Penniman (ed.), *Britain at the Polls, 1979* (Washington DC: American Enterprise Institute, 1981), pp. 95–6; Morgan, *Callaghan*, p. 636.

8   Leonard, 'The Labour Campaign', p. 96.

9   H. Young, *The Hugo Young Papers* (London: Allen Lane, 2008), p. 123.

10 Morgan, *Callaghan*, p. 638.

11 *Ibid.*, pp. 639–42.

12 T. Benn, *Conflicts of Interest: Diaries 1977–80* (London: Hutchinson, 1990), p. 334.

13 Leonard, 'The Labour Campaign', p. 97.

14 B. Donoughue, *Downing Street Diary: Volume Two – With James Callaghan in No. 10* (London: Pimlico, 2009), p. 359.

15 Morgan, *Callaghan*, p. 644.

16 M. Foley, *The Rise of the British Presidency* (Manchester: Manchester University Press, 1993).

17 J. Callaghan, Leader's Speech, Labour Party Conference, 1978: http://www.britishpoliticalspeech.org/speech-archive.htm?speech=176

18 Benn, *Conflicts of Interest*, pp. 356, 355.

19 Donoughue, *Downing Street Diary: Volume Two*, p. 370.

20 Morgan, *Callaghan*, p. 661.

21 Benn, *Conflicts of Interest*, pp. 480–84, 487.

22 M. Scammell, *Designer Politics: How Elections are Won* (Basingstoke: Macmillan, 1995), p. 78.

23 C. Moore, *Margaret Thatcher: The Authorized Biography, Volume One: Not for Turning* (London: Allen Lane, 2013), pp. 402–3.

24 Donoughue, *Downing Street Diary: Volume Two*, p. 477.

25 M. Pinto-Duschinsky, 'Manifestos, Speeches and the Doctrine of the Mandate', in Penniman, *Britain at the Polls, 1979*, p. 309.

26 W. Shawcross, *Rupert Murdoch: Ringmaster of the Information Circus* (London: Pan Books, 1993), p. 154.

27 Donoughue, *Downing Street Diary: Volume Two*, p. 481.

28 I. Crewe, 'Why the Conservatives Won', in Penniman, *Britain at the Polls, 1979*, pp. 284–7.

29 R. Rose, 'Towards "Normality": Public Opinion Polls in the 1979 General Election', in Penniman, *Britain at the Polls, 1979*, p. 198.

30 'How Britain Voted Since October 1974', Ipsos MORI: https://www.ipsos.com/ipsos-mori/en-uk/how-britain-voted-october-1974

31 R. Johnson, 'Regional Variations in the 1979 General Election Results for England', *Area* (1979), vol. 11, no. 4.

32 Crewe, 'Why the Conservatives won', pp. 273–4.

33 H. Wilson, *The Governance of Britain* (London: Weidenfeld & Nicolson, 1976), p. 38.

34 D. Butler and D. Stokes, *Political Change in Britain*, 2nd edn (London: Macmillan, 1974).

35 Donoughue, *Downing Street Diary: Volume Two*, p. 484.

PART TWO
POLICIES

7

ECONOMIC POLICY

Wyn Grant

O N T H E D A Y T H A T he became Prime Minister, James Callaghan was given a 'state of play' report by the Cabinet Secretary
on the major issues likely to face him in the coming months. Unsurpris-
ingly, there was a significant emphasis on economic policy. The opening
message was that there was considerable uncertainty about the economic prospects.[1] Despite the confidence expressed in Treasury forecasts,
'in fact, nothing is certain. The world has been through the worst boom
and slump and the worst inflation since the war. We currently have a
major imbalance in our economy but we don't know what will happen
when the world and United Kingdom recovery gets fully into stride.'

Nevertheless, the overall prospect was a miserable one: 'The
Treasury forecast is that the United Kingdom recovery in the short
term and the medium term presents a depressing prospect: employment, inflation and the balance of payments all look very gloomy.'
Depreciating the currency was one policy option,

...but the recent experience of a sharp fall in sterling showed that the international reaction to a major depreciation might well be severe. Thus it looks as if all the measures which might possibly be used to help the British economy through this prospective very bad period of imbalance would be very painful and damaging internationally.

The going was 'likely to be very rough indeed'. However, Treasury advice seemed to offer little help:

> We are sailing in a largely unknown sea, and it could be damaging to take decisions based largely on the Treasury's computer prediction of where we shall end up if the economy behaves as it has done in the past. The moral of this is probably that Ministers should avoid any radical changes of economic policy in the next few months (during which the Treasury could again be shown to be too pessimistic) but should monitor the evolving situation very carefully indeed.

It may be that 'wait and see' was the best advice that could be offered, but it was not very helpful as a guide to action for which there would be continuous political pressure.

Incomes policy was at the centre of economic policy, and its political accompaniment was neo-corporatism – in particular, the need to gain the consent of the TUC to enact economic policy decisions. This was exemplified by the importance attached to the so-called 'Neddy Six', the group of key trade union leaders with seats on the National Economic Development Council. 'The Cabinet heard this morning how the Chancellor hopes to present his Budget to do as much as possible to obtain TUC support for a stringent pay policy.' However, it was admitted that 'there is a delicate path to be trodden here'. It was thought that the increase in the Retail Price Index by the end of 1976 would be down to 10–12 per cent, 'nearly, but not quite, on target'. In fact, the outturn was 16.5 per cent.

Discussions on prices and incomes policy were expected to

continue 'with increasing intensity through April and May'. It was considered that 'a successful outcome is crucial both for the fight against inflation and for tackling the medium-term difficulties. Discussion will be needed on two levels (a) the broad issue of the level of the norm; (b) the more detailed issues like exceptions, increments, low pay.' Officials were to prepare papers on these issues which would then be discussed with the TUC.

However, there were also problems with the other corner of the tripartite triangle, the employers' organisation, the CBI. 'The Price Code is under attack by the CBI who wish to see it abolished; but some continuing price restraint will be essential if the TUC is to be persuaded to play ball on incomes.'

It was hoped to devise some sleight of hand through adjustments to the Price Code 'which would permit the higher profits to be earned which will be necessary if industry is to be able to finance – and have a motive for undertaking – the new investment on which our ability to benefit from an upturn (and thus to increase employment) depends'. A further complication was higher incomes, where delay in implementing recommendations of the Top Salaries Review Body was making it difficult to fill vacancies on the boards of nationalised industries and in a range of public sector posts with satisfactory candidates.

It was thought that public expenditure, in line with prospects for the economy, had to be kept 'more or less flat, so that it takes a decreasing proportion of national output, leaving resources available for investment and for exports'. Almost as an afterthought it was noted that 'Ministers may need to consider during the year the degree of success which attends the new technique of imposing cash limits on a wide range of public spending'. They placed a limit on the net amount of cash that could be spent on a particular service within a financial year. This turned out to be a very effective means of restraining public expenditure. It also had the political advantage of pushing awkward decisions down to programme managers.

THE CHANGE IN POLICY DIRECTION
AND THE IMF CRISIS

Callaghan did not particularly want to get involved in economic
policy. After leaving office he told Peter Hennessy:

> I hadn't intended to get myself immersed in economic affairs. I'd had
> enough trouble with that when I was Chancellor of the Exchequer,
> and we had a very experienced Chancellor in Denis Healey ... I just
> thought my job would be to support him and allow him to get on with
> it while I did other things.[2]

This hope was not, of course, realistic, and as Callaghan later admitted, 'the economy is always there, like Banquo's ghost, to haunt you.'[3]

The relationship between the Prime Minister and the Chancellor
is crucial to the successful conduct of economic policy, and Callaghan
and Healey, despite certain disagreements, had an effective working
relationship, with Callaghan always supporting his Chancellor when
the chips were down. Callaghan's original intention had been that,
at a later date, 'Healey and Crosland [the Foreign Secretary] would
swap jobs, a plan which was thwarted by Crosland's sudden death'.[4]
Healey for his part regarded Callaghan as 'the best of Britain's post-
war prime ministers after Attlee'.[5]

What Callaghan did realise was that the conventional Keynesian
orthodoxy no longer worked and there needed to be a new approach
to the conduct of economic policy. His speech to the Labour Party
conference in 1976, written by his son-in-law Peter Jay, who was a
convert to monetarism, contained some passages about the futility of
Keynesian demand management. He stated:

> We used to think you could spend your way out of a recession by
> cutting taxes and boosting Government spending. I tell you in all

candour that that option no longer exists, and in so far as it ever did exist, it only worked on each occasion since the war by injecting a larger dose of inflation into the economy followed by a higher level of unemployment as the next step.[6]

The change in the course of economic policy was embedded in the decisions taken in the IMF crisis of the autumn of 1976, which represented a defeat for the left of the Labour Party, although it subsequently emerged that the decisions taken were based on flawed and overly pessimistic forecasts. Having fallen below two dollars in March 1976 sterling continued to lose value in the summer, reaching a record low against the dollar in June. On 28 September, as the Chancellor and the Governor of the Bank of England arrived at Heathrow on their way to the annual IMF conference, it fell by a further 4.5 cents to $1.64. This was seen as a signal that the downward fall was out of control. Healey broke off his journey and on 29 September a formal application was made to the IMF for support amounting to $3.9 billion, the largest amount ever required of them. The IMF demanded heavy cuts in public expenditure and the budget deficit in return for the loan. 'Application to the Fund was … made on the basis that an agreement with the IMF was essential if Britain was to bridge its external financing gap, and while it was recognised that borrowing from the Fund would involve cuts, officials were in favour of them.'[7] Indeed, one interpretation of events is that Treasury officials used the crisis to advance their traditional policy remedy of public expenditure restraint.

An IMF team visited the UK in November, an event which the press and the Conservative opposition presented as a national humiliation worthy of a banana republic. These discussions were initially not very productive because civil servants were told to discuss only procedural and technical matters and not questions of policy. However, the gap between the two sides eventually narrowed, in large part because the IMF had a lower Public Sector Borrowing Requirement (PSBR) forecast and consideration was given to the implications of three different scenarios involving levels of the PSBR at £8.5 billion, £9 billion and £9.5 billion. The Prime Minister told the Cabinet towards the end of the month that

> the IMF now fully understood that the Cabinet was not convinced of the need for deflationary measures; and they understood the nature of the dilemma facing the government in which if the action taken was unduly severe the government would lose the present co-operation of the trade unions, whereas if it was too mild it would fail to carry conviction in the markets.[8]

It was evident that a number of Cabinet members were unhappy about being forced to either accept or reject proposals put forward jointly by the Prime Minister and the Chancellor and wanted to discuss a wider range of options. It was felt that there should be an opportunity to consider papers setting out alternative proposals, including the more radical Alternative Economic Strategy which had already been discussed in the Cabinet committee on economic strategy. This was based on the ideas of the 'New Cambridge School', which, in effect, advocated pulling Britain out of the international financial system and imposing substantial import controls to create a siege economy.

On the one hand, the government had to satisfy the IMF, and more importantly the markets, for which an IMF agreement was a Good Housekeeping seal of approval. On the other hand, it had to arrive at a package that could secure the support of the Labour Party and the House of Commons.

> On the former count, it was argued that the alternative strategy was quite impracticable, and that it was essential to avoid negotiating the IMF into a package which the markets would reject as inadequate. On

the latter count it was argued that any package which involved cuts in public expenditure and a continuation of the rising trend in unemployment would not work, and would destroy the social contract.[9]

In a worst-case scenario, 'it was not impossible that the insistence of the IMF on hard terms could lead to the government losing office'. In terms of practical politics, this would seem to be an unlikely situation as it is difficult to see how it would come about. However, it could be used as an argument against waverers both in the Cabinet and the parliamentary party. Moreover, while a tough package might encounter resistance from the Labour Party, it might be more difficult to persuade them to accept a repeated series of smaller doses because the market was unconvinced by the adequacy of the initial measures. The underlying problem was that the country 'had been spending, and continued to spend, more than it earned. This was true of both the nation and the Government.'[10] In an open economy, spending more than was earned made the country dependent on foreign borrowing.

'It would be essential to convince the Government's supporters that these were facts of life which had to be faced.' Of course, for the opponents of a strategy of fiscal restraint, such an approach represented an uncritical application of market logic and a failure to consider more genuinely socialist approaches. What was evident was that the government was stuck between a rock and a hard place and, as so often is the case in government, there had to be a search for a least bad alternative. In his summing up of the 25 November Cabinet, the Prime Minister 'said that none of the courses facing the Cabinet was attractive or certain in its effect. In the following week they would have to decide which course was least unpalatable and least risky, and then seek the maximum support for it.'[11]

When Cabinet met in a key meeting on 1 December, the Prime Minister asked ministers to concentrate on the key strategic options, leaving the details for the following day. The Cabinet had four papers

before them: one by the Chancellor of the Exchequer; one by the
intellectually formidable Foreign Secretary, Tony Crosland; one by
the Energy Secretary, Tony Benn; and one by the Environment Secretary, Peter Shore. Callaghan's strategy throughout had been 'to sit
back and let the heavyweights talk themselves into exhaustion, acting
as a benevolent, unflappable umpire while they slugged it out'.[12] His
highly effective tactic in the Cabinet meeting was to let the dissenters
present their case, often digging a hole for themselves, and allow critical colleagues to come in and demolish their arguments.

Although his import control measures were more modest than
those advanced by Tony Benn, Shore quickly shot his bolt, losing
'all chance of support when he had to admit this would require at
least as much unemployment and as many spending cuts as the IMF
would demand'.[13] Moreover, Healey pointed out that it was a short-
term policy designed to last only until the balance of payments was
in surplus and involved all the short-term disadvantages without any
of the longer-term prospects of improvement. As for Tony Benn, 'a
siege economy of the kind envisaged by the Secretary of State for
Energy implied also a command economy, which was contrary to the
maintenance of the mixed economy to which the government was
committed'.[14]

Tony Crosland was the most formidable opponent and had a
stronger argument that the situation was already under control,
which indeed it was. The problem was that the markets didn't believe
it. Crosland's view was that the government should call what he saw
as the IMF's bluff and threaten a siege economy, withdrawing troops
from Germany and threatening to leave the EEC. The more dramatic
his suggestions, the less his Cabinet colleagues found them credible.
The Prime Minister had met Crosland privately and had also invited
him to a breakfast with West German Chancellor Helmut Schmidt,
who made it clear that he would not ask the IMF to change his position. While he enjoyed developing his arguments as an intellectual

exercise, Crosland was also a political realist and took the view that the Prime Minister and Chancellor could not be overridden on a central issue of economic policy. The political imperative was to keep the Cabinet together and Labour in power. Once he had capitulated, the Prime Minister and the Chancellor were able to secure the solution they favoured.

In his summing up, the Prime Minister said that 'it was clear that the majority were not in favour of adopting a strategy which would involve quota restrictions on imports; and that they would support the continuation of efforts to reach agreement with the IMF on the loan'. As for the political climate, 'he observed that in his view the state of the Labour Party was not, perhaps, as bad as some had suggested, and that there was a growing understanding of the situation which had to be faced and an increasing will to come together in a closer unity'.[15]

Callaghan had been uncertain throughout about the economic and political desirability of further public expenditure cuts and had cast about internationally for alternatives, although he came to realise that the United States and West Germany were not prepared to exert pressure on the IMF on Britain's behalf. When Cabinet met on 2 December, he admitted that 'he himself had earlier been uncertain what was the best course to adopt, but the time had now come to take decisions, and he had been asked to make his position clear'. In terms of the political costs, he believed

> that the country was better informed about the nature of the problems they faced than was sometimes thought ... The package proposed by the Chancellor of the Exchequer would probably have an adverse effect both on the government's supporters in the House of Commons; but not, he would judge, on the public at large.[16]

The Prime Minister made it clear that he supported £1 billion of public expenditure cuts (a further £500 million would be raised by selling BP shares, which was the first significant act of privatisation).

On the major issue before Cabinet, the reduction in the PSBR to be put in the offer to the IMF, the majority view was that there should be an adjustment of £1.5 billion in 1977–78 which would then lead to one of £2 billion in 1978–79. There was 'a group of members of Cabinet who regarded a £1.5 billion cut as unacceptable, and for whom some elements in the total would be repellent. That group, however, was in a minority'.[17] Further meetings had to be held to discuss the shape of the package, with the last one on 13 December, and it was then presented to Parliament on 15 December. Consultation with the TUC throughout the process had been constrained by the necessity to maintain secrecy, although discussions had been held with the General Secretary, Len Murray, on Privy Council terms. There were also discussions with Jack Jones of the Transport and General Workers' Union.

One thing that is evident is that Callaghan handled the Cabinet with patience and consummate skill, while also keeping the Parliamentary Labour Party and the TUC broadly in line amid much grumbling. He achieved all this without losing a single minister. He thus achieved a political victory and displayed his skill as a political tactician, although at the cost of damage to his government's reputation for economic competence.

One of the paradoxes was that 'in a sense, the whole affair was unnecessary'. Britain did not need to draw on the full loan from the IMF. 'The Treasury had grossly overestimated the PSBR, which would have fallen within the IMF's limit without any of the measures they prescribed.'[18] Nevertheless, 'the IMF and the money markets were looking for a change of spending policy on the Labour government's part and would have demanded reductions to an even lower figure even if the Treasury's forecast had been more realistic'.[19]

The IMF crisis did represent a significant change in economic policy and methodology that paved the way for the more radical changes introduced by the Thatcher government. There was less emphasis on full employment and social welfare as policy objectives and a greater emphasis on the control of inflation and public expenditure. Keynesianism was not abandoned, but its intellectual hegemony was significantly weakened. These changes were not the result of deliberate policy choices, but rather a measured response to the pressure and drift of events.

ECONOMIC RECOVERY

The period after the IMF crisis saw the beginning of a recovery in the economy which should have yielded a political dividend, although there was popular resentment at the compression of differentials brought about by incomes policy and the small gap between those on low earnings and those receiving social security benefits. The April 1977 budget was not received well, although it changed very little apart from making unpopular increases in taxes on cigarettes, petrol and vehicle excise duties. Its most distinctive feature was a pledge to cut the basic rate of income tax by 2 per cent if the unions agreed to a new pay policy, underlining the centrality of incomes policy to economic policy at the time, and the weight placed on the relationship with the trade unions.

Nevertheless, an extended period of stagnation, high inflation and large current external deficits which had lasted since the first oil crisis came to an end with an improvement in economic performance which began around mid-1977 and continued in 1978. Inflation fell back from a peak of 24 per cent in 1975 to 8 per cent in 1978. The minimum lending rate fell to just 5 per cent by October 1977, giving considerable relief on mortgage payments to those buying houses who, in any case, had seen the real value of the outstanding mortgage eroded by inflation. The value of the pound against the dollar increased from $1.70 in January 1977 to $1.93 at the end of the year. This is all too often seen as a measure of economic success, particularly in the financial services sector. In fact, manufacturing industry would have benefited from a lower pound giving a boost to exports. The government was, however, preoccupied with holding down inflation to which imported goods contributed and this perspective was reinforced by the preferences of the financial services sector.

With the improvement in the balance of payments and the fall in the rate of inflation, it was possible to modify economic policy in the latter part of 1977 to stimulate demand and reduce the high level of unemployment. Reflecting these policy measures, and the increased funds in the pockets of mortgage payers, domestic demand rose markedly in 1978. There was a particularly strong recovery in private consumption and investment and a continuous decline in unemployment. The potential inflationary effect of a sharp increase in average earnings was offset by a reduction in import prices as a result of currency appreciation and a fall in seasonal food prices. North Sea oil production came on stream at significant levels of output, making a positive contribution to the balance of payments. Demand management had to be tightened a little in 1978.

THE WINTER OF DISCONTENT

Incomes policies can work in the short run in an emergency as a means of restraining wage-driven inflation, as happened with the £6-a-week policy instituted in 1975. However, in the longer run, anomalies and distortions multiply and there are unintended consequences, such as the growth in the number of company cars in the 1970s. Unions resent the erosion of collective bargaining. Designing an exit strategy from an incomes policy is not an easy task and it was one that the Callaghan government approached in a mood of over-confidence, insulated from the realities of industrial politics.

The government had an economic justification for the 5 per cent pay limit they set in 1978. If the objective was to keep inflation down, and to ensure that it was not significantly higher than in competitor countries, then a 5 per cent limit meant that, after taking account of wage drift, actual increases should be around 8 per cent. This should make it possible to keep inflation down to single figures, although a second oil crisis was looming because of events in Iran. This could then be sold to the electorate as a political victory, demonstrating that Labour was the only party that could deliver a working relationship with the trade unions.

However, a number of obstacles stood in the way of this hoped-for achievement. Workers had seen a cut of 13 per cent in real wages since 1974. Union leaders were therefore not disposed to support another period of stringency, and the retirement of Jack Jones had deprived them of an authoritative voice who was often prepared to lend his decisive support to the government. However, even if the union leaders had been prepared to go along with the government's plans, there were limits to their ability to control a highly decentralised trade union movement. The shop stewards, the real authority on the shop floor, were in a militant frame of mind. There was particular discontent among public sector workers, for whom the pay policy had been more rigorously applied without any of the loopholes available in the private sector. Healey subsequently admitted that he had set the target too low: 'I think, if rather than going for 5 per cent, I had said single figures we would have had settlements of around 11 per cent.'[20]

After Ford workers had broken through the pay limit in the autumn, the government then permitted a generous settlement just before Christmas to BBC workers where a dispute had led to blank television screens. This was said to be the first time government policy had been influenced by the threat of the absence of *The Sound of Music* on Christmas Day. More worryingly, a series of strikes broke out in the public sector, including trouble on the railways, and the walk-outs of not only ambulance workers but, most notoriously, grave diggers in Liverpool. Rubbish piled high in the streets as refuse collectors withdrew their labour. 'Since most strike activity took place in the public services and in transport it created a degree of dislocation not felt since the 1947 fuel crisis.'[21] Parents had to cope with school closures created by a lack of oil for heating while they searched for petrol for their cars.

If the lived experience was bad enough, matters were not helped from a presentational point of view when Callaghan breezed back in January 1979 from the Guadeloupe Conference where he had been pictured enjoying the Caribbean sunshine while Britain froze in a cold winter and tried to cope with the absence of basic commodities. On his return Callaghan tried to be avuncular, but ended up sounding smug and self-satisfied, with no idea of the privations that the country had been experiencing. He never said 'Crisis? What crisis?', but the newspaper headline so aptly captured his mood that people came to believe that he had.

It may be that there was a sense in which the Winter of Discontent was a constructed or manufactured crisis, as Hay argues. It 'came to be understood in terms of a crisis of a state overloaded by the demands of sectional (union) interests'.[22] The advantage that the Callaghan government had been able to claim of an effective working relationship with the trade unions thus instead became a burden. An initial poor judgement was compounded by an inability to manage the crisis itself in a competent way, which damaged the government's reputation in relation to economic policy and more generally.

CONCLUSION

As Peter Hennessy notes, it 'was the economic factor which came swiftly to dominate the political, governmental and global weather systems that buffeted and shaped the Callaghan administration and its policies and which eventually led to the loss of office at the polls'.[23] There was, however, a lack of understanding at the time of the extent to which structural changes in the economy were causing economic and political disruption. Their impact was understood much later and, although they may have been unavoidable and necessary, the process of transition was painful.

The first of these was the shift from an industrial-based to a service-based economy. Manufacturing in England and Wales declined from around 38 per cent of jobs in 1961 to around 22 per cent in 1981. Those employed in manufacturing formed the bedrock of trade union membership and support for the Labour Party. When those with specific manufacturing skills lost their jobs, it was difficult for them to find alternative employment, certainly at a similar rate of pay.

The government's response to this challenge took the form of an industrial strategy largely based around sectoral schemes which in effect propped up or slowed the decline of industries that had poor prospects. A more ambitious policy might have sought to pursue the positive impact that generic technologies could have on manufac-turing industry, such as emergent information technology. It could also have invested more heavily in the labour force, providing it with new skills. However, manufacturing industry was seen in terms of the strengths of the past rather than new opportunities.

The second was the advent of globalisation. This was more diffi-cult to counter through national policy. One reason for the decline in manufacturing jobs in the 1970s was the emergence of newly indus-trialising countries in East Asia that could compete on costs for basic labour-intensive products (which were characteristics of much of British manufacturing) and were able to take advantage of the remov-al of tariff barriers under the General Agreement on Tariffs and Trade (GATT). If there was one lesson to be learned from the IMF crisis it was that Britain could not stand aside from international influences.

James Callaghan's conservative outlook did not equip him to

comprehend these changes and the new challenges they brought to economic policy, although not many other people did either. The alternative and more radical economic policy proposals did not get much of a hearing, although in their more moderate form as advanced by Crosland and Shore, rather than Benn, they had merit. The Callaghan–Healey approach based on confidence and crowding out was not the only option, but it was crowded out politically by the Treasury and the Bank. The Treasury's policy preferences centred on fiscal restraint and they were able to frame the debate in these terms, making opportunistic use of the IMF crisis to advance their agenda. The Bank of England's conservative preferences were also influential.

Callaghan's approach to economic policy was essentially reactive, although he was open to advice and aware of the broad contours of a 'sea change' in economic policy. His approach was generally a cautious one which allowed him to deploy his skills as a political tactician. He placed great store on relations with the trade unions in line with his reputation as 'keeper of the cloth cap', and made no move away from incomes policy, which eventually was his undoing. He was not in command of economic policy, nor did he particularly wish to be, but he showed some (though not enough) capacity to move away from inherited orthodoxies. It was poor political judgement rather than a lack of understanding of economics that brought his tenure as Prime Minister to an end.

NOTES

1   These and subsequent quotations are from National Archives, PREM 16/908, 5 April 1976.
2   P. Hennessy, *The Prime Minister* (London: Allen Lane, 2000), p. 387.
3   Quoted in *ibid.*, p. 382.
4   D. Leonard, *A Century of Premiers* (Basingstoke: Palgrave, 2005), p. 293.
5   D. Healey, *The Time of My Life* (London: Penguin, 1990), p. 447.
6   *Report of the 75th Annual Conference of the Labour Party* (London: Labour Party, 1976), p. 188.

7   C. Rogers, 'The Politics of Economic Policy Making in Britain: A Re-assessment of the 1976 IMF Crisis', *Politics and Policy* (2009), vol. 37, no. 5, pp. 971–94, 983.

8   National Archives, CAB 128/60/12, Limited Circulation Annex, CM(76) 34th Conclusions, Minute 3.

9   *Ibid.*, p. 2.

10 *Ibid.*, p. 3.

11 *Ibid.*, p. 4.

12 D. Sandbrook, *Seasons in the Sun: The Battle for Britain 1974–1979* (London: Allen Lane, 2012), p. 490.

13 Healey, *The Time of My Life*, p. 431.

14 National Archives, CAB 128/60/13, CM(76) 35th Conclusions, Limited Circulation Annex, p. 6.

15 *Ibid.*, p. 7.

16 National Archives, CAB 128/60/14, CM(76) 35th Conclusions, p. 3.

17 *Ibid.*, p. 7.

18 Healey, *The Time of My Life*, p. 432.

19 Hennessy, *The Prime Ministers*, p. 387.

20 Quoted in H. Davies, *The Chancellors' Tales* (Cambridge: Polity Press, 2006), p. 61.

21 K. Jefferys, *Finest and Darkest Hours: The Decisive Events in British Politics, From Churchill to Blair* (London: Atlantic, 2015), p. 203.

22 C. Hay, 'Chronicles of a Death Foretold: The Winter of Discontent and Construction of the Crisis of British Keynesianism', *Parliamentary Affairs* (2010), vol. 63, no. 3, pp. 446–70, p. 467.

23 Hennessy, *The Prime Minister*, p. 382.

8

INDUSTRIAL RELATIONS

Andrew Taylor

INTRODUCTION

THE CALLAGHAN GOVERNMENT'S IMPACT on industrial relations (defined as the institutions, norms and processes structuring and managing the workplace) was nothing when compared to the impact of industrial relations on the government. Callaghan did not add to the Wilson government's 1974 Trade Union and Labour Relations Act (TULRA) and the 1975 Employment Protection Act (EPA), key components of the social contract, but 'our main claim to power is that we can deal with the unions to curb inflation. If we cannot do that, then we shall be thrown out.'[1] By the time Callaghan became Prime Minister in April 1976 the social contract was under strain, and he relied on his close personal relations with the TUC and union leaders, combining appeals to the solidarity of TIGMOO ('this great movement of ours') and concessions with warnings about the threat from the Conservative opposition.

Permeating his approach were two assumptions: first, that union leaders controlled their members; and second, that when faced with the 'facts', they and their members would support a Labour government. Both these assumptions proved unfounded.

THE KEEPER OF THE CLOTH CAP

In a peroration to his first Cabinet meeting as Prime Minister, Callaghan expressed the wish that his government 'work very closely with the Party and the Trades Union Congress'; a positive working relationship with the unions was essential for the government's survival and success.[2] Callaghan believed he was in a unique position to retain union support and cooperation. Chapter 2 of Morgan's biography is titled *Union Man* and this appellation is central to Callaghan's behaviour as Prime Minister.[3] Employed as an Inland Revenue officer, Callaghan became an activist in the Association of Tax Officers and was elected a national assistant general secretary of the newly created Inland Revenue Staff Federation (IRSF) in 1936.[4] Morgan writes: 'His experience with the IRSF left Callaghan with an instinctive commitment to negotiation, arbitration and conciliation, and a resistance to strike action. He developed early on an intuitive bargaining style, adapted later in life to running government departments or handling international conferences.'[5]

Elected to Parliament in 1945, Callaghan was not, and did not see himself as, a union 'voice' in the party. This changed when he was elected party treasurer in 1967, holding this position until he became Prime Minister, and also thereby becoming an *ex-officio* member of Labour's NEC. The party treasurer was traditionally regarded, given Labour's historic reliance on trade union money, as having a special role vis-à-vis the unions. In the Wilson Cabinet Callaghan was – ironically, given future events – sceptical about incomes policy and he supported the TUC's arguments in support of voluntarism in industrial relations. Voluntarism

> ...reflected a belief that it is better in the long run for the law to interfere as little as possible in the settlement of questions arising between employers and workmen ... Parliament has long been committed to the view that the best means of settling such questions in voluntary collective bargaining and has equipped government in various ways to support, assist and promote collective bargaining.[6]

Callaghan's ascension to the role of 'the keeper of the cloth cap' came with his opposition to the Labour government's industrial relations reform proposals derived from 'In Place of Strife'.[7] Callaghan's stance, as reported by Richard Crossman, was unequivocal: 'I think it absolutely wrong and unnecessary to do this.'[8] Callaghan believed Barbara Castle and her supporters (including Harold Wilson) were ignorant of workplace realities and Callaghan's opposition presaged a split in the movement, but he quickly metamorphosed into the 'common sense' unity figure, thereby strengthening his position in the party and convincing many union leaders (as well as himself) of his special understanding. However, in March 1969, as Home Secretary, Callaghan contemplated how to neutralise left-wing union leaders Jack Jones (the TGWU general secretary) and Hugh Scanlon (the AUEW general secretary), dubbed 'the terrible twins', who were to become key figures in the social contract and the Callaghan government.[9] Under the second Wilson government, Barbara Castle (unceremoniously sacked by Callaghan when Prime Minister) complained about Callaghan's 'Cassandra act' and his belief in his 'special' relationship with the unions, which, he claimed, allowed him to be frank with them, warning them of growing middle-class disenchantment with their behaviour and their 'real fear of the power of the unions'.[10] However, as Callaghan told the House of Commons, 'I have always insisted that whatever the difficulties in a democratic society like ours we shall not succeed without the support of the trade unions…'[11]

Callaghan remained convinced of the unions' centrality to the Labour Party and government and of the necessity of a positive relationship with the TUC, and Jack Jones conceded Callaghan 'had a greater understanding than most ministers of the difficulties facing trade union officials'.[12] Callaghan's approach was captured by Tony Benn, the Energy Secretary, in a meeting with Joe Gormley, the NUM president, discussing a potential miners' wage claim:

> Jim said, 'perhaps we had better tell your chaps not to press for it, and rely on their loyalty to carry the ballot against.' Joe said, 'it was a very narrow ballot last year.' Jim said, 'perhaps you're going to bring a third government down … perhaps you'll bring us down.'
> 'We're politicians, we don't want to do that…'[13]

However, he failed to recognise, or preferred to ignore, the scale of the changed relationship between union leaders and their members. Callaghan relied on sentiments of solidarity, personal persuasion and self-interest to sustain cooperation but he was conscious that appealing to solidarity was a wasting asset to be deployed carefully.[14] In both 1968–69 and as Prime Minister, his stance 'relied on the unions behaving as they had done under the loyalist regime of Deakin and Lawther [in the 1940s and 1950s], and on reforming themselves, and their leaders arousing the same kind of deference…' and 'he had taken his authority over the union leaders … for granted, and assumed that respect could be equally assumed from the rank and file. It was a very serious miscalculation, from which the roots of his downfall could be eventually traced.'[15]

In his memoirs Jones recognises Callaghan's desire to work with the unions: 'More approachable than Harold Wilson, he had a friendly attitude that broke down barriers. On the whole he was well liked by most of us in the unions...'[16] Personal chemistry, however, could only go so far. In February 1977, for example, David Basnett of the GMWU warned Bernard Donoughue that union leaders 'were having great difficulties in holding the rank and file. He does not see how a deal can be made', and later Basnett opined that 'one could almost physically see the power ebbing away from Jack Jones and Hugh Scanlon', key government supporters.[17] The problems facing Callaghan's government were worsened by the structural fragmentation of the unions and industrial relations. In 1978 the Cabinet noted:

> There was support for the government's policy amongst the trade union rank and file generally and the problem often lay with the extent to which union power had fallen, or been given to shop stewards who were not in line with the thinking of either the rank and file of that of senior union leaders.[18]

The Donovan Commission had identified two industrial relations systems, the *formal* (embodied in official institutions) and *informal* (produced by actual behaviour), which, when combined with multi-unionism and the rise of shop stewards, led to a decline in industry-wide bargaining and a reduction in union leaders' power over members, producing fragmented bargaining that proved highly resistant to external influence.[19] A theme in Jack Jones's memoirs is of Labour politicians failing to grasp the realities of shop-floor organisation, which led ministers to have unreasonable and unrealistic expectations of what union leaders could deliver. Equally, ministers argued union leaders (and their members) had an imperfect understanding of the pressures on the government. Callaghan believed the problem was that 'the influence of the TUC with the government had increased at a faster pace than its influence with their own member unions', with the result that the unions (and employers) 'were [not] able to practise a form of self-discipline for a period long enough to

have a lasting effect'.[20] Hence the importance of the TUC–Labour
Party Liaison Committee (TUCLPLC) and the social contract to
both the government and the TUC.[21]

Confronted by the tension between the formal and informal industrial relations systems, Callaghan's influence as Prime Minister was
strongest in the formal system where he relied on his personal political
relationships with trade union leaders.[22] Donoughue sees Callaghan's
speech to the 1978 TUC (the one including the infamous Vesta Victoria
song) as a clear example of Callaghan's self-image vis-à-vis the unions
and his determination to exploit it: 'He wants to be personal, accessible,
a former trade union official and not a Prime Minister surrounded by
aides and civil servants.'[23] His original intention was to leave economic
management largely to Denis Healey (the Chancellor) and the TUC
to Michael Foot (the Employment Secretary) but his identifying the
'supreme importance' of agreement with the unions on inflation drew
Callaghan into the day-to-day political management of the TUC. This
involvement became so extensive that Callaghan lamented in February
1979: 'I spend 80 per cent of my time on pay…'[24]

Particularly important to Callaghan were the 'Neddy Six', the
six members of the TUC General Council who sat on the National Economic Development Council (NEDC) and constituted the
TUC's 'inner Cabinet'. As Prime Minister, Callaghan instituted
small working dinners monthly that continued throughout his government. Originally composed of Jack Jones (TGWU), Hugh Scanlon (AUEW), David Basnett (GMWU), Geoffrey Drain (NALGO),
Alf Allen (USDAW) and Len Murray (TUC General Secretary),
the Neddy Six met primarily with Denis Healey, Michael Foot and
Callaghan. The meetings 'gave Ministers the chance to explain our
problems and prospects, and the "Neddy Six" the opportunity to
respond and tell us where the shoe was pinching'.[25] As time went on
it became increasingly difficult for élite-level meetings or Callaghan's
appeals to solidarity to deliver union support.

On the day after the 1977 TGWU biennial conference called for a return to free collective bargaining, Callaghan told the Cabinet he still hoped for agreement and that Jones and Scanlon would 'continue to do their best to prevent the situation getting out of hand'.[26] When a modus vivendi was put together, Callaghan confessed to having been 'impressed by the air of sobriety and realism amongst the trade union leaders ... and this gave some assurance that the policy would succeed, despite the undoubted militancy of some trade union members'.[27] In November 1978, the government negotiated an agreement on pay with the TUC Economic Committee which was subsequently rejected by the General Council (described by Benn as 'a real kick in the teeth for the corporate state') but the Cabinet – including the Prime Minister – believed the agreement's value lay not in its *content* but in its *existence*:

> It was worth having because it kept the special relationship with the TUC and meant that we could take on an individual rogue union without taking on the whole TUC. Most important is that it provides the basis on which the TUC can stay in contact with the government ... enabling it not to support individual unions in conflict with the government and committing it to further talks on long-term incomes policy.[28]

Despite the General Council's rejection, Callaghan nonetheless deemed it essential that nothing be said or done that 'implied that the TUC were being shut out of the government's counsels', decreeing that 'every effort should be made to reassure the TUC that the government still valued and wished to maintain the informal working relationship which had served well in the past'.[29] Even in the depths of the Winter of Discontent, he strove to convey the message that current difficulties did not constitute a fundamental shift (though he thought somewhat differently in private), telling the Cabinet:

that the balance of power between employers and trade unions had shifted significantly in the last 10 years. The only way to deal with the new situation was by co-operation with the unions. The [TUC] must be brought to recognise that a new agreement with the government was essential, if they were to avoid having their powers greatly reduced by an incoming Conservative government.[30]

Convinced there was no practical alternative to the 'tripartism-lite' of post-war British politics, his chief difficulty was that 'the corporate relationship, negotiated in private conclave ... seemed both ineffective and profoundly undemocratic'.[31] This relationship's weakness was a repeated theme in Callaghan's career, but in the absence of an alternative he had no option but to try to revivify a relationship careering towards disaster. Callaghan was conscious that other countries managed their industrial relations differently; he was, for example, impressed with the West German model, based on co-determination and social partnership.[32] The Callaghan government sponsored two initiatives – industrial democracy and a concordat with the TUC – that hint at his diagnosis of the 'industrial relations problem', while their failure points to the limitations of 'tripartism-lite'.

INDUSTRIAL DEMOCRACY

Industrial democracy was an original element of the social contract and in September 1975 the government appointed a commission of inquiry under Lord Bullock. The commission was soon perceived to be running into 'lots of trouble' and seemed 'fated to fail from the beginning'; it reported in June 1977.[33] The majority report recommended companies with 2,000-plus employees elect worker representatives (solely by union members – 'the single channel') to the main board; shareholders would have equal representation (the

$2x+y$ formula), with an independent group holding the balance (the minority report, written by the commissions' three industrialists, proposed instead a second tier board elected by all employees). The government accepted the majority report, which had been endorsed by Jack Jones and partly written by Dave Lea, the secretary of the TUC economic department, and Lea stressed Bullock's wider importance: 'After the cuts there is so little left of the social contract ... We must give it a positive and fair wind,' but in Cabinet, Callaghan described the report as an 'explosive political issue'.[34] The Conservatives were hostile; the CBI opposed, and despite welcoming the report the TUC was not united. Neither was the Cabinet. Edmund Dell, the Industry Secretary, for example, opposed Bullock, fearing union-dominated industrial democracy would damage business confidence and investment. Callaghan, who sympathised with Dell, felt his only option was further consultation. Callaghan correctly described the issue as explosive, but industrial democracy was part of the social contract and so he proposed 'to make it clear that the government is committed ... to a radical extension of industrial democracy ... and to the essential role of trade unions in this process'. His professed intention was 'a fundamental change which should make a major contribution to an improvement in labour relations and industrial efficiency'.[35] Tony Benn reports, however, that Callaghan feared Bullock 'would be like the Tory Industrial Relations Act. [Callaghan] was afraid it would cause polarisation.'[36] It did.

Board representation was the missing link in the architecture of the unions' integration into the structures of industrial politics. At the workplace level, integration had been promoted by the growing autonomy of workplace organisation, and traditional union participation in policy-making had been enhanced by the social contract, so the extension of union influence at the board level would give unions a significant presence at all levels of the power structure. Employers saw it as a major infringement of the right to manage, and control, unlike wages, was non-negotiable. Lord Watkinson, the CBI president, made it clear at the NEDC that the CBI 'could not accept the majority report ... legislation would be divisive and unworkable and would prevent economic growth...'[37] The responsibility for preparing the government's proposals passed to Shirley Williams as Callaghan feared that Dell's proposals, which largely abandoned Bullock, would antagonise the TUC. Dell, Williams and Callaghan were concerned, however, about any proposals' impact on business and investor confidence; Benn argued the fundamental question to be addressed was 'how to handle the increased power of the unions', and he identified three ways. First, reduce union power by increasing unemployment; second, head it off by participation, which he thought was window-dressing; and third, by 'shifting the balance of power and responsibility in favour of labour', the original intention of the social contract, which meant implementing Bullock in full.[38] Over the next year a Cabinet committee consulted and prepared a draft White Paper, but a consensus between the CBI and TUC was impossible as industrial democracy was a zero-sum issue: 'To satisfy one would mean the rejection of the other...'[39]

While adhering to the 'single channel', but with safeguards, Callaghan favoured a voluntary system, concluding his government 'would not force employers to move down the road of industrial democracy if they did not wish to do so'. Characteristically, he believed compromise was still possible. Some in Cabinet felt conceding to the CBI would antagonise the TUC, 'so every effort should be made to reduce the prospect of criticism from the TUC which could be much more damaging politically'.[40] The TUC, however, 'rejected the Prime Minister's suggestions of a compromise, with some modest reforming legislation, demanding all or nothing. So it is nothing.' Benn had earlier dismissed the government's proposals as 'a corporatist huddle'.[41] Williams had concluded that any 'arrangements for industrial democracy should be consistent with the established system of collective representation in British industry', and the resulting White Paper, 'Industrial Democracy', shifted dramatically away from Bullock. Further progress was ended by the Winter of Discontent and the general election.[42]

THE CONCORDAT

In November 1978, the government and the TUC finally agreed a joint statement on pay. The negotiations had been 'very long and very tough', and the TUC conceded no ground on the government's 5 per cent wage increase target, but ministers hoped to persuade the TUC to issue guidance on pay to negotiators and further meetings were arranged on, inter alia, prices, low pay and public sector comparability. 'If obtained, it would mean the TUC was moving into a position of helpful neutrality [but] it would be represented by their opponents as a sell-out to the unions.'[43] Approved by the TUC economic committee in the morning, the General Council in the afternoon split 14–14 (two government supporters were absent; one was on holiday) and the chair, Tom Jackson (UPW), was forced to declare the motion lost. Thereafter events slid inexorably into the Winter of Discontent.[44]

Confronted by wage dispute after wage dispute, Callaghan struggled to maintain relations with the TUC while remaining committed to pay restraint, although these seemed incompatible as initiative lay with individual unions, not the TUC. Nevertheless, meetings with the TUC continued. At Cabinet on 18 January 1979 Callaghan reported on the meetings with Len Murray and members of the General Council. These had focused on identifying common ground and the coming election, where it was apparent union power would be a major – if not *the* – issue, but this created an opportunity 'to persuade the unions to adopt a more co-operative attitude in their own interests'. A code of practice on picketing was agreed with Len Murray and Moss Evans but the TGWU had little authority as 'negotiations were conducted by a series of regional committees which were not wholly within the control of the union leaders'.[45] During January, as the crisis deepened, the prospect of some form of agreement beyond pay increased in likelihood. On 29 January the General Council offered six items for discussion, 'without moving too far away from the present pay policy, without any promise of a new [pay] norm, but with assurances about union conduct of negotiations to ensure a period of industrial calm, and a plan for reducing inflation 5 per cent by the spring of 1982'.[46]

On 1 February Callaghan circulated the draft text of an agreement. On pay it was described as 'deeply disappointing', but greater positivity was believed likely on a second agreement dealing with industrial relations. There was, however, evidence of straw-grasping – phrases such as 'still some chance of a useful outcome', 'useful passages', 'phrases on which it might be possible to build' were highlighted as positive results – but serious industrial disruption continued.[47] Callaghan welcomed the talks but conceded any agreement would not be 'worth a lot … But we cannot afford *not* to have it', and described the eventual document as crucial not just for the immediate situation but for the next three years, seeing in it the potential for a new relationship with the unions.[48] Critics dismissed it as an élite stitch-up with little wider significance. The statement, written largely by Dave Lea of the TUC and Kenneth Stowe, Callaghan's principal private secretary, was dubbed 'the concordat', the 'social contract Mk II' and the 'St Valentine's Day agreement' (it was published on 14 February) in preference to its inelegant official title. Callaghan saw it as an opportunity to re-launch the government–TUC relationship, believing it 'represented a favourable outcome' and possibly a new way of conducting industrial politics.[49] It contained two key proposals intended to align the formal and informal industrial relations systems: a tripartite national economic assessment, influenced by West German practice, that sought to promote an economic consensus; and second, a permanent comparability commission to de-politicise public sector pay bargaining. This emerged in March 1979 as the Clegg Commission. Given the climate in which it was launched, comment was dismissive: it had been 'rushed out to placate an electorate turned sour by a wave of post-income policy strikes'; Mrs Thatcher described it as a 'boneless wonder', the CBI as 'too little, too late', and the TUC greeted it with a lack of enthusiasm.[50] Though superficially pleasing, and inspired by electoral considerations, its fourteen pages articulated a continued belief in tripartism and the value of a close government–TUC relationship. Both were fundamental to Callaghan's world-view, but putting aside the temper of the times, which Callaghan conceded was against this style of politics, its inescapable weakness was that it gave no intimation as to how, or why, it would find acceptance in the workplace.[51]

CONCLUSIONS

In February 1979 Callaghan told Tony Benn 'he was more depressed as a trade unionist now about the future of this country than he had been for fifty years. He never believed it would come to this.'[52] The final months of his government signalled the demise of the post-war political regime – what I have termed 'tripartism-lite' – and the traditional mode of British social democracy. In his memoirs, Callaghan captured this shift thus:

> In my youth we used words like 'fellowship' and 'solidarity' to express ... the ethical basis of our belief in socialism. Socialism should concern itself with the weak and under privileged [but] we were always conscious that the idealism of the Labour Movement could come into conflict with its materialistic aspect – but we claimed it was the aim of socialism to reconcile the two.[53]

Callaghan's difficulties were exacerbated by this conflict and by the structural tensions inherent in the co-existence of (and overlap between) the formal and informal industrial relations systems that neither the Labour movement's concept of solidarity, nor the style of governance, could hope to bridge. Callaghan's rise, Morgan writes, 'was a perfect model of traditional Labour and the kind of region-al/industrial solidarity which Callaghan embodied'.[54] Callaghan's understanding of solidarity and governance was formed in an ear-lier era and retained a strong faith in the unions' collective common sense and the ultimate victory of consensus politics. Both relied on, in this case, reaching an accommodation with senior union leaders who were then expected to deliver their members. Many observers comment on the co-existence of, first, a hard-headed appreciation that his government's fate would be determined by the unions; and second, an optimism that, in the end, the traditional solidarity would be maintained. These same observers describe Callaghan in the latter part of his premiership as depressed and even angry, which, given the foundations of his political life, is hardly surprising.

Callaghan was well aware of the challenge to his government posed by industrial relations, but tradition and circumstance meant he could do little to mitigate that challenge. Aspects of his govern-ment – industrial democracy and the concordat – hint of different ways of organising and conducting industrial politics. Both of these efforts were stillborn because of the temper of the times and the con-tradictions inherent in British social democracy and the system of industrial relations.

NOTES

1   B. Donoughue, *Downing Street Diary, Volume Two – With James Callaghan in No. 10* (London: Jonathan Cape 2008), p. 179 – entry for 18 April 1977. Bernard Donoughue was head of the Downing Street Policy Unit from December 1976 until May 1979.

2   National Archives, CAB 128/59, Cabinet Conclusions, 13 April 1976. Callaghan was a member of the General and Municipal Workers Union (GMWU).

3 K. Morgan, *Callaghan: A Life* (Oxford: Oxford University Press, 1997).

4 For Callaghan's union career see J. Callaghan, *Time and Chance* (London: HarperCollins, 1987), pp. 40–45.

5 Morgan, *Callaghan*, p. 38.

6 Royal Commission on Trade Unions and Employers' Association 1965–1968, Cmnd 363 (London: HMSO, 1968), para 40, 10.

7 The phrase 'keeper of the cloth cap' is from P. Jenkins, *The Battle for Downing Street* (London: Knight, 1970), a contemporary account of Labour's battle over reform. Chapter 5 focuses on Callaghan's role. For Callaghan's own account see *Time and Chance*, pp. 274–7. P. Dorey, *Comrades in Conflict: Labour, the Trade Unions and 1969's In Place of Strife* (Manchester: Manchester University Press, 2020) is an extensive academic account.

8 R. Crossman, *The Diaries of a Cabinet Minister, Volume Three: Secretary of State for Social Services, 1968–1970* (London: Hamish Hamilton/Jonathan Cape, 1977), p. 305.

9 'Wilson government used secret unit to smear union leaders', *The Guardian*, 24 July 2018: https://www.theguardian.com/politics/2018/jul/24/wilson-government-used-secret-unit-to-smear-union-leaders

10 B. Castle, *The Castle Diaries, 1974–1976* (London: Weidenfeld & Nicolson, 1980), p. 194 – entry for 15 October 1974.

11 Hansard, HC Deb, 1 December 1977, vol. 940, col. 716.

12 J. Jones, *Union Man: An Autobiography* (London: Collins, 1986), p. 307.

13 T. Benn, *Against the Tide: Diaries 1973–76* (London: Arrow, 1989), p. 622 – entry for 7 October 1976.

14 Callaghan, *Time and Chance*, p. 417. After the 1976 IMF crisis Benn warned the Cabinet that 'loyalty is the only thing you are going to be living off from now on'. Benn, *Against the Tide*, p. 686 – entry for 7 December 1976.

15 Morgan, *Callaghan*, p. 343 and p. 649.

16 Jones, *Union Man*, p. 309.

17 Donoughue, *Downing Street Diary*, p. 141 and p. 152 – entries for 2 February and 23 February 1977.

18 CAB 128/64, 26 October 1978, p. 15.

19 Royal Commission report, para 105, 27. An evocative picture of mass production workplace relations in this period is H. Beynon, *Working for Ford* (Harmondsworth: Penguin, 1973).

20 Callaghan, *Time and Chance*, p. 273 and p. 467.

21 For the development of the social contract see A. J. Taylor, *The Trade Unions and the Labour Party* (London: Croom Helm, 1987), pp. 6–46. An insider's account is B. Donoughue, *Prime Minister: The Conduct of Policy under Harold Wilson and James Callaghan* (London: Jonathan Cape, 1987).

22 A revealing instance of his intimacy with Labour's culture can be seen in Callaghan singing ('doing a turn'), 'I am the fat man, the very fat man, who waters the workers' beer' taped by Tony Benn at a Durham miners' dinner. See 'Tony Benn on James Callaghan singing', BBC News, 17 March 2014: https://www.bbc.co.uk/news/av/magazine-26587298/tony-benn-on-james-callaghan-singing

23 Donoughue, *Downing Street Diary*, p. 353 – entry for 1 September 1978.

24 Morgan, *Callaghan*, p. 526 and T. Benn, *Conflicts of Interest: Diaries 1977–80* (London: Arrow, 1991), p. 464 – entry for 28 February 1979.

25 Callaghan, *Time and Chance*, p. 470, p. 521. The Neddy Six became less effective with the retirement of Jones and Scanlon in 1978. Callaghan described it as 'divided and increasingly ineffective' and said that he could not trust, for example, Moss Evans, who followed Jones as TGWU General Secretary.

26 CAB 128/62, 7 July 1977, p. 2. For steady unravelling of the social contract see Taylor, *The Trade Unions and the Labour Party*, pp. 93–106.

27 CAB 128/62, 14 July 1977, p. 1.

28 Benn, *Conflicts of Interest*, p. 391 – entry for 14 November 1978; and Donoughue, *Downing Street Diary*, p. 388, 13 November 1978. Despite the rejection Callaghan remained optimistic.

29 CAB 128/64, 16 November 1978, pp. 2–4.

30 CAB 128/65, 15 January 1979, pp. 2–3.

31 Morgan, *Callaghan*, p. 344.

32 See, for example, Callaghan, *Time and Tide*, p. 474.

33 Donoughue, *Downing Street Diary*, p. 90 – entry for 28 February 1976; *Report of the Committee of Inquiry on Industrial Democracy*, Cmnd 6706, June (London: HMSO, 1977).

34 Donoughue, *Downing Street Diary*, p. 124 – entry for 17 December 1976. CAB 128/61, 20 January 1977, pp. 1–4.

35 Industrial Democracy. Note by the Prime Minister, 19 January 1977. CAB 129/149/9, p. 1 and p. 3. See also Callaghan, *Time and Chance*, p. 425.

36 T. Benn, *Conflicts of Interest: Diaries 1977–80* (London: Arrow, 1991), p. 80 – entry for 20 January 1977.

37 Benn, *Conflicts of Interest*, p. 22 – entry for 2 February 1977.

38 Benn, *Conflicts of Interest*, pp. 141–2 – entry for 20 May 1977.

39 Memorandum. Draft White Paper on Industrial Democracy, 26 April 1978. CAB 129/200/23.

40 CAB 128/63, 27 April 1978, pp. 6–8, p. 2.

41 Donoughue, *Downing Street Diary*, p. 295 – entry for 28 February 1978; Benn, *Conflict of Interest*, p. 267 – entry for 22 December 1977.

42 Cmnd 7321, May 1978 and Industrial Democracy. Memorandum by the Secretary of State for Education and Science and Postmaster General, 19 March 1979, p. 3. CAB 129/201/21.

43 CAB 128/64, 9 November 1978, p. 2.

44 For recent accounts see J. Shepherd, *Crisis? What Crisis? The Callaghan Government and the British Winter of Discontent* (Manchester: Manchester University Press, 2015) and T. Martin López, *The Winter of Discontent: Myth, Memory, and History* (Liverpool: Liverpool University Press, 2014).

45 CAB 128/65, 18 January 1979, pp. 6–7.

46 CAB 128/65, 30 January 1979, p. 1. See also Callaghan, *Time and Chance*, pp. 538–40.

47 CAB 128/65, 1 February 1979 Limited Circulation Annex, pp. 1–4 and Morgan, *Callaghan*, pp. 670–74.

48 Donoughue, *Downing Street Diary*, p. 441 – entry for 8 February 1979.

49 Department of Employment, 'The Government, the Economy and Trade Union Responsibilities: Joint Statement by the TUC and the Government' (London: HMSO, 1979), and CAB 129/65, 15 February 1979, p. 4. Its publication is conventionally taken as marking the end of the Winter of Discontent, although disputes continued.

50 B. Weekes, 'The TUC–Government "Concordat": The Economy, the Government and Trade Union Responsibilities', *Industrial Law Journal* (1979), vol. 8, no. 1, p. 114.

51 Donoughue, *Prime Minister*, p. 197.

52 Benn, *Conflicts of Interest*, p. 450 – entry for 1 February 1979.

53 Callaghan, *Time and Chance*, p. 396.

54 Morgan, *Callaghan*, p. 475.

9

SOCIAL POLICY[1]

Ben Williams

INTRODUCTION

J AMES CALLAGHAN HAD A resolutely working-class upbringing, and during it he experienced genuine poverty and
hardship. The early death of his father as the main breadwinner left
his family reliant on charity at a time (the 1920s) when the UK welfare
state was far more limited and conditional than the more universalised model introduced from 1945. Pension improvements for widows
under the first Labour government in 1924 eased the family's burden
somewhat, and this personalised benefit of a welfare policy reform,
experienced first-hand, would play a significant role in the young
Callaghan's initial politicisation. This challenging family upbringing could therefore certainly be said to have shaped his formative
commitments to the egalitarian focus of the Labour Party, while also
reflecting the potentially very positive impact of government social

policy on everyday lives. It subsequently strengthened Callaghan's political commitment to a more comprehensive and paternalistic welfare model that aspired to keep the poorest members of society out of the clutches of desperate poverty. As his political career took shape, this made Callaghan naturally sympathetic to those social groups who relied on the welfare state to maintain the basic standards of everyday living, and this attitude was further consolidated by him representing a working-class area of Cardiff in Parliament from 1945 right up until his retirement as an MP in 1987. Such experiences certainly influenced his burgeoning political outlook in the immediate post-war years, and after serving as a junior minister in the trailblazing 1945–51 Attlee government that established the modern welfare state, he got a major opportunity to put his values and beliefs into practice during the 1960s as Chancellor of the Exchequer (1964–67). In this more senior ministerial role, he had major responsibility for delivering Labour's manifesto commitments to increase old-age pensions and abolish some charges for medicines, actively contributing to the ongoing expansion and evolution of the British welfare state in the process.

SOCIAL POLICY: AIMS AND ASPIRATIONS

Yet it would be as Prime Minister between 1976 and 1979 that Callaghan would have the greatest opportunity to craft a social policy direction that would potentially establish a personalised legacy for the class of people he originated from. As outlined in his autobiography, Callaghan was driven throughout his political career by admirable social principles for high public office that stemmed from his upbringing, as he summarised: 'Central to the purpose of a Labour

Government is responsibility for eliminating social wrongs and promoting social well-being. The class system had grown less rigid during my lifetime but it was still a millstone that hampered progress, as was gross inequality.'[2]

The tone of these above comments reflects a sense of Callaghan's deep commitment to addressing social injustices that stemmed from the class system, yet which was also aligned with a pragmatic awareness of the unerring resilience of various long-term socio-economic issues that were difficult to eradicate from British society. Such comments also highlighted the difficulties facing Labour governments in particular when it came to resolving deep-rooted poverty and social inequality, which was a long-standing cause and priority associated with that particular party. In terms of outlining broader social policy goals, in May 1976 Callaghan mapped out his longer-term objectives for the forthcoming decade (yet which he never came to fully deliver), and he wrote down that his goals for 1980 were to 'resume our social aims in housing, education, health and welfare to build a cohesive society'.[3] This clearly indicated his desire to strengthen the effectiveness of the welfare state and broader social policy, in alignment with the principles of the universalised model of 1945. Yet to what degree he was likely to fulfil such positive aims in the late 1970s remains a matter of significant conjecture, and they arguably faded away and were drowned out by the somewhat chaotic and crisis-ridden ending of his premiership in the spring of 1979.

THE CONTEXT FOR DELIVERING WELFARE PROVISION AND SOCIAL EQUALITY

Consequently, as Prime Minister in the very testing economic conditions of the mid-1970s, Callaghan's strong personal commitment to maintaining the required levels of welfare support in the name of delivering a fairer and more equal society became a much more difficult circle to square. The welfare state was the key engine to lever these social goals, but on a longer-term scale, demographic changes had placed considerable and growing pressures on the country's welfare provision, evident in the fact that between 1945 and 1975, 'the proportion of GDP spent on the main welfare services rose from just 5 per cent to around 20 per cent'[4] (incorporating all core elements of the welfare state). In addition to this, approximately one sixth of the population had moved above the pensionable age due to a rise in life expectancy (fuelled by improved welfare provision), and NHS spending had risen from an estimated £500 million in 1951 up to £5,596 million by 1975[5] (a tenfold increase). In short, Beveridge and the architects of the post-1945 welfare state had perhaps not factored in such demographic trends and improved levels of public health, which entailed that the financial costs of maintaining the post-war welfare settlement had risen significantly over three decades up until the point that Callaghan's premiership commenced. Within the context of such longer-term trends and an increasingly sluggish economy, Callaghan came to 10 Downing Street in the spring of 1976 amid an atmosphere of significant economic strains impacting on the government's capacity to deliver core public services, and which culminated in his administration taking a loan from the IMF later that year. Some have described this bleak scenario as representing a prevailing environment of 'stagflation'– specifically a combination of a stagnant economy, rising unemployment and surging inflation.[6]

This turbulent atmosphere placed tremendous pressure on the maintenance and delivery of the post-war model of welfare provision that Callaghan believed was vital for the well-being of the poorer social classes from which he originated. The most urgent challenge was arguably to reduce the scourge of inflation, which impacted on the costs of everyday goods for ordinary people, but also crucially on the costs of delivering the welfare services that the government provided, namely in terms of purchasing materials and paying wages. Yet this drive to reduce public expenditure costs and to instil greater economic stability had tough implications for social policy, potentially further worsening the everyday living conditions of the poorer classes, and therefore making Callaghan's aspirations for a more equal and socially just society far more difficult to fulfil. Within this context, and in the shorter term at least, the first obvious signs of trouble in meeting such social policy aspirations were the demands imposed by the IMF loan, which would cast a major economic cloud over most of 1976,[7] and which was undoubtedly one of the most serious crises of post-war British politics. On this basis, one of Callaghan's first notable instructions to his Cabinet, via the calculations of his often-besieged Chancellor Denis Healey, was to tackle such spiralling public spending levels by asking ministers to identify approximately £1.5 billion of total spending cuts in order to meet the initial IMF loan requirements of $3.9 billion dollars.[8] Callaghan himself observed that his ministers 'were obviously concerned to protect their cherished programmes',[9] including Secretary of State for Health and Social Services David Ennals. Indeed, in such key departments, at the heart of the government's social policy agenda, such cutbacks would have an inevitably negative impact on both welfare recipients and the public sector workforce, despite attempts to curb bureaucratic costs rather than frontline welfare provision. Difficulties in dealing with the workforce saw ministers like Ennals facing an ongoing battle over pay with disgruntled NHS workers in particular during the 1976–79 period. Yet the need to address the spiralling levels of public spending remained the political priority for Callaghan's administration, and the narrative of economic retrenchment and wage restraint to 'balance the books' was particularly epitomised by his often-quoted 1976 annual Labour Party conference speech where he declared that 'we used to think you could spend your way out of recession', before warning delegates that such an option no longer existed due to the country's weakened economic state.

This speech appeared to mark an initial admittance by senior Labour figures that the country had reached the end of the so-called 'post-war consensus', and Callaghan went on to declare in this speech that if such an expansive 'Keynesian' option was pursued as some of the Labour left wanted, those who suffered most would be 'the poor, the old and the sick'[10] due to the further public raft of expenditure cuts that he claimed would have to follow. Yet, in delivering his speech, Callaghan appeared to be making a symbolic retreat from the interventionist commitment towards full employment and a more egalitarian society, and in doing so left-wing critics could claim he was departing from the fundamental principles of the 1945 Beveridge welfare settlement. While Callaghan was conscious of some relative short-term pain for the heavily unionised public sector workers in terms of pay reductions caused by this economic squeeze, on an electoral level this also ran the risk of alienating some of Labour's key voting groups in the build-up to the next general election, due in 1979. Indeed, what had notably hampered Callaghan's government in this specific policy area was the fact that the escalation of the welfare state in both size and cost over the course of the post-war era had 'generated massive new lobbies of political interest (of both consumers and producers) who had an active interest in seeing the size and resources of the public sector expand'.[11] This meant that both the producers (workforce) and the users and recipients of the welfare state had a vested interest in seeing it continue to expand, thus benefitting them in terms of both employment and social rights respectively. A specific criticism to consequently emerge from the political right was that the producers (notably the unions) had too much power and control, at the ultimate expense of the users. Such a scenario put the Callaghan administration in a particularly difficult position when it came to making cutbacks in the social policy sphere, creating the potential for it to antagonise some significant bodies of public opinion – namely welfare recipients and those working in the welfare system, both of whom formed key components of the Labour electoral coalition. Yet Callaghan nevertheless firmly believed that it was only by taking such harsh but responsible economic decisions that in the longer term his government could maintain 'the living standards of the sick, the poorest, the unemployed and the pensioners',[12] which again reflected both the social welfare policy priorities and practical political calculations at the heart of his political agenda. This suggests that amid the tough economic decision-making by his administration during its first year in office in particular, it was society's most vulnerable who (for varying reasons) appeared to be at the forefront of Prime Minister Callaghan's thoughts.

ANALYSIS OF CALLAGHAN'S SOCIAL POLICIES – TACKLING POVERTY AND INEQUALITY

Consequently, as economic conditions gradually improved throughout 1977 and 1978, Callaghan could claim that his government's capacity to invest in core areas of social and welfare policy improved likewise. Yet while particularly conscious of cultivating the support and loyalty of welfare users, Callaghan's administration increasingly appeared to lose patience with another core group of traditional Labour supporters, the trade unions, and history tells us that in resisting the more extreme wage demands of the welfare state's workforce he ultimately sealed his own political fate. Yet despite Callaghan's sense of justification for his course of action in this specific policy area, academic policy experts from the left continued to criticise what they perceived to be the ongoing failure of the 1945 Beveridge settlement in tackling persistently stubborn levels of poverty and inequality, and highlight how Labour governments (such as this one) particularly struggled to address what was one of their core policy priorities. Brian Abel-Smith was one such prominent figure from this tradition, and his background in social policy had been developed in research work with Professor Richard Titmuss of the London School of Economics, and then in a further research capacity on the Guillebaud Enquiry (1956), which explored the ongoing cost of the National Health Service. Following on from his 1950s conclusions that the NHS established from 1948 was indeed an affordable public service model, Abel-Smith would argue that governments should be doing more in the welfare policy sphere, particularly those that were Labour-led, with more interventionist and welfarist political instincts. In partnership with sociologist Peter Townsend, Abel-Smith was also responsible for establishing a new so-called 'poverty line', which appeared to prove that despite the extension of a more comprehensive welfare state after 1945, poverty had actually increased in Britain from the 1950s onwards, specifically for the most vulnerable groups unaffected by the 'era of prosperity'. This 'poverty line' would form the basis for the somewhat controversial and damaging argument that even under Labour governments after 1945, poverty had risen. Within such a context, there were various key welfare policy areas that provided Callaghan's government with the potential to notably benefit poorer citizens during a relatively short period of time in office, namely child benefit, housing and the NHS.

CHILD BENEFIT

Abel-Smith and Townsend were therefore advocates of a more effective and expanding welfare state, and they authored the 1965 book *The Poor and the Poorest*, which in its focus on the impact of poverty on children in particular inspired the formation of the Child Poverty Action Group (CPAG) in 1965. The director of this organisation between 1969 and 1979 was Frank Field, who went on to become a Labour MP for forty years and was briefly minister for welfare reform during Tony Blair's first administration in the late 1990s. During the Callaghan era, Field emerged on the political left as a critic of this administration's social policies, and in this specific role he gained much of his welfare policy expertise, while formulating various criticisms of government fallings in this policy sphere in the process.[13] Abel-Smith went on to become a special (expert) advisor to Secretary of State Ennals between 1976 and 1978, and in 1977 he was influential in instigating 'The Black Report', which reported back in 1980 and formally concluded that the post-war welfare state had so far failed to tackle long-standing socio-economic inequality. All such developments reflected ongoing concerns on the political and academic left with how the post-war welfare model was performing for those that needed it most, both during Callaghan's government and under the Wilson administrations that preceded it during the 1960s and earlier 1970s. Nevertheless, some positive social policy innovation did take place during the period between 1976 and 1979, but its implementation proved to be problematic and the government gained limited credit for it. As an example, under significant pressure from charities such as the CPAG in particular, Callaghan inherited responsibility for implementing the 1975 Child Benefit Bill. This involved the merging of existing state allowances, replacing family allowance with a benefit for each child (which was more generous in terms of working to the advantage of larger families in particular). This innovation marked a further widening of the scope of the original 1946 Family Allowances Act, which had introduced the payment of an allowance directly to the mother, while being universal in its application and not means-tested. Yet by the time Callaghan took office, this generous manifesto pledge had encountered some resistance in terms of cost, as well as concerns about removing an existing child tax allowance for men to fund an in-flated level of child benefit paid directly to women. Some feared this would be electorally unpopular, including Chancellor Healey, who observed its potential to 'cost us male votes because it would mean a switch from the wallet to the handbag'.[14] Frank Field exposed these various objections with support from sympathetic (anonymous) leaks from a civil servant named Malcolm Wicks, who would later become a Labour MP. Field (who maintained the identity of his anonymous source until after Wicks's death) recalls:

> Child benefit was a commitment in the two 1974 manifestos ... I was incensed at the whips alleging that backbenchers were against the scheme [and] this purported survey was used to convince trade union leaders that, without backbench support, they should withdraw their support for a reform that had been prominent in two party manifestos. Once the anonymous article I wrote was published in *New Society*, under the headline 'Killing a Commitment', [it led to] the embar-rassment of the Prime Minister and Chancellor misleading their col-leagues in Cabinet, in the unions and on the backbenches.[15]

Economic conditions certainly created some political resistance, and this ultimately played a part in the way this social policy was introduced. The government's image was consequently damaged in terms of its apparent commitment to progressive welfare reform, yet while this particular pol-icy's roll-out was delayed, it was eventually phased in between 1977 and 1979,[16] representing a notable welfare expansion and contributing to the 'biggest increase in real family income for a long time'.[17]

SOCIAL HOUSING POLICY

In the housing domain, providing and constructing significant levels of state-subsidised council houses had been a staple of Labour governments since the 1920s in terms of addressing social hardship, poverty and providing minimum standards of housing. Callaghan's government was able to maintain its provision of this social policy to a degree amid difficult economic conditions, but its rate of construction did steadily fall throughout the administration (see Table 1), which can be viewed as a failure to meet social needs in this area. As an example, the approximate 85,000 council properties built in 1979 compared poorly to almost 200,000 a year built during the mid-1960s. The government would defend its record in social housing policy by highlighting expenditure cutbacks required after 1976, but concerns about the volume of social housing built were also fuelled by concerns about quality (which had plagued previous Conservative governments also). This was related to the fact that during this period, various issues and problems were being highlighted regarding the quality and durability of many of the high-rise 'futuristic' council housing blocks that were being built (so-called 'streets in the sky'). Influenced by European trends in architecture, many such high-rise structures appeared to have been built cheaply, and would quickly prove to be unpopular with tenants and have limited lifespans in most cases. As a further complication for this policy area, there had also been a steady growth in the number of council tenants buying their properties from the early 1970s, as had been encouraged by the Heath government of 1970–74. Callaghan's environment minister (with responsibility for housing) Peter Shore felt that Labour should react to such a trend which reflected some degree of popular demand, and in 1977 he issued a government Green Paper acknowledging that home ownership was a 'strong and natural desire' for many citizens, and that such aspirations 'should be met' by the government.[18]

Table 1: Council house dwellings built between 1974 and 1979 (approximate thousands)

Year	England and Wales	Scotland	Total
1974	99.4	16.2	115.6
1975	122.9	22.8	145.7
1976	124.2	21.2	145.4
1977	121.2	14.3	135.5
1978	96.8	9.9	106.7
1979	75.0	7.9	82.9

Source: John English (ed.), *The Future of Council Housing* (1982) and ITV News, 'Key events in history of UK council housing' (19 September 2018), https://www.itv.com/news/2018-09-19/key-events-in-history-of-uk-council-housing/

However, perhaps reflecting the more collectivist instincts of the left, Shore explored the prospect of shared equity and shared ownership schemes, encouraged the development of housing associations and also housing provision via charities or other (non-state) social bodies, hoping such measures would provide the catalyst for much-needed inner-city regeneration. Yet Labour's social housing policy at this stage ultimately remained aligned with the conventional Beveridge model which emphasised that the bulk of council housing would be primarily maintained by the state via local authorities, and there remained approximately 6.5 million council-owned houses when Labour left office in 1979, representing an estimated third of all housing occupancies in the country. However, in tough economic conditions, the ongoing cost of providing such housing stock to the required standards remained a problem that needed addressing. Consequently, this post-war social housing equilibrium would be transformed by Thatcher's populist 'right to buy' policy, which began to significantly deplete local authority housing stock from 1980 onwards. It could be argued that in adopting this policy, Thatcher radically tackled the longer-term affordability issue of how the government could deliver such a volume of social housing within the welfare state, yet in a much bolder and often destabilising way (for both ideological and political reasons) than the Callaghan government ever did.

NHS FUNDING AND EXPENDITURE

The creation of the NHS has been viewed as perhaps the most enduring and monumental legacy of the Attlee administration of 1945–51, and subsequent Labour governments in particular viewed this core public institution with a degree of both reverence and awe. Its socially egalitarian implications have therefore been a significant challenge for successive governments, particularly those of the political left, to maintain. The Department of Health and Social Security was at this time a fused ministerial portfolio at the hub of social policy-making, so on this basis the NHS also came under the remit of David Ennals. As already alluded to, healthcare workers were a key part of the public sector workforce, and during this decade were involved in ongoing pay disputes with the government amid a turbulent period of industrial relations. However, in the Callaghan government's defence, spending levels on the NHS were reasonably maintained by the historical standards of the decade. Although measured by a percentage of GDP the rate did fall slightly compared to the Wilson administration (1974–76), it was favourable compared to the Conservative government of Heath between 1970 and 1974. Nevertheless, the annual rate of NHS spending growth during the Callaghan government did significantly drop after 1976 (see Table 2).

Table 2: Annual changes in NHS spending

Year	Per cent annual change
1975–76	+7.4
1976–77	+0.3
1977–78	–1.5
1978–79	+1.5
1979–80	+0.7

Source: The King's Fund, John Appleby, *How does this year's NHS budget compare historically?* (11 May 2016), https://www.kingsfund.org.uk/blog/2016/05/how-does-this-years-nhs-budget-compare-historically

Yet this trend again has to be seen within the context of the more stringent economic conditions imposed in the wake of the IMF loan, which evidently impacted on the government's public spending commitments. While this can be viewed as a negative in terms of the funding levels required to meet the inexorable and unlimited service demands of the NHS, the rate of the spending fall as a percentage of GDP was relatively slight (see Table 3), and service levels could therefore be seen to have been maintained to sufficient standards to benefit the poorer social groups who used and needed it most. However, both the trade unions and wider public always wanted more, while a steadily rising and ageing population placed ongoing strains on the service.

Table 3: NHS spending during the 1970s

Year	UK population (millions)	NHS spending as a percentage of GDP
1970	55.6	3.6
1971	55.9	3.7
1972	56.0	3.6
1973	56.2	3.7
1974	56.2	4.2
1975	56.2	4.5
1976	56.2	4.4
1977	56.1	4.2
1978	56.1	4.1
1979	56.2	4.0

Adapted from sources: John Appleby, Nuffield Trust, *70 years of NHS spending* (21 March 2018), https://www.nuffieldtrust.org.uk/news-item/70-years-of-nhs-spending and UK Public Spending, https://www.ukpublicspending.co.uk/uk_national_healthcare_analysis

CONCLUSION – SUCCESS OR FAILURE?

Callaghan undoubtedly inherited something of a political 'poisoned chalice' in 1976, with a whole range of challenging socio-economic policy problems piled up on his in-tray from the moment he became Prime Minister. He would later claim that despite the economic and industrial turmoil that dominated his premiership, the continuous Labour government of 1974–79 had in fact managed some notable social policy successes amid very difficult circumstances: 'We had protected the weakest in the country during our period of office, and in some areas had increased benefits, notably those of children.'[19] In re-emphasising his pragmatic political streak, Callaghan would refer to this political approach as 'practical Socialism ... ensuring the nation met the needs of those who were unable to help themselves'.[20] He could also point out that the Labour vote in 1979 had actually numerically risen since the October 1974 general election, although as a national percentage it had dropped, and the Conservative opposition vote had of course improved even more. Callaghan himself argued that despite his electoral defeat, the consolidation of reasonably solid Labour electoral support suggested some degree of success on various policy fronts since 1976, most notably in relation to the ongoing delivery and protection of key public services and social policy, which reflected 'how much steady understanding and support existed for what we tried to do'.[21] Indeed, the post-war era up until 1979 saw Britain becoming a more equal society, and the 1970s as a decade is now viewed as arguably the most egalitarian of the entire twentieth century; Callaghan could rightly claim that his government played a part in maintaining this status.[22] Subsequently, in the years that have followed this administration the gap between rich and poor in the UK has consistently widened. As the IFS has commented, the 'general pattern is of increases in social equality during the 1970s, followed by rising inequality in the 1980s and 1990s',[23] so on this basis perhaps the Callaghan administration deserves some credit when it comes to the question of how it managed social inequality and wealth variations within British society. This may well be its most positive enduring legacy in this specific policy area.

It is also true that by the late 1970s an improving economy and falling inflation rate had allowed core public services to be secured and maintained in the longer run, but on a political level increasing numbers of voters were clearly dissatisfied by the continuing sense of crisis and the inexorable growth and ongoing cost of the welfare state. Indeed, the overall welfare (or social security) budget had consistently risen throughout the 1970s, from approximately just over 7 per cent of GDP in the early 1970s to 9 per cent by the early 1980s.[24] While some of this increase could be linked to the IMF loan and a subsequent rise in unemployment benefit, the ongoing costs of social security had been on a steadily upward spiral since 1945 due to longer-term factors such as population growth, increased eligibility and more generous payments. Notable free-market bodies such as the Institute for Economic Affairs (IEA) had been arguing since the 1950s that expanding welfare costs were ultimately unsustainable in the longer term and would prove to be a drain on the country's economic performance, and it was during the 1970s that such warnings seemed to be coming to fruition. On this premise, the flourishing New Right agenda, and some of its key figureheads such as Sir Keith Joseph and Margaret Thatcher (inspired by the writings of Hayek), offered a libertarian critique of British welfare provision, and saw the opportunity for a radical and ideologically driven restructuring and eventual 'shrinking' of what they viewed as a bloated and inefficient welfare state if the Conservatives could win the 1979 general election. This focus on expenditure retrenchment was a key element in how they eventually secured the electoral victory that ended Callaghan's premiership, and it reflected the Conservatives' ability 'to tap into a growing (if inarticulate) strain of popular disenchantment ... about the state of the welfare state'[25] and specifically its ongoing cost and affordability. This more economically prudent and neoliberal analysis chimed with the country's mood after the IMF crisis, and aligned with fears of 'dependency' and people getting 'something for nothing' that were prevalent among financially stretched skilled workers in particular. This socio-economic group would go on to form a vital component of the Thatcher electoral coalition in the years ahead.

Other recurring criticisms continued from the left, including claims that while the Callaghan government staved off the most destructive potential cuts affecting social policy, in practical terms this meant that by engaging in such 'firefighting' it lost any coherent focus on tackling inequality and redistributing wealth. Some left-wing critics could also validly question whether Callaghan's paternalistic tendencies were wholly compatible with greater egalitarianism and redistribution. Anti-poverty campaigners and charities like the CPAG, advised by academics such as Brian Abel-Smith, continued to lament that unacceptable rates of poverty still existed in one of the world's strongest economies and richest nations, and by implication this was a condemnation of Labour's consistent failings in this policy sphere.[26] As a specific negative observation, one commentator has remarked that during this embattled administration of 1976–79, the 'poor saw little improvement in their lot. Child Benefit, introduced in 1976, appeared to be a big spending increase, but in reality it largely replaced child tax allowances. Then the economy just went off the rails.'[27] David Piachaud, an academic and another advisor to this government, claims that 'previous Labour governments failed to make any real impact on poverty because they were knocked off course by the macro-economy', and that 'under Callaghan, any redistribution ground to a halt because the IMF stepped in'.[28] Piachaud also had links with Abel-Smith, and both had been a source of expertise and knowledge to successive Labour governments during the 1960s and '70s in the field of social security and child poverty in particular.

In addition, the sense of prolonged economic crisis had in turn created a stagnant welfare state environment which became complacent and lacked dynamism, and which has been described as existing in 'a routinised pattern of incremental growth and institutional torpor'.[29] The nature of these varying criticisms highlight the dilemma faced by the Callaghan government when it came to social policy delivery – specifically that the left argued it was not spending sufficient money on tackling poverty and inequality, whereas the right claimed it was spending too much and in an inefficient and bureaucratic manner. This had been a long-standing and recurring pattern of simmering debate since the establishment of the post-1945 Beveridge welfare settlement, and in the context of a crippling economic crisis it appeared to peak during Callaghan's three-year tenure as Prime Minister, before further evolving in a markedly different direction under a Thatcherite policy agenda during the 1980s. Given the various globalised political and economic trends of the 1970s, it is perhaps doubtful whether any government of the left, conspicuously tiring after five continuous and difficult years in office since 1974, could have stopped the advent of New Right ideology and its more radical alternative solutions for both the British economy and associated welfare delivery. This could perhaps cushion some of the criticisms and negativity that have been directed at Callaghan's social policy record, as his government did manage to avoid the more volatile levels of socio-economic instability that various vulnerable groups experienced during the next decade.

NOTES

1   I would like to thank my mother, Christine Williams, for the primary historical information and knowledge provided by her as a beneficiary of the Callaghan government's child benefit reforms in the late 1970s.

2   J. Callaghan, *Time and Chance* (London: Collins, 1987), p. 395.

3   *Ibid.*, p. 398.

4   C. Pierson, 'Social Policy', in D. Marquand and A. Seldon (eds), *The Ideas that Shaped Post-War Britain* (London: Fontana, 1996), p. 151.

5   *Ibid.*

6   First said to have been used by Conservative frontbencher Iain Macleod, Hansard, HC Deb, 17 November 1965, vol. 720, col. 1165.

7   See K. Hickson, *The IMF Crisis of 1976 and British Politics* (London: I. B. Tauris, 2004).

8   See Callaghan, *Time and Chance*, p. 423.

9   *Ibid.*, p. 434.

10 James Callaghan, speech to Labour Party conference, Blackpool, 28 September 1976: http://www.britishpoliticalspeech.org/speech-archive.htm?speech=174

11 Pierson, 'Social Policy', p. 151.

12 Callaghan, *Time and Chance*, p. 447.

13 See F. Field, 'How the Poor Fared', in K. Coates (ed.), *What Went Wrong? Explaining the Fall of the Labour Government* (Nottingham: Spokesman, 1979).

14 D. Healey, *The Time of My Life* (London: Michael Joseph, 1989), p. 448.

15 'My Life with Malcolm Wicks' Secret', *The Guardian*, 19 January 2014: https://www.theguardian.com/politics/2014/jan/19/frank-field-secret-life-malcolm-wicks-identity
    See also 'Late Labour MP Malcolm Wicks admits child benefit leak', BBC News, 20 January 2014: https://www.bbc.co.uk/news/uk-politics-25807245

16 See the National Archives, Cabinet Papers, 'The Beveridge Report and child benefit': https://www.nationalarchives.gov.uk/cabinetpapers/themes/beveridge-report-child-benefit.htm

17 Healey, *The Time of My Life*, p. 449.

18 'A history of social housing', BBC News, 14 April 2015: https://www.bbc.co.uk/news/uk-14380936
    K. Hickson, J. Miles and H. Taylor, *Peter Shore: Labour's Forgotten Patriot* (London: Biteback, 2020), pp. 97–100.

19 Callaghan, *Time and Chance*, p. 511.

20 *Ibid.*

21 *Ibid.*, p. 564.

22 See House of Commons Library, 'Income Inequality in the UK', 20 May 2019: https://researchbriefings.parliament.uk/ResearchBriefing/Summary/CBP-7484
    R. Joyce, *Fifty Years of Income Inequality*, Institute for Fiscal Studies, 16 May 2017: https://www.ifs.org.uk/publications/9231

23 D. Dorling et al., *Poverty and Wealth Across Britain, 1968 to 2005*, Joseph Rowntree Foundation, 17 July 2007: https://www.jrf.org.uk/report/poverty-and-wealth-across-britain-1968-2005

24 A. Hood and L. Oakley, *The Social Security System: Long-Term Trends and Recent Changes*, Institute for Fiscal Studies (November 2014): https://www.ifs.org.uk/uploads/publications/bns/BN156.pdf

25 Pierson, 'Social Policy', p. 152.

26 See N. Bosanquet and P. Townsend, *Labour and Equality* (London: Fabian Society, 1972).

27 A. Browne, 'How give-away Gordon is robbing the rich by stealth', *The Observer*, 19 September 1999: https://www.theguardian.com/politics/1999/sep/19/labour.labour1997to993

28 D. Piachaud, cited in *ibid*.

29 Pierson, 'Social Policy', p. 150.

10

EDUCATION: POLITICS AND POLICY-MAKING WITH THE INTELLECTUALS OF 'OLD' LABOUR

Jane Martin

There is no virtue in producing socially well-adjusted members of society who are unemployed because they do not have the skills. Nor at the other extreme must they be technically efficient robots. Both of the basic purposes of education require the same essential tools. These are basic literacy, basic numeracy, the understanding of how to live and work together; respect for others, respect for the individual. This means acquiring certain basic knowledge and skills and reasoning ability. It means developing lively minds and an appetite for further knowledge that will last a lifetime.[1]

INTRODUCTION

JAMES CALLAGHAN DELIVERED A defining speech of his premiership at Ruskin College, Oxford, in October 1976.

He talked about complaints from industry that schools were not
adequately preparing children for the world of work and expressed
concerns about the methods and aims of informal instruction, as well
as the need to bring curriculum matters into the public domain and
monitor the use of resources in order to maintain a national standard
of performance. It was unusual for a Prime Minister to devote a full
speech to education and Callaghan's approach was rooted historically in his own early struggles and personal commitment to access
and opportunities for working people. Using newly available diaries,
memoirs and personal papers, this chapter offers an original account
of political conflicts during the lead-up to Callaghan's intervention
and the series of events that surrounded it. In so doing, I provide
a critical overview of education politics and policy-making between
1976 and 1979, focusing on particular sets of relations and sites that
had some kind of influence upon Labour's reform agenda.

My storyline begins with Callaghan's childhood in an era when
nearly 90 per cent of people went to work at fourteen, only 10 per
cent achieved passes in public examinations and less than 5 per cent
went into higher education. It considers the provision of universal
secondary education in the mid-1940s and the development of comprehensive education from the 1960s. Second, I map and describe a
set of 1970s policy networks and highlight some of the intellectuals
and politicians within specific power–knowledge relations before
moving on to examine struggles over the generation and circulation
of key policy ideas disseminated and reiterated by individuals before,
during and after the 'Great Debate' on education Callaghan sparked
in 1976/77. I use the term 'intellectual' in a sociological and cultural
sense to refer to people who have consciously drawn upon 'ideas' as
solutions to social problems and enjoy a level of 'cultural authority'
in society. I conclude with some reflections on Callaghan's legacy.
The recent availability of the personal papers of Caroline Benn
(1926–2000), adult education lecturer and founder member of the

comprehensive education campaign group, provdes an opportunity for deeper understanding of what was at stake in this era.[2]

Non-fee-paying secondary schools did not exist in 1920s England when Callaghan was a boy. An avid reader, he passed a competitive examination at the age of ten and won a scholarship, but his impoverished, widowed mother had to send his reports to the Ministry of Education at Whitehall to make sure that he had done sufficiently well to have his fees paid for another term. Going to university was simply impossible and this denial of opportunity influenced his thinking a great deal.[3] It meant he cherished education as something precious and demonstrated a sense of inferiority. 'I haven't even got a degree,' he exclaimed on hearing he was victorious in the Labour leadership contest.[4] On meeting Bernard Donoughue, head of the prime ministerial Policy Unit at Downing Street, he drew a contrast between himself and Harold Wilson. In the second volume of his political diaries, published in 2009, Donoughue recalled Callaghan saying at their first meeting, 'I am not very clever, as you will know from the newspapers. I don't have Harold's brain for bright ideas.'[5]

COMPREHENSIVE STRUGGLES AND THE INTELLECTUALS OF 'OLD' LABOUR

The 1944 Education Act created universal free secondary education. Claims made in the Norwood Report of 1943 that it was possible to identify three types of children with three types of mind supported the separation of pupils into three sorts of secondary school – grammar, technical and modern, each in theory enjoying parity of esteem. The new grammar schools would offer a curriculum that emphasised PE, 'character' and the English language as opposed to anything more practical or contemporary. Cyril Burt, the country's foremost educational psychologist, at that time held that 'intelligence', and therefore learning capacity, were fixed and innate. For two decades, belief in IQ testing sanctioned the rigidly streamed and competitively selective system that developed. In practice, technical schools accounted for less than 5 per cent of the age group, and while some local authorities established comprehensive schools in opposition to government advice, the issue became whether a child 'succeeded' and went to a grammar school or 'failed' and went to a less well-resourced secondary modern.

Government reports and sociological surveys soon evidenced the realities behind secondary education for all. It was obvious that middle-class offspring dominated grammar intakes, owing to advantages imbued by family background, and social class remained a major influence on educational achievement. From 1946, the secondary modern schools and bottom streams of the grammar schools were full of working-class children who had largely negative experiences. Defenders of selective education argued only a small number of children had the academic ability to attend grammar schools, but research showed that coaching and intensive tuition, used by the middle classes, improved test scores. Added to which, successes secured by fifteen- and sixteen-year-old secondary modern school candidates for the new 'O' level examination exposed the fallibility of a selection process that made it acceptable for around 80 per cent of mainly working-class children to 'fail'.[6]

Michael Young intended his 1958 book *The Rise of the Meritocracy* to warn against an imagined future society in which individual merit, based on a narrow understanding of intelligence, determines social station. In Young's book, women and 'populists' emerge as critics – resisting the gradual extension of sifting and segregation that denies all opportunity to the rest – who eventually, goaded by the constant reminders of their inferiority, rise in angry revolt. While the rising tide of elitist stratification in British schools during the 1950s in part prompted Young's work, other conceptions of the term 'meritocracy' presumed an equal start, unencumbered by well-documented class inequalities. In 1961, the headmaster of Manchester Grammar School told the journalist Anthony Sampson:

> If you want to have equality of opportunity you inevitably have a meritocracy: but you can mitigate the dangers, by producing essentially *humane* meritocrats. The grammar schools must have their own *noblesse oblige* – but in order to have that, they have to *know* that they are a new kind of aristocracy – as Etonians know it.[7]

By the 1960s, the new emphasis on human capital theory, the need for more public expenditure in science and technology, which sustained economic growth and development, and rejection of deterministic theories of intelligence translated into support for comprehensive education. Labour won the 1964 general election and the new government made the introduction of comprehensive secondary schools a priority, issuing Circular 10/65, which requested that all local authorities submit plans for reorganisation. Outside Whitehall, 'policy intellectuals' who thought it a mistake for the government to request, not require, launched the Comprehensive Schools Committee (CSC) on 24 September 1965. Key 'interlockers',[8] as they are sometimes called in network analysis, who acted as bridges and brokers, included Caroline Benn, CSC Information Officer and editor of *Comprehensive Education*, wife of the then Postmaster General Tony Benn, who joined the Wilson Cabinet as minister of technology in July 1966.

There was substantial overlap in membership between CSC and urban think tanks like the Institute of Community Studies (ICS) and the Advisory Centre for Education (ACE). Thus, Michael Young (who founded both), Brian Jackson (who co-founded ACE) and Michael Armstrong (ICS and Nuffield researcher) all joined the CSC. Academics included Peter Townsend (formerly at ICS; co-founder professor at the University of Essex), Robin Pedley and Brian Simon, who held posts at the University of Leicester and co-founded the journal *FORUM* to promote the development of comprehensive education. Edward Blishen (*FORUM* editorial board), who in 1950 starting teaching at Archway Secondary Modern School in North London – and published an unflinchingly realistic autobiographical novel, *Roaring Boys*, five years later – and future Conservative politician Rhodes Boyson, then head at Robert Montefiore Secondary Modern School in Stepney, were both supporters.

Dennis Marsden (formerly at ICS; part of the Sociology team at Essex), who researched and wrote a 1962 book on grammar schools and social mobility jointly with Brian Jackson, outlined three views at the heart of Labour's public political debate in a 1971 Fabian pamphlet. First, the idea of meritocracy. Second, the 'social engineering' approach. Third, the 'community school' orientation. The ideology of meritocracy troubled Brian Simon, who envisioned comprehensive education embodying humanist objectives with science and technology for all. He noted the shortcomings of grammar schools, with their record of B- and C-stream failure and narrow curricula. 'We have new methods which lay emphasis on learning rather than didactic teaching, a new educational technology,' he said. 'There is an opportunity to try out what secondary education can do to develop human powers, as opposed to channelling them from an early age, and it is in the general interest that this opportunity be taken.'[9]

When Callaghan took over as Prime Minister in April 1976, Bernard Donoughue's inclusion of restoring values and standards to Britain's education system on a 'shopping list' of possible areas of intervention enabled him to indulge an old inclination to be education minister. In his autobiography, he wrote:

> I have always been a convinced believer in the importance of education, as throughout my life I had seen how many doors it could unlock

for working-class children who had begun with few other advantages, and I regretted my own lack of a university education. I was also aware of growing concerns among parents about the direction some schools were taking and I was anxious to probe this.[10]

Donoughue set his own perspective out in his political diaries and 2003 autobiography. Three things influenced him: the experience of his wife, then working at the headquarters of what he saw as the 'appalling' National Union of Teachers (NUT); the experience of his children in the state school system in Islington; and Harold Wilson's assessment of the Department of Education and Science (DES) as 'little more than a post-box between the teachers' unions and their local authority employers'.[11]

Between 1965 and 1976, the percentage of pupils in comprehensive secondary schools in England and Wales grew from 8.5 to 75.6.[12] Critics saw non-selective education as a formula for decline. A series of 'Black Papers' published by right-wing academics and policy groups between 1969 and 1977 was an important focus upon which arguments were built, individuals and campaigns were connected up and a political identity was forged. The first targeted progressive methods in primary schools as the root of a period of liberal anarchism and levelling down. The second appeared just before the 1969 Conservative Party conference and attacked comprehensive education as social engineering and as a destruction of high academic standards. In 'The Rise of the Mediocracy', Eysenck claimed people of *'mediocre* ability' would submerge 'people of *superior* ability' (Eysenck's emphasis). The fourth quoted the shadow education minister Norman St John-Stevas, who claimed that a quarter of a century's left-wing possession of the educational initiative had caused 'unprecedented worry and alarm among parents' about quality within education.[13]

In the midst of a Conservative offensive, including a carefully orchestrated 'parental' campaign in the case of the rebellious Tameside local authority over the 'threat' to local grammar schools, Callaghan felt the time was ripe for a public debate on education. Briefed by Donoughue, when he met with Secretary of State Fred Mulley in May, he asked what he wanted to do and what stopped him. Mulley undertook to prepare a memorandum on basic standards and teaching methods at primary level, curriculum choice, examinations and provision for sixteen- to nineteen-year-olds. Concurrently, Callaghan approved the appointment of a new permanent secretary at the DES to strengthen central authority. James Hamilton, transferred from Trade and Industry, brought with him an awareness of industrialists' criticisms that schools were not adequately preparing children for work. Meanwhile, officials produced a 'Yellow Book' or briefing paper that reached Callaghan in July. Recommendations included the identification and definition of minimum standards of attainment and a proposal to examine the workings of the Schools Council for the Curriculum and Examinations, which, with a majority of teachers' representatives on its governing council, had greater importance as a symbol of the ideology of 'teacher control' than in anything it actually did.[14]

Callaghan illustrated his general cast of thinking in his leader's speech at the party conference that autumn. Drawing on Labour's legacy as a party of social reform, he suggested a need to gear education more efficiently towards the 'needs of industry', and referenced 'the anxiety amongst parents at some aspects of the education of their children', but described positive visits to schools that had impressed him 'by their innovation and their experiment'. He appeared ambivalent towards 'new ways of learning that were unknown to us, vouched for by the teachers', and re-emphasised 'that the greatest gifts a teacher can give to a child are the basic tools of learning and a desire for knowledge. A literate and a numerate child has the key to open the door of learning and the key to the freedom of the mind.'[15]

A series of leaks to the press marked the lead-up to the formal announcement of a public debate on priorities, but Donoughue welcomed the chance this afforded 'to feed in some of my personal prejudices'.[16] Tony Benn's diary entry for 14 October 1976 is revealing. In Cabinet, Benn had asked the new Education Secretary, Shirley Williams, what she knew. Her note read, 'Tony, no question of any change of emphasis on comprehensives. It's mainly on maths, why not enough kids are doing engineering, etc. A bit about standards. Curriculum will be the main row.' Back at home, Caroline Benn suggested the aim was 'to root out the "lefties" who are teaching the social sciences'.[17] Then, on 18 October at Ruskin, Callaghan attacked what he called the 'educational establishment'. In so doing, he reiterated points about parental unease over new informal methods of teaching, low standards of numeracy for school leavers, the many girls abandoning science at an early age, vacancies in science and technology courses and the unwillingness of graduates to join industry.[18]

CALLAGHAN'S POLICY AGENDA

A week later, Tony Benn heard reactions during the TUC–Labour Party Liaison Committee. Callaghan said, 'We may need a core curriculum; to talk about the three Rs can't be reactionary. We should be thinking about education and employment in engineering, about exams.' Len Murray, TUC General Secretary, put it that education was not training. Benn welcomed the fact that Callaghan had opened the debate 'because there was a massive attack on comprehensive schools and we had to reject it'. In a speech Caroline helped prepare, he stressed the divisiveness the 1944 Act engendered, as did the binary system in higher education and exams,

> whereby working-class kids get CSEs and the others get GCEs. We
> must turn away from the idea that working-class kids should be given

technical training and shunted into industry. We have to deal with the massive subsidies to private education, and we must end the strangle hold of the universities over the school exam.

Shirley Williams warned of a backlash, repeating concerns about teaching methods and unaffordable duplication of provision in the sixteen-to-nineteen age group. 'We must look at the basics again and at the big comprehensives and avoid the mistakes of the past.'[19]

Simultaneously, negotiations about the extent and nature of the IMF loan to support the British economy and the size of the public expenditure cuts demanded as one condition of the lending dominated the news. As a discourse of education as training garnered publicity, Britain's premier post-war industrialist, Arnold Weinstock, suggested teachers were featherbedded, inefficient and putting young people off industry. The Director General of the Confederation of British Industry wanted a shift in balance from the arts to the sciences, greater weight to applied studies, more encouragement and opportunities for girls in science and engineering, better, more relevant maths and science teaching, and a stronger commitment to careers education and guidance for every pupil.[20]

A month after Ruskin, the media unleashed a ferocious attack on performance at Holland Park comprehensive school in West London. 'Showpiece school in exam flop' captures the tone of the reporting, which called into question school policy to operate a non-selective sixth form and give all pupils the chance to sit external examinations. Critically, this was the school the Benns chose, withdrawing their children from the private sector in order to 'go comprehensive' in 1964. Caroline Benn had been Holland Park's chair of governors since 1970, when school governance was less open to women and Inner London one of a minority of authorities with school governing bodies. Tony Benn recalls several mentions of her name at the 1976 Labour Party conference and sources in her archive show the fallout from events at William Tyndale Primary School in Islington, which hit the headlines in 1975, with almost daily national coverage between October 1975 and February 1976.[21]

Teachers at Tyndale operated a progressive curriculum and a subsequent inquiry called into question their behaviour and methods and encouraged calls for greater teacher accountability. One of the Tyndale staff had connections with Rhodes Boyson, a newly appointed MP and a leading voice in the Conservative critique of state education. Boyson presented the affair as an educational disaster in which left-wing ideology had taken over from good teaching and blighted the opportunities of working-class children. In his 1975 publication *The Crisis in Education*, he declared 'the intellectual deprivation of children occurs at the moment of conception in the dance of the chromosomes', and urged that the 'malaise' in British schools had followed from a breakdown in the organisation, curriculum and values of British traditional education.[22]

During the period of her governorship, Caroline Benn dedicated her life to building effective comprehensive education at Holland Park. The school implemented unstreaming and a common core curriculum and gave all pupils previously written off academically the chance to sit an exam at sixteen and stay on beyond the years of compulsory schooling. Holland Park pass rates reflected this policy and the problem of unemployment meant fewer left school as soon as they could (at the end of the term in which they became sixteen) and more took GCE 'O' levels in the summer of 1976 (75 per cent compared with 44 per cent from comprehensives nationally). Staff and students defended the school's reputation for attainment, participation and retention. 'My old school just dismissed me as dumb,' one student said. 'They wouldn't let me try for any exams there.' Another feared labelling them as 'tearaways' meant local employers would not welcome applications from the school's alumni.[23]

Two Conservatives helped stir the controversy over Holland

Park's results in 1976–77: Robert Vigars, leader of the opposition on
the Labour-controlled Inner London Education Authority (ILEA)
and Holland Park governor, and borough councillor Muriel Gumbel,
a former mayor of Kensington and Chelsea who sent her son to Eton.
In 1975, Vigars organised a visit to Holland Park by St John-Stevas.
Now Vigars made direct comparisons between events at Holland Park
and the Tyndale school. Angry parents called for his dismissal, but
the Authority proved reluctant to remove him from the ruling body
of a school in his ward. Holland Park's head teacher asked Gumbel
to explain the link between Holland Park's exam results and who the
husband of the chair of governors was. She 'exposes by her innuendo
the political background to the whole smear campaign against the
school...' he wrote in a letter to the press. 'Its "unique catchment
area" includes the worst slums in London, which are, need I say it,
the responsibility of the borough council on which Mrs Gumbel has
the honour to sit.'[24]

Inside Parliament, a new Education Act received royal assent on
22 November 1976. It defined comprehensives as schools not entered
as the result of selection tests (which was also true of secondary mod-
erns) and, unlike legislation in other countries, it did not insist that
all authorities had the duty to provide comprehensive education by a
set date. Nor did it bring the private sector into reorganisation. Pro-
comprehensive campaigners urged the Secretary of State to make
local authorities observe the law, end selection and refuse permission
for place-buying in private schools. Certainly, the retention of grammar schools (with their power to reject and select on social as well
as academic grounds) in some areas meant the debate on attainment
took place on a systematically sloping playing field. Yet measures of
performance at sixteen, university entrance, and percentages in full-
time education at seventeen or eighteen did not show a system 'in
crisis'.[25]

Next spring, energies funnelled into Callaghan's 'great debate' because of his insistence that the government needed to take the public and the teaching profession with them. In an early example of something Williams noted became fashionable later on – consultation with the users of public services[26] – there were eight regional conferences (invitees only), each attended by a minister and about 250 people from within education and without. The issues for discussion were: one, the curriculum for five- to sixteen-year-olds; two, the assessment of standards; three, the education and training of teachers (Boyson suggested the calibre had fallen); and four, school and working life.

The Comprehensive Schools Committee put forward the case that a common core curriculum without the immediate introduction of a single examination at sixteen and without support on unstreaming would be less effective than it could be in overcoming disadvantage and raising standards. In their view, all young people were capable of acquiring the knowledge and skills, albeit in different ways and to degrees, from the major activities or disciplines of secondary education (humanities, sciences, languages, arts, crafts and physical education) up to the age of sixteen plus. Thus, they fought for a system of education that did not make distinctions in terms of provision, resources and opportunities for reasons that could not be justified except in terms of relevant differences. Theirs was an argument against the orthodoxy that 'certain types' start work at sixteen and have no further education, while others 'naturally' stay on for higher education. Indeed, 'Labour's Programme '76' argued university entrance requirements had too great an influence upon secondary school curricula, which should reflect the educational needs of the community as a whole. Instead of cuts, it proposed using the opportunities afforded by the fall in the birth rate to improve the quality of schools, and teacher–pupil ratios, particularly in areas of greatest need, and urged a halt to proposed cuts in teacher supply.[27]

Teacher demoralisation was one result of Callaghan's intervention. NUT President Max Morris thought Callaghan 'focussed attention

on the alleged shortcomings of everyone in the service except those
responsible for organising, administering, paying for it, and for deciding policy at top level'. All 'skilfully designed to divert attention
from the massive cuts imposed on the schools and further and higher
education by all governments from December 1973 on'.[28] Shirley
Williams said later that her intention was to secure consent through
public participation, which was why she supported legislation to give
parents a legitimate say in the management of schools through representation on governing bodies. However, the abortive Education
Bill she brought before Parliament was contentious.

In her 2010 autobiography, Williams said she 'wanted to see diversity among schools, as distinct from a selection-based pecking order'.
In her view, parental choice on grounds of faith or internal organisation (progressive versus traditional, mixed versus single-sex) 'would
strengthen support for comprehensive schools', but the Labour
left and the NUT disagreed. 'Led by Tony and Caroline Benn and
quietly supported by one of my junior ministers, Margaret Jackson,
they opposed my proposals in the Party and in the Parliamentary
Party.'[29] Sources show Caroline Benn was then a co-opted expert on
the education and science subcommittee of Labour's national executive. In the winter of 1977–78 she met with the parliamentary party's
Education and Science Group to discuss parental choice, which she
thought would exaggerate rather than reduce inequalities between
schools, as well as between children of parents who are knowledgea-
ble and those who are not. Those who had fundamental issues with
the way fixed 'ability' thinking and discourse regards children were
alarmed to find protection of admission 'based wholly or partly on
selection by reference to ability or aptitude' enshrined in the proposed legislation. Caroline Benn spotted the proposals by chance
while chairing Labour's subcommittee in the absence of Joan Lestor
(who was ill). As another co-opted education expert, Tyrell Burgess,
put it, 'the Labour Government could not find a way to legislate to

end selection in twelve years, but in twelve days it has found a way to bring it back'.[30]

At this point, press leaks from the DES suggested a desire to include an Education Bill in the next session of Parliament. Shirley Williams raised it at Cabinet. 'She said that every other bill that people wanted was included in the Queen's Speech except hers, which would be popular.' Told by Caroline that 'it was contrary to the whole tradition of allocation and would create chaos in the local authorities', Tony Benn intervened. His warning of electoral damage was not popular with Williams, but Callaghan said Benn was entitled to raise it in Cabinet. 'I stopped the bill from going into the Queen's Speech,' Benn noted, 'not that I think it would have gone in anyway, but I may have helped to kill it.'[31] The Bill's absence seemed to beg the question of who exactly was Education Secretary, as *The Guardian* reported on 5 November 1977:

Obviously, late developer Callaghan feels some paternal responsibility for his great debate on standards and rumour has long detected a difference between Portsmouth Northern Secondary's Jim and Somerville College's Shirley. There is also the question of winning votes on education, to which Mr Callaghan has no great objection in principle. Yesterday we listened to Mrs Williams rattle rapidly through the government's achievements; defend herself against Mr St John-Stevas's charge of bullying over comprehensives (very stern about her duty at this point) and insisting that standards have not fallen.[32]

What has happened to the missing Education Bill? asked the opposition. Armed with a cutting from the *Times Educational Supplement* headed 'Choice Row Splits Labour', St John-Stevas moved to a picture: 'It does not do her justice, but it is not bad – underneath which there appears "*Shirley Williams: 'I will'*". On the other side, there is another picture, rather more unflattering, underneath which there appears "*Caroline Benn: 'You won't'*".' He called it 'bad enough' having 'Macbeth in the Cabinet, we do not want Lady Macbeth around as well'. The nub of the matter was to present Williams as a weak minister 'unable or unwilling to take the decisive action needed in education', but he rather undermined his appeal with a smug peroration in Latin, which he declined to translate, 'since standards have not fallen'. As Callaghan stoutly declared, 'I don't know what it means', it fell to Labour's Bryan Davies to ask whether achievements in Latin were the new measuring rod.[33]

CONCLUSION

We remember Callaghan today for the contribution he made to a policy area for which he never held direct ministerial responsibility. Looking back on the Ruskin legacy for the Open University's Education Bulletin radio series in 1993, Callaghan explained his speech made waves. "'Oh, the PM, he was clearly too political to talk about education, what on earth does he know about it anyway?", which might have been true, but at least I'd got the interest of lots of parents and children at heart, and they could correct me if I was wrong.' Some thought he did change the agenda; 'that now the focus was on a particular section of the school population, which, in terms that he might have used, were the "non-academic" pupils', as Caroline Benn put it. Stuart Maclure, who had become editor of the *Times Educational Supplement* in 1969, called it a 'watershed' when a 'proactive' Ministry of Education was going to go out and start making some change.[34]

From the perspective of 2020, Callaghan's distrust of what he called 'progressive education', support for meritocratic selection and emphasis on accountability measures helped prepare the ground for an active restructuring of the educational system that reinforced a hierarchy of schools just as Caroline Benn predicted. Unlike the double standards embedded in much of the media reporting of allegations about educational decline, she and Brian Simon did present detailed evidence from both sides about comprehensive education. The 1977 Green Paper made it clear that there was no evidence that standards in schools had fallen. The pity is that the psychosocial cost of Callaghan's personal self-identification as 'uneducated', due to lack of a degree, may have manifested itself in an unreflective conservatism that never understood the arguments and values of Labour intellectuals who made the educational case against segregation based on so-called 'ability'.

NOTES

1   'The Prime Minister's Ruskin speech', *Education*, 22 October 1976, p. 332.
2   Caroline Benn papers, UCL Institute of Education, 'Caroline DeCamp Benn: a comprehensive life, 1926–2000', British Academy/Leverhulme: SG131085. I appreciate the financial support of the British Academy/Leverhulme Trust.
3   J. Callaghan, *Time and Chance* (London: Collins, 1987), p. 35.
4   S. Williams, *Climbing the Bookshelves* (London: Virago, 2010), p. 176.
5   B. Donoughue, *Downing Street Diary, Volume Two – With James Callaghan in No. 10* (London: Pimlico, 2009), p. 15.
6   O. Banks, *Parity and Prestige in English Secondary Education: A Study in Educational Sociology* (London, Routledge and Kegan Paul, 1955); D. Reay, *Miseducation, Inequality, Education and the Working Classes* (Bristol: Polity, 2017); B. Simon, *Intelligence Testing and the Comprehensive School* (London: Lawrence & Wishart, 1953).
7   M. Young, *The Rise of the Meritocracy* (London, Thames & Hudson, 1958); A. Sampson, *Anatomy of Britain* (London: Hodder & Stoughton, 1962), p. 190.
8   S. J. Ball and S. Exley, 'Making Policy With "Good Ideas": Policy Networks and the "Intellectuals" of New Labour', *Journal of Education Policy* (2010), vol. 25, no. 2, p. 152.
9   D. Marsden, *Politicians, Equality and Comprehensives* (London: Fabian Society, 1971); B. Simon 'What is a Comprehensive School? Replies to Dennis Marsden', *Comprehensive Education* (1970), vol. 14, no. 1, pp. 6–8.
10 J. Callaghan, *Time and Chance*, p. 409.
11 B. Donoughue, *In the Heat of the Kitchen* (London: Politico, 2003), p. 240.
12 B. Simon, *Education and the Social Order, 1940–1990* (London: Lawrence & Wishart, 2010), p. 443, p. 586.
13 *Ibid.*, pp. 396–9, p. 443.
14 CCCS, *Unpopular Education: Schooling and Social Democracy in England since 1944* (London: Hutchinson, 1981), p. 217; Callaghan, *Time and Chance*, p. 409; C. Chitty, *Towards a New Education System: The Victory of the New Right?* (Lewes: Falmer, 1989).
15 J. Callaghan, Leader's Speech, Blackpool 1976: http://www.britishpoliticalspeech.org/speech-archive.htm?speech=174
16 Donoughue, *Downing Street Diary, Volume Two*, p. 82.

17 T. Benn, *Against the Tide: Diaries 1973–76* (London: Arrow, 1990), p. 626.

18 Blackpool 1976; 'The Prime Minister's Ruskin speech, *Education*, 22 October 1976, pp. 332–3.

19 T. Benn, *Against the Tide*, p. 631.

20 A. Weinstock, 'I Blame the Teachers', *Times Educational Supplement*, 23 January 1976; J. Methven, 'What Industry Wants', *Times Educational Supplement*, 29 October 1976.

21 T. Benn, *Against the Tide*, p. 616.

22 R. Boyson, *The Crisis in Education* (London: Woburn, 1975), p. 98.

23 *The Sun*, 11 November 1976; *Evening Standard*, 12 November 1976; Caroline Benn (CB) papers, UCL Institute of Education, Box 41/1, Holland Park School 1970–78.

24 *Kensington News and Post*, 19 November 1976; 25 March 1977; CB Box 41/1.

25 C. Benn, 'The Comprehensive Reform: All Over But the Reorganising', *FORUM* (1976), vol. 19, no. 1, pp. 2–7.

26 Williams, *Climbing the Bookshelves*, p. 234.

27 Campaign for Comprehensive Education, 1977, p. 5; CB Box 1/5 Labour Party (LP) Science and Education Subcommittee.

28 M. Morris, quoted in R. V. Seifert, *Teaching Militancy: A History of Teacher Strikes, 1896–1987* (London: Falmer, 1987), p. 136.

29 Williams, *Climbing the Bookshelves*, p. 237.

30 C. Benn to B. Simon, n.d., CB Box 1/5 Labour Party Science and Education Subcommittee.

31 T. Benn, *Conflicts of Interest: Diaries 1977–80* (London: Arrow, 1991), p. 232.

32 'In the Gallery: Opposing Schools of Thought', *The Guardian*, 5 November 1977, CB Box 3/5 LP Science and Education Subcommittee.

33 Hansard, HC Deb, 4 November 1977, vol 938, col. 165–270: https://api.parliament.uk/historic-hansard/commons/1977/nov/04/education-and-social-services

34 'Witness to Change', BBC/Open University, 20 June 1993.

11

DEVOLUTION AND LOCAL GOVERNMENT

Neil Pye

IN APRIL 1976, WHEN James Callaghan became Prime Minister, replacing the retiring Harold Wilson, his Labour government inherited a devolution policy which he both politically and personally opposed. During the 1960s, Callaghan's predecessor had established two Royal Commissions, the first of which looked at the pattern of local governance and the second of which explored the nature of national and regional devolution. The creation of those commissions was in response to demands from nations within the British union, as well as some of the English regions, whose politicians felt that the Westminster and Whitehall model of governance had become too detached and remote from the needs of both their citizens and places. Further, the devolution debate under the Callaghan administration came about during a period of great social, economic and political turbulence, when questions were being raised about whether the United Kingdom had become ungovernable following the turmoil that brought down Edward Heath's Conservative administration in 1974.

For three years, the Labour government of James Callaghan tried
to tackle the devolution question cautiously and continued with the
manifesto pledges that Harold Wilson's Labour government was
elected on at the February and October 1974 general elections. This
policy agenda was pursued in accordance with the core aims of the
Labour Party, for which the notion of Scotland being governed by
Scotland had been championed previously by Labour's founding
leader, Keir Hardie, and was a major reason for the party's existence.
The rise of nationalism in both Scotland and Wales during the post-
war era had forced Labour to revisit Hardie's home rule policy. This
chapter will tell the story of how James Callaghan's administration
tentatively attempted to implement a divisive devolution policy that
would eventually cost the Labour Party the right to govern, and ultimately lead to eighteen years in opposition, which, at the time, very
few politicians and pundits predicted.

SCOTLAND AND WALES

Amid foreign competition and financial indebtedness to the United
States following the Second World War, from 1964 to 1970, the Labour
government led by Harold Wilson tried to solve Britain's poor economic and industrial performance through the 'white heat of technology'. In doing so, devolution and regional development were seen
as a way forward.[1] The first of the two Royal Commissions Wilson's
government set up during May 1966 examined the constitution, and
the second, the Scottish question.[2]

Beginning with the long-standing issue of home rule, in 1969 the
Kilbrandon Commission was charged with the task of examining
the constitution, along with the intention of both finding ways of
strengthening democracy and making government more accountable
to the people.[3] For five years, an extensive consultation process took

place with representatives from Scotland and Wales, and it was later extended to the English regions. In October 1973 the commission, chaired by Lord Kilbrandon, produced its findings, which unanimously rejected separatism and federalism, and recommended directly elected Scottish and Welsh assemblies, 'without damaging the unity of the United Kingdom'.[4]

For a number of years, politicians in both Scotland and Wales had become quite critical of the Westminster and Whitehall model of governance. In Scotland's case, the demands for devolution and separation could be traced back to the 1880s over disputes about poor housing and the Crofters Acts.[5] With regard to Wales, the demands for devolution were mainly due to the need for greater decision-making power for politicians in the south and south-west of the country over its own economic and industrial affairs, and in the north, cultural needs that included the preservation of its language.[6]

In Scotland, many inhabitants were quite critical about the failure of successive post-war Westminster-based governments in tackling the country's 'brain drain' and the economic problems of the Central Lowlands, for which it was felt that the discovery of North Sea oil would produce employment for all in Scotland and better wages. This gave rise to suggestions that Edinburgh rather than Westminster should be its natural seat of government.[7] A poll conducted by the *Scotsman* newspaper on 3 June 1975 showed substantial dissatisfaction among Scottish people as 69 per cent of those asked felt that the system of governing Britain either 'could be improved quite a lot' or needed 'a great deal of improvement'.[8]

On the back of Winnie Ewing's stunning by-election victory for the SNP at Hamilton in 1967, Margo MacDonald's wipe-out of a 16,000 Labour majority at the Govan by-election in 1973, and triumphs for Plaid Cymru at a local government level in traditional Welsh Labour heartlands during the early to mid-1970s, the October 1974 general election was seen as 'a take-off point' for both parties, where the SNP gained eleven seats and Plaid Cymru three seats.[9] For the very first time, the SNP exhibited the traits of a truly national party as every constituency in Scotland was contested, and support for its candidates rose from between 4,000 and 6,000 votes to roughly 9,500 votes.[10] A similar trend occurred in parts of Wales, which frightened the Labour Party.[11]

In August that year, James Callaghan had been so vehemently opposed to the idea of devolution and the creation of National Assemblies for Scotland and Wales that he tried to stop Labour's National Executive Committee from publishing the policy document entitled 'Bring Power Back to the People'.[12] On becoming Prime Minister in April 1976, it was quite clear that Callaghan did not have the stomach to pursue such a divisive policy agenda, and nor did the Labour Party. Many pundits felt that the pursuit of devolution was a high-risk strategy.[13]

The devolution question caused divisions among Welsh Labour politicians. Elystan Morgan felt that an elected Welsh Assembly was needed for the democratic scrutiny of day-to-day matters in Wales, which the centralised and top-down Westminster system of governance had failed to achieve. Morgan said that if devolution was not delivered then Wales would lurch into 'a miserable retreat of defeatism and despair'. Opposing that view was future Labour leader, Neil Kinnock, who warned that devolution would lead to 'a process of disintegration' and cautioned that Welsh rights that existed through being an integrated part of the UK would be diminished.[14]

At the time, a crucial question being asked was how much the devolved assemblies, along with a system of governance for Scotland and Wales, would cost in monetary terms, and also whether such public spending could be justified. For instance, in terms of capital costs, in the case of Wales, during 1978 it was estimated that the refurbishment of the Exchange Buildings in Cardiff's docklands as the location of the Welsh Assembly would cost in the region of £3 million. The creation of the Welsh Parliament would have also entailed extra costs for the Welsh Office, in terms of office space and staffing, which would have amounted to another £1 million. Also, setting up an assembly would have meant moving and relocating civil servants to Cardiff, for which the cost of doing so was estimated to have been in the region of £1.25 million. Further, the cost to the Labour government of holding the referendum in Wales amounted to £500,000, and on the establishment of the Assembly, the cost of staging its first elections would have cost £750,000. On Wales alone, the total capital costs amounted to £6.5 million, and that was before the Welsh Assembly had sat for its first-ever meeting. It was estimated that the administrative costs of both Scottish and Welsh Assemblies would amount to £35 million.[15]

In terms of the layout of the Scottish and Welsh devolution referendums, the basic question was just 'Yes' or 'No', but the system was not as simple as it appeared, as a number of wrecking amendments had previously been included in the legislation by opponents of devolution.[16] The Scottish and Welsh referendums were framed by a rule, whereby a minimum of 40 per cent of voters had to vote 'Yes' if an assembly was to be established automatically. For example, in Wales, 40 per cent of the people who were entitled to vote had to vote 'Yes' in order to settle the referendum, and likewise in Scotland. Therefore, out of roughly two million potential voters, 800,000 inhabitants had to vote 'Yes' to gain a devolved assembly for Wales.[17]

The referendum was also complicated by the proviso that there had to be a majority of more than half the people voting 'Yes' for devolution to succeed. This arithmetic was confused by the fact that voting registers being compiled in November did not come into force until the middle of February, which meant that they did not account for the deaths of voters, or those voters who were under eighteen in November and therefore were ineligible to vote on the day of the referendum in March 1979. Another anomaly was the fact that a number of students who lived and attended universities in either Scotland or

Wales could have been twice registered to vote, both where they lived and where they studied. The students could only vote once, but their second registration could count towards the overall total required to make the 40 per cent threshold. Also, at the ballot box, Welsh voters were asked, 'Do you want the provisions of the Wales Act 1978 to be put into effect?', and likewise for Scottish voters, which confused many people over the actual exercise.[18]

The referendum took place on St David's Day, which was supposed to inject a sense of patriotic fervour, but the Welsh population seemed indifferent about devolution. On 2 March 1979, the results were declared, and when they all came in, not a single Welsh county had voted in favour. By a majority of four to one, the people of Wales said 'No' to devolution. Out of 1,203,422 votes cast, the total number of 'Yes' votes amounted to 243,048, while those who voted 'No' amounted to 956,330. This was a crushing defeat for the supporters of a devolved assembly for Wales. In Scotland, there was a majority of 52 per cent to 48 per cent for setting up a Scottish parliament, but it was not enough of a majority to cross the threshold.[19]

Despite suffering a heavy defeat, James Callaghan refused to shelve Labour's Scottish and Welsh Assembly proposals.[20] The government had clearly misunderstood the mood of the Welsh people and, likewise, the people of Scotland, for which the issue would come back to haunt Labour many years later. Politically, the result of the referendum posed many problems for Plaid Cymru, which had supported Labour's proposals, and for the SNP in Scotland in the long-term, for this was a huge blow to its self-confidence.

On 22 March 1979, James Callaghan appeared on television and insisted that Britain's unity depended upon providing devolved government for Scotland, although at the time, eleven SNP MPs at Westminster had met and agreed upon the terms of a motion of no confidence in the government.[21] Callaghan's intervention prompted further debates about the 'West Lothian question', regarding which,

during a 1977 parliamentary debate, the Scottish anti-devolution politician Tam Dalyell had previously argued that it would be unfair for
Scottish MPs to have equal rights to vote on English-only legislation.
This is a question that has reverberated for many years, and one for
which Labour has failed to arrive at a solution.[22]

ENGLAND

The second major plank of James Callaghan's devolution policy involved tackling the problems associated with the UK's regions, which
was closely interlinked with its national devolution strategy for Scotland and Wales. In 1966, Harold Wilson's Labour administration
established the Royal Commission on Local Government, chaired by
Lord Redcliffe-Maud, which looked at the pattern of local government, as it had not undergone any major reform since measures were
introduced in 1888 and 1894.[23] At the time, there were roughly 1,400
local authorities and 19,000 councillors in existence. The commission report recommended the creation of sixty-one unitary authorities and local government areas outside Greater London, for which
in fifty-eight of those, one single authority would be responsible for
all services.[24]

Prior to 1974, the system of local government was not only 'complicated and uneven' but also 'a relic of the late-Victorian age', which
had failed to take into account shifts in population and the widespread growth of communications. Under the system created in 1888,
each county was divided into urban and rural county districts with
some of the former being boroughs. Many of the large municipalities
were given the position of county boroughs, for which their councils
combined the powers of both county and district councils, and were
wholly autonomous unitary authorities. However, where the two-tier
system prevailed, the division of functions between separate levels of

authority created difficulties for the efficient administration of services, and many authorities were far too small in size for the functions they were called upon to fulfil.[25]

When the Redcliffe-Maud Commission produced its findings in 1969, had Labour won the June 1970 general election, it would have implemented its recommendations.[26] However, the Wilson administration lost out to Edward Heath's Conservative Party, which for four years grappled with the policy. Until 1972, a problem which faced the Secretary of State for the Environment, Peter Walker, and his Parliamentary Under-Secretary of State, Michael Heseltine, was that the system of local government, particularly within the counties and districts, was mainly controlled by Conservative councillors who were also the officers of Conservative Associations. On that basis, Peter Walker had to find an alternative solution to significantly reduce the number of local authorities, from 1,400 to roughly 400, but not to the sixty which the Redcliffe-Maud Commission had specified.[27]

The 1972 Local Government Act led to the creation of a two-tier system of counties and districts throughout England and Wales, with fewer and larger authorities than previously. This legislation gave rise to the abolition of county boroughs and, as a consequence, the special characteristics of metropolitan areas were recognised through the allocation of more functions to the metropolitan districts than to their non-metropolitan counterparts. Metropolitan districts were made responsible for education and social services, which in non-metropolitan areas were still county functions. Further, all county councils were allowed to retain their strategic functions.[28] According to Michael Heseltine, the solution that Peter Walker had achieved was not 'intellectually clever' but more representative of real politics.[29]

Both in opposition and after returning to power in 1974, the Labour Party was unhappy with the reorganisation that had taken place. On 5 November 1976, shortly after being appointed Secretary of State for the Environment by Prime Minister James Callaghan, Peter Shore tried to establish an interdepartmental working group to study organic change in local government. The Welsh Office criticised the 1974 reorganisation of local government because it had created a number of shortcomings and 'particularly strong' discontent in Wales.[30] Shore was hugely critical of the Constitution Unit's consultation document. His 'colourful and dramatic' focus of attack was about the 'appalling' style of the document. Second, Shore felt that it did not clearly state whether the government was prepared to contemplate major constitutional changes, and third, the document had only originated from the need to get the Scottish and Welsh Bills through, for which Shore believed that the idea of an English Development Agency should have been 'more sharply postulated'.[31]

While Peter Shore's views lacked support, Shirley Williams felt that the consultation document did not face up to the real political difficulties for England of substantial devolution to Scotland and Wales. However, the Constitution Unit document did receive support from Merlyn Rees and junior ministers from the Treasury, Industry and DHSS, as well as in writing by the Welsh Office.[32] Two consultation documents produced by Peter Shore and John Smith were later put before the Ministerial Committee on Devolution Strategy; of the two, junior ministers found Shore's draft 'more cogent and appealing'.[33]

When discussing the possible impact of the Labour government's devolution policies, which would have given the Scottish and Welsh Assemblies a wide range of devolved powers, under the proposals, both assemblies would not have been given taxation powers to raise revenues. The main source of finance for the Scottish and Welsh Assemblies would have been a block grant negotiated annually from Westminster. The Labour government had plans to put in place a separate ceiling for borrowing for capital investment by local authorities and public corporations for devolved purposes. In relation to the block grant, the main principle which would have determined this was whether the devolved administrations could provide comparable standards of public services to those in England, based upon an objective assessment of needs. The method of working out the size of the block grant would have been determined by scrutiny and political debate.[34]

As the Labour government tried to push its devolution legislation through Parliament, eight north-east Labour MPs opposed this. Outside the National Enterprise Board (NEB), which had previously been set up by the recent Wilson administration in 1975 to support industries, what they wanted was the establishment of regional development agencies in England. At the time, there was support for the measure on the basis of the success of the Scottish Development Agency, which supported small and medium enterprises. However, the Secretary of State for Industry, Eric Varley, opposed such demands on the basis that he feared the creation of a number of them across the UK would result in fragmentation and rivalry between agencies, which in turn would 'make any coherent regional policy extremely difficult'.[35] Further, he felt such measures would affect the role of the NEB and diminish it to that of a state holding company for very large companies established in more than one region.[36]

From those discussions, an official group on Regional Policy and Devolution was created and chaired by the Cabinet Office, having arisen from a ministerial committee about devolution strategy on 20 October 1976. This was due to concerns that people in the English regions would possibly press for constitutional change as 'the best way of protecting their economic interests'.[37] The terms of reference for this group were:

> to identify those aspects of existing and contemplated regional policies likely to cause concern to the English regions in the context of devolution; to make recommendations about adaptations to those policies or new policy departures which might alleviate that concern; and to advise Ministers accordingly.[38]

As the group began its work, many circumstances changed, namely through the defeat of the timetable motion on the Scotland and Wales Bill. Further, the creation of the Lib–Lab Pact in 1977 caused uncertainty about the future of devolution proposals and their direction. The group doubted whether it was practical to give public opinion in certain English regions adequate reassurances about the maintenance of effective regional policies. As a consequence, an interim report was submitted which called on the government to strengthen its regional policy through increasing the role of Regional Economic Planning Councils, the establishment of development agencies in the north and north-west regions and a general review of assisted area boundaries.[39]

Within the English regions, there were differences over devolution due to the feeling that they 'lacked muscle' within government and that when important decisions were taken, their case was treated as a default position. This meant that their voice at the government table appeared 'fragmented', but there was much agreement, along with wider calls for the strengthening of Regional Economic Planning Councils and the establishment of an English Development Agency or Agencies in some of the English regions.[40] Varley believed that the best approach did not involve the creation of regional development agencies, but in the NEB putting 'increased effort and resources behind its regional activities', especially in relation to support for small and medium firms. He cited that the NEB's operations in the north-east and north-west had been 'relatively modest', amounting to 'half a dozen investments in all' that involved the creation of 2,500 jobs.[41]

Taking on board those views, Peter Shore realised that the structure of local government set up in 1974 was 'not universally admired' and recognised that many people were 'genuinely confused' about its allocation of functions, which prompted a need for change. Shore cited the dismantling of the former county boroughs (FCBs) as the least popular aspect of the reorganisation, and his main proposal involved the transfer of responsibility for education and personal services (PSS) from the counties concerned to the nine largest FCBs.[42]

At the time, what Peter Shore wanted was not a 'root and branch' review, but rather an adjustment of what was seen as being an unequal situation between the district authorities in metropolitan areas and the district authority in non-metropolitan areas. He also wanted all FCBs to have equal status with metropolitan authorities, insofar as the 1974 changes had stripped a number of cities of key functions.[43] At the same time, the Environment Secretary felt that too much emphasis had previously been placed on the development of new towns at the expense of the inner cities, and wanted the implementation of the 1968 Seebohm Committee recommendations, which advocated that services such as housing, education and social services be integrated.[44]

In early 1978, Prime Minister James Callaghan asked Cabinet ministers with relevant functional responsibilities to examine Shore's proposals.[45] Following lengthy discussions, on 3 August 1978 the Labour government recognised that there was a good case for 'organic' or limited change in the distribution of some functions between county and district councils. Those changes did not imply any major alterations to boundaries, but minor amendments to the structure of local governance. In essence, 'organic change' involved both tweaking and refining the functions of local authorities in districts that required such intervention. However, there were some anomalies, insofar as Greater London would not have been affected by the changes proposed, and nor would Wales, where under the 1978 Wales Act, the Welsh Assembly would have been required to review local government structures and functions. It was to this end that the government's proposals for each of the principal functions were determined:

1. For personal social services, the case for transferring the function to the larger districts that wanted it (in particular those that had it before the 1974 reorganisation) was in principle strong. The definition of districts which might properly have this function and the processes by which decisions on individual cases would be reached were to be considered further, but the districts would need to have a population of at least 100,000, and it would be necessary to pay full regard to any recommendations the Royal Commission on the National Health Service might make about the structure of the service and its relationship with personal social services.
2. For education, transfer would be considered only in respect of the nine largest former county boroughs; and reviews would be made individually, case by case, for any seeking transfer.
3. The government would consider the possibility that some districts could exercise highways and traffic powers in their own right, while preserving the county's proper responsibilities for planning and for allocating resources effectively.
4. In the field of town and country planning, all district councils should be solely responsible for development control decisions on all but a narrow group of matters.[46]

By the time James Callaghan's government tried to introduce its policy measures for 'Organic Change in Local Government' during early 1979, they had become mired by the Winter of Discontent and fighting losing battles with various trade unions over pay claims. This followed the disastrous introduction of a 5 per cent limit on public sector wage increases as an anti-inflationary measure during the autumn of 1978, and at a time when political pundits felt that Callaghan should have gone to the country.[47] As a result, Shore's measures became lost following Labour's general election defeat in May that year.

THE INNER CITIES

Directly linked to the problems of governing the UK's regions was the state of Britain's inner cities, which from the immediate post-war era had fallen into steep decay. Liverpool's economy, for instance, which was heavily reliant upon its port and port-related industries, had experienced massive unemployment once it fell into decline. As well as the poor quality of the city's housing stock and anti-social behaviour, an exodus of the inner-city population to neighbouring new towns such as Skelmersdale, Runcorn and Kirkby exposed the failings of Liverpool's education provision. This led not only to a rapid decline in the number of students attending schools within its city boundaries but also to declining standards – all of which would later come to a head through the Croxteth Comprehensive School dispute in 1982, where parents staged a lock-in to keep the school open. Around the same time, tensions emerged between the police and ethnic communities which needed urgent solutions.[48]

During the summer of 1977, Labour launched a White Paper titled 'Policy for the Inner Cities'. This document outlined many initiatives that were designed to give local authorities new powers to help arrest the decline of urban areas. The paper was later criticised on several fronts as it did not address what was seen at the time as the 'inherent problems' of using the Rate Support Grant as a financial means of delivering urban renewal and failed to recognise the central importance of the collapse of the inner-city economy.[49] A further criticism outlined the lack of coordination at central government level in dealing with inner-city problems, for which the proposals lacked a regional dimension.[50]

Despite this, Prime Minister James Callaghan promised an assault on the 'vast problems of our inner cities on a huge scale'. On visits to some of the worst areas, which were bleak, empty landscapes littered with shattered buildings and vandalised houses, Callaghan said that 'the people who remain there and who exist in this desolate

environment are all too often the same people who suffer from poverty and face acute social problems'. The Prime Minister argued that
some of the damage had been inflicted through previous redevelop-
ment policies which had ruined many small businesses and firms.[51]

With regard to Liverpool and its city region, during 1978 and 1979
Callaghan and Shore met two delegations consisting of MPs, local
councillors, council officials and business leaders, first in April 1978,
and second in February 1979. Callaghan and Shore listened to a range
of opinions which included calls from the Walton MP Eric Heffer for
the appointment of a 'Minister for Merseyside' who would have a seat
in government and act as a link between central and local government
to coordinate policy responses to the problems associated with the
conurbation.[52] Another idea discussed was the creation of Regional
Development Agencies (RDAs), which both the Prime Minister and
Shore seemed more receptive to.[53] However, it would not be until
1997, with the election of a Labour government led by Tony Blair,
that RDAs would eventually come about as a vital link between the
central and local government, even though Michael Heseltine had
previously set up the Merseyside Development Corporation (MDC),
which performed a similar role.[54]

On the subject of a 'Minister for Merseyside', although this later
came to fruition in the immediate aftermath of the 1981 inner-city
disturbances which affected the Toxteth, Liverpool 8 area of the city,
in 1978 Callaghan had refused to appoint a Cabinet minister for the
region on the basis that it would lead to many similar claims from
other cities and regions.[55] An alternative measure which had already
been introduced by Shore in 1978 was the Inner City Partnership,
through which a minister was put into a personal relationship with
a city leader. Shore ran the initiative with a special interest in Liverpool, and on becoming Secretary of State for the Environment
when Margaret Thatcher's Conservative Party were elected into
office in May 1979, Michael Heseltine retained what he saw as being

'quite a commendable scheme', as well as taking on Shore's previous responsibilities.[56]

Becoming personally involved with Liverpool, Heseltine said that prior to the creation of the partnership, the city and its conurbation had lacked leadership and that there was 'no great strategy or no great plan'.[57] All of which, according to Michael Parkinson, would later play a huge role in Liverpool's steep decline during the early years of Margaret Thatcher's premiership, which saw mass unemployment, rioting and the total breakdown of community relations, all of which Heseltine later had to address on becoming Minister for Merseyside in October 1981.[58] As a result of the Inner City Partnership created by Peter Shore from within James Callaghan's Labour administration, the strong links between central and local governance still exist to this day. This has spawned many innovations, including 'City Challenge' during the early 1990s, which involved local authorities developing ideas and strategies for transforming inner city areas on the basis of public and private sector partnerships, as well as more recently the creation of metro mayors under the 2010–15 Conservative–Liberal Democrat coalition government, with the intention of rebalancing the UK economy and developing the city regions.[59]

CONCLUSION

According to John Shepherd, who in 2013 penned the book *Crisis? What Crisis?* examining the 1978–79 Winter of Discontent, devolution proved to be the undoing of Callaghan and the Labour government.[60] The infamous vote of no confidence on 28 March 1979 in which, ironically, eleven Scottish Nationalist MPs played their part in bringing down the government, paved the way for a general election in May that year, which propelled Margaret Thatcher's Conservative Party to power and brought about eighteen years of opposition for

Labour. According to the former deputy leader of the Labour Party, Roy Hattersley, the fall of the Callaghan administration also heralded the end of Old Labour in government as a party of nationalisation, redistributive taxation and trade union power.[61] Over eighteen years later, it would take a New Labour government led by Tony Blair and then Gordon Brown between 1997 and 2010 to introduce devolved assemblies for Scotland and Wales, along with many other policy innovations for the regions and inner cities, building upon those once devised by Shore. Both Callaghan and Keir Hardie had promised devolution, which New Labour eventually delivered.

NOTES

1   'Harold Wilson's "white heat of technology" speech 50 years on', *The Guardian*, 19 September 2013: https://www.theguardian.com/science/political-science/2013/sep/19/harold-wilson-white-heat-technology-speech

2   PREM 16/460, Annex A, 'Democracy and Devolution – Proposals for Scotland and Wales', Introduction, p. 1, 17 September 1974.

3   PREM 16/460, Statement by Edward Short, Lord President of the Council, presenting the White Paper on Democracy and Devolution in *London Today*, 17 September 1974.

4   *Ibid.* and 'Democracy and Devolution – Proposals for Scotland and Wales', 17 September 1974.

5   Stephen Mason, MP for Mid-Lanarkshire, speaking about the '1886 Crofters (Scotland) Act – Inadequacy of the Act', Hansard, HC Deb, 31 August 1886, vol. 308, cols 898–990; 'Home Rule for Scotland', Hansard, HC Deb, 9 April 1889, vol. 335, cols 68–124.

6   'Mr Evans on the dual-language road to rule', *The Guardian*, 23 October 1970.

7   'Scottish choice', *The Observer*, 8 August 1976.

8   *The Scotsman*, 3 June 1975; PREM 16/462 in 'Devolution, Meeting: 16 June 1975', Bernard Donoughue to Harold Wilson, 13 June 1975.

9   PREM 16/463, 'Political aspects of devolution in Wales', pp. 2–3; 'Scottish Nationalist ousts Labour at Glasgow while Tories retain Edinburgh and Hove', *The Times*, 9 November 1973.

10 PREM 16/126, 'A Take-Off Point; The Political Situation in Scotland Today: The Rise of the Scottish National Party', Alex Neil, Scottish Research Officer, June 1974.

11 *Ibid.*

12 'Change could hinder plans for Scottish devolution', *The Guardian*, 17 March 1976.

13 'Callaghan hints at referenda for Scots and Welsh', *The Guardian*, 14 December 1976.

14 *Ibid.*; 'Devolution issue splits Wales Labour Party', *The Guardian*, 22 May 1978.

15 'Initial administrative cost will be total of £35.3m', *The Times*, 1 December 1976; 'Blueprint for warfare between departments', *The Times*, 11 December 1976; 'Scotland and the tartan tariff', *The Guardian*, 14 January 1977; *Devo 79*, BBC Two, 1 October 2007: https://www.bbc.co.uk/programmes/b00803fc

16 'The bread and circuses of devolution', *The Times*, 14 November 1977; 'Labour rebels aim to wreck devolution Bills in guillotine vote', *The Times*, 15 November 1977; 'The Scottish devolution dilemma', *The Times*, 14 March 1978; 'Confusion hits Wales Bill after Government defeats', *The Guardian*, 20 April 1978; 'Government defeated twice on Wales Bill', *The Times*, 14 June 1978.

17 *Devo 79.*

18 'One question gets the wrong answer', *The Guardian*, 1 February 1977; *Devo 79.*

19 *Devo 79*; 'Wales votes No to assembly by four to one', *The Guardian*, 3 March 1979.

20 'Callaghan in no hurry to axe devolution plans', *The Guardian*, 7 March 1979.

21 'Callaghan sticks to devolution as SNP ponder vote', *The Guardian*, 22 March 1979.

22 'What is the West Lothian Question?', *New Statesman*, 19 September 2014: https://www.newstatesman.com/politics/2014/09/what-west-lothian-question; 'BBC Scotland Investigates, The Fall of Labour', BBC Scotland, 5 July 2015: https://www.bbc.co.uk/programmes/b060dwn3

23 PREM 13/2762, Statement by the Prime Minister on the Redcliffe-Maud Report, 9 June 1969.

24 *Ibid.*

25 PREM 16/2158, White Paper: 'Organic Change in Local Government', 19 January 1979.

26 PREM 2763, 'Note of a meeting between Minister without Portfolio and Sir Mark Henig on 23 July 1969, on the Redcliffe-Maud Report'.

27 Lord Michael Heseltine speaking at RIBA North, Liverpool, 17 October 2018.

28 'Organic Change' pp. 1–2.

29 Lord Heseltine speaking at RIBA North.

30 PREM 16/1359, Peter Shore MP to the Rt Hon. John Morris QC MP, Welsh Office, 30 November 1976.

31 PREM 16/1359, Robert Armstrong to Prime Minister James Callaghan, 'Devolution and England', 30 November 1976.

32 PREM 16/1359, Robert Armstrong to Prime Minister James Callaghan, 'Outcome of Monday's DVY', 24 November 1976.

33 PREM 16/1359, Robert Armstrong to Prime Minister James Callaghan, 'Devolution and England', 30 November 1976.

34 PREM 16/1359, John Hunt to Mr Meadway, 21 July 1977.

35 *Ibid.*

36 *Ibid.*

37 PREM 16/1359, John Hunt to Prime Minister James Callaghan, 10 May 1977.

38 *Ibid.*

39 PREM 16/1359, John Hunt to Prime Minister James Callaghan, 10 May 1977.

40 PREM 16/1359, John Hunt to Mr Meadway, 21 July 1977.

41 PREM 16/1359, Miss Anna Butterworth, Private Secretary to Eric Varley to John Meadway, Private Secretary to Prime Minister, James Callaghan, 19 July 1977.

42 PREM 16/1359, J. W. Stevens, Private Secretary to J. W. S. Dempster, Principal Private Secretary of State to the Environment, 4 August 1977.

43 *Ibid.*

44 PREM 13/1359, 'Organic Change in Local Government: Memorandum by the Secretary of State for the Environment', 10 December 1976.

45 PREM 16/2158, White Paper: Organic Change in Local Government, 19 January 1979.

46 *Ibid.*

47 See J. Shepherd, *Crisis? What Crisis? The Callaghan Government and the British 'Winter of Discontent'* (Manchester: Manchester University Press, 2013).

48 See PREM 16/2164, Unemployment on Merseyside, 1975–8; AT 81/289, Secretary of State's initiatives on Merseyside; ET 16/6, Ethnic Minorities in Liverpool.; 'Alarm as survey sees big drift from city', *Liverpool Echo*, 3 September 1979.

49 'Minutes of the Town and Country Planning Sub-Committee', Transport House, 13 September 1977, in Labour NEC Minutes, 23 November 1977.

50 *Ibid.*

51 'Mr Callaghan promises vast help for inner cities', *The Times*, 31 January 1977.

52 PREM 16/1750, 'Notes of a meeting held in the Prime Minister's room in the House of Commons at 1600 hours on Thursday 27 April 1978 with representatives of the City of Liverpool'; PREM 16/2218, 'Note of a meeting held in the Prime Minister's room at the House of Commons at 1600', 8 February 1979.

53 PREM 16/2218, M. J. Vile, Cabinet Office to Peter Mason, Department of Industry, 26 February 1979.

54 See AT 81/248, Secretary of State initiative on Merseyside: The Role of Merseyside Development Corporation; D 15/79 Regional Development Agencies.

55 PREM 16/2218, 'Note of a meeting held in the Prime Minister's room at the House of Commons at 1600', 8 February 1979.

56 'City backs £2.5m for improving the inner areas', *Liverpool Echo*, 2 February 1978; Lord Heseltine speaking at RIBA North, Liverpool, 17 October 2018.

57 *Ibid.*

58 See M. Parkinson, *Liverpool on the Brink: One City's Struggle Against Government's Cuts* (Cambridge, MA: Burlington Press, 1986); 'Now ... A Supremo for Merseyside', *Liverpool Echo*, 9 October 1981.

59 'Councils to vie for Tarzan cash – £750m is City Challenge glittering prize', *Liverpool Echo*, 18 February 1992; 'A vision of the future from the "Minister for Merseyside"', *The Times*, 20 October 2011; 'Now ... A supremo for Merseyside', *Liverpool Echo*, 9 October 1981.

60 Shepherd, *Crisis? What Crisis?*, p. 156.

61 'The Party's Over', *The Observer*, 22 March 2009: https://www.theguardian.com/politics/2009/mar/22/james-callaghan-labour-1979-thatcher

12

CALLAGHAN AND
NORTHERN IRELAND

Kevin Bean and Pauline Hadaway

SPEAKING IN JULY 1981 during a debate about the renewal of emergency powers in Northern Ireland, James Callaghan
made a highly significant intervention, in which he admitted to the
exhaustion of British policy in the region since the late 1960s. While
supporting the emergency powers, Callaghan argued that the situation had reached 'an almost total stalemate' whereby twelve years of
'well-intentioned and well worked-out proposals ... to create a stable
political structure' had been rejected 'by one community or the other,
and sometimes by both'. The resulting deadlock suggested that

> [t]he time has come when we in Westminster must remove any
> lingering belief among the two communities that it is the duty and
> the responsibility of the British Government alone to overcome the
> obduracy of whichever community is in opposition to what British
> Ministers propose. I believe that this would mark a sea change in our
> relationship with the Province.[1]

Going beyond the familiar exasperation of British politicians when confronted with the intractable nature of the communal conflict in Northern Ireland, Callaghan questioned whether 'our dual policy of direct rule combined with firmness' could ever lead to a permanent political solution. He argued instead that the ultimate responsibility for achieving a permanent reconciliation between nationalists and Unionists lay not with Britain alone but with 'the people of Northern Ireland'. Despite ambiguities in meaning about the precise nature of Britain's 'duty and responsibility', Callaghan in 1981 had shifted from his position in the early years of the Troubles, when he stated that 'the cardinal aim of our policy must be to *influence* Northern Ireland to solve its own problems' [our italics].[2] Drawing on his own failures and the failures of successive governments during the intervening years, significantly Callaghan was now questioning Britain's authority, capacity and obligation to play a positive role in directing any future settlement.

The implications of Callaghan's words become clearer in the context of the immediate challenges facing Britain in July 1981, both in Northern Ireland and elsewhere. The Hunger Strikes, the election of Bobby Sands and deepening divisions between the communities pointed to the continuing failure of British policy in Northern Ireland. Meanwhile, amid mass unemployment, growing social polarisation, riots and civil unrest, it seemed that the disintegration of the state in Northern Ireland may have been but a harbinger of a wider crisis in British society. This unravelling of established relationships between the rulers and the ruled on both sides of the Irish Sea posed wider questions about legitimacy and authority in state and society.[3] Echoes of these contemporary concerns can clearly be heard in the frankness of Callaghan's admission of past failures and future impotence. Extending his focus beyond the conduct of individual ministers and governments, the speech points to deeper anxieties about the ability of the state to command consent and exert its authority, whether

in Belfast or in Brixton. Viewed in this way, Callaghan's words cast
doubt on many of the underlying assumptions of the post-war consensus that had both shaped and been shaped by leaders of his political generation. In this reflective mood, the question he posed for
Britain and Northern Ireland at the start of the 1980s was whether the
old certainties of that post-war project could continue to apply in the
less certain times they were now entering.

SHORING UP A DIVIDED HOUSE

As Home Secretary, Callaghan had been closely involved with attempts to contain the unfolding disintegration of the Stormont
regime between 1968 and 1970. Adhering to the long-established
bi-partisan consensus on British policy in Ireland, Harold Wilson's
government had attempted to manage the crisis by pressurising the
Unionist government to carry out a policy of 'reform from above'.
Even before the intervention of British troops in August 1969, this
arm's-length policy was coming under pressure as the Unionist government dragged its heels in the face of rising Catholic anger and an
emerging Protestant reaction.[4] There was broad agreement between
the Labour and Conservative leaderships at this stage about the need
to normalise Northern Ireland by bringing it into the fold of British
liberal democracy. However, while Conservatives emphasised the
restoration of law and order, Labour politicians like James Callaghan
saw the sectarian divisions of 1960s Northern Ireland as an affront
to the social democratic project that they regarded as the normative
basis of a good society.[5]

From the beginning of the crisis, the Labour government pledged
to 'restore normality to the Northern Ireland community so that economic development can proceed at the faster rate that is vital for social
stability'.[6] Reflecting the ideological assumptions and distinctive

features of Labour's social democratic tradition, James Callaghan's response to the crisis represented an attempt to apply British post-war models and standards to remedy outstanding abuses in housing, policing and local government.[7] There were also tentative proposals to strengthen regional development strategies aimed at tackling unemployment blackspots. These policies rested on the assumption that there was a direct connection between social and economic factors – such as deprivation, inequality and unemployment – and political conflict.[8] In this way, Callaghan was laying down a framework that would guide thinking on the central role of the social and economic instrument in the policy repertoire of all future governments.[9] The link between peace and prosperity was held to be self-evident. However, rather than radical reform or direct rule, Callaghan's approach in the late 1960s was limited to manageable changes designed to make Stormont work for the whole community.[10] The problem he faced was fundamental: in such a divided society as Northern Ireland, politics could never simply be framed around assumptions of a single, unified political community or *demos*. Consequently, the prospect of implementing any change acceptable to the whole community appeared unlikely. It was inevitable that British ministers seeking to stabilise the situation from London would ultimately find themselves drawn directly into responsibility for the government of Northern Ireland.

The Labour government's appeal to 'all citizens of Northern Ireland to use their influence to *restore* harmony between all sections of the community' (our emphasis) was accompanied by the reassuring pledge, reiterated by successive British governments since the partition of Ireland, that 'Northern Ireland should not cease to be part of the United Kingdom without the consent of the people of Northern Ireland ... the border is not an issue.'[11]

Callaghan's emphasis on social and economic policy thus relied on an assumption that it was both possible and desirable to return Northern Ireland to a modified status quo ante.[12] The nature and extent of that modification would remain a major point of contention between Unionists and nationalists. The balance of communal forces and the likelihood of a 'Protestant backlash' in the event of significant change or direct rule weighed heavily on the minds of Labour ministers in these early years. The possibilities of a 'Rhodesia' on Britain's doorstep or the threat of a sectarian civil war that might spill over from Northern Ireland into the rest of the United Kingdom were very much to the fore in the thinking of the Wilson government.[13] Having adopted the role of the 'honest broker' appealing for a cooperative response, these fears indicated an awareness of the existential threat that the breakdown of social order in Northern Ireland might pose to the British state.[14]

When James Callaghan became Prime Minister in 1976, Northern Ireland's political landscape had fundamentally changed. While Britain's direct responsibilities had grown significantly, its policy options were narrowing. In the face of widespread civil disorder and a republican insurgency that challenged state legitimacy, Stormont had disintegrated, forcing the British to impose direct rule from Westminster in 1972. Four years on, however, the sense remained of Northern Ireland being overwhelmed in the chaos of an all-consuming conflict, which had grown to encompass every area of life. While the headlines understandably focused on the intensity of violence and growing communal polarisation, British policy-makers were attempting to develop workable solutions to 'restore normality to the Northern Ireland community'.[15] British troops would be deployed to contain the immediate security threat posed by the Provisional IRA, while more lasting peace would be achieved by incorporating moderate sections of the nationalist population into a reformed, stable and economically viable Northern Ireland.

Emerging from talks between the British and Irish governments and the Northern Ireland parties, the 1973 Sunningdale Agreement attempted to put direct-rule strategy into political effect. With its inter-dependent elements of Unionist consent, power-sharing and the 'Irish dimension', Sunningdale represented both a re-statement of British policy in Northern Ireland and a radical departure. On the one hand, it allowed Britain to assert sovereignty through the principle of Unionist consent; on the other it proposed replacing the majoritarian Stormont system with power-sharing structures that gave the nationalist minority a role in government. Even more radically, the recognition of the Irish dimension entailed the establishment of a 'Council of Ireland', composed of representatives of the two parts of Ireland.[16]

Sunningdale was defeated through widespread Unionist opposition culminating in the Ulster Workers' Council (UWC) general strike in May 1974, which forced the resignation of the power-sharing executive. The failure of Sunningdale was underscored the following year, when an elected constitutional convention with a Unionist majority rejected power-sharing and the Irish dimension, and simply called for the restoration of Stormont. In the rather confused period that followed, the Wilson government had put forward various options for British withdrawal. For example, in what appears to be an unauthorised public intervention, Roy Mason, in his role as Secretary of State for Defence, had floated the idea of reducing Britain's military commitment in Northern Ireland.[17] Meanwhile, Harold Wilson set up a Cabinet working group to explore different models for British withdrawal, including the idea of an independent Ulster with dominion status.[18] Running alongside these initiatives, government representatives raised the possibility of British withdrawal in discussions with members of the IRA during a truce that formally lasted between 1975 and 1976.[19] In this way, the Sunningdale crisis and its muddled aftermath exposed the impotence and lack of determination of Harold Wilson's government in the face of Unionist intransigence.

However ingenious the strategy, the fundamental problem British policy-makers faced was one that had been identified at the

very beginning of the experiment in direct rule: how to resolve the
contradictions inherent in the 'artificially constructed constitution'
imposed by the Government of Ireland Act 1920.[20] The central
contradiction arose from the political reality that Northern Ireland
did not constitute a unified political *demos* upon which a stable relationship between state and civil society could be built. As Foreign
Secretary and Secretary of State for Defence respectively between
1974 and 1976, James Callaghan and Roy Mason had experienced
the intractable nature of the constitutional problem at first hand. The
frustrations and failures arising from these unresolved contradictions
would colour their policies in the following years when they assumed
direct responsibility for Northern Ireland.

BACK TO THE FUTURE

How to normalise Northern Ireland remained the central dilemma
facing the Callaghan government in 1976. The concept of normalisation proceeded from two underlying premises established at the outset
of direct rule: that Britain was a neutral arbiter or 'honest broker' of
the conflict and that the destabilising effects of the conflict had to be
contained *within* Northern Ireland. The failure of Sunningdale had
once again raised the thorny question of what constituted a normal
state and by whose authority citizens should consent to be governed.
While many Unionists may have accepted the need for some reform,
they largely understood normalisation in terms of the restoration of
Northern Ireland to its previous condition. Nationalists, on the other
hand, understood normalisation in terms of a transformation from
a previously aberrant state. After 1974, the government was left with
two broad options: either to persevere with a power-sharing initiative
that would deliver the essential elements of Sunningdale or to regu-
late and manage existing structures and imbalances of power.

In September 1977, in a significant conspectus of problems and
policy options based on his first year in office, Roy Mason restat-
ed Labour's long-term priority of achieving 'a system of devolved
government ... which the majority of all parts of the community can
support and sustain'. Adopting an almost vice-regal tone, Mason
characterised the exceptional nature of the problems he faced as 'a
cauldron of serious ... difficulties – a unique "Irish Stew". In no
other region of the United Kingdom is there such a mixture of political, religious, industrial and terrorist problems, all of which must be
vigorously tackled.'[21]

Recognising that all these problems were 'inevitably interlinked',
Mason promoted a vision of direct rule as a positive vehicle for managing and ultimately reconfiguring power relations in Northern Ireland. Standing aloof from what he described as local 'political squab-
bles', Mason prioritised 'security as a matter of primary concern',
while identifying economic and industrial policies as instruments for
creating 'a stable and law-abiding society'.[22] However, by placing the
contentious issue of constitutional change on 'the backburner' and
bringing security and economic policy to the fore, Mason earned the
lasting opprobrium of bien pensant historians, obituarists, sections
of his own party and almost the entire nationalist population of Ireland.[23] Criticisms focused on Mason's supposed colonial attitudes,
pro-Unionist orientation and enthusiasm for aggressive security policies, which earned him the reputation of 'the true political thug of the
Callaghan administration'.[24]

Criticisms of Mason's destructive influence usually focused on the
immediate and long-term impacts of his security policies: Ulsterisa-
tion, criminalisation and normalisation. These coercive approaches,
which included the much-trumpeted deployment of the SAS, the
militarisation of policing and the ending of special category status for
prisoners convicted of terrorism offences, led to systematic human
rights abuses, which were detailed in the 1978 Bennett Report. In

attempting to impose a military solution that rode roughshod over human rights, the Callaghan government stood accused of betraying fundamental Labour values.

Whatever the immediate success, either in reassuring the Unionist community or reducing actual levels of violence, the boastful rhetoric that 'we are squeezing the terrorists like rolling up a toothpaste tube … we are squeezing them out of society and into prison' was interpreted negatively, even by moderates, as a declaration of war on the whole nationalist community.[25] With the benefit of hindsight and in the aftermath of the peace process, some argued that the Callaghan government's policies in Northern Ireland were overwhelmingly retrograde, in the way that they had radicalised the nationalist population, undermined the moderate nationalism of the SDLP and thus contributed to the rise of Sinn Féin as an electoral force in the 1980s.[26] In other words, by abandoning political initiatives for bringing the nationalist population into a power-sharing government in Northern Ireland, the Callaghan government had opened the door to more than a decade of political stalemate.[27] From this perspective, attempts at developing the economy were often dismissed as a mere sideshow or, even worse, as a cynical political calculation to distract attention from the government's lack of political progress.

Far from relegating it to the periphery, however, the Callaghan government promoted economic development as a vital tool for achieving political stability. Published in September 1976 by a team of civil servants, the Economic and Industrial Strategy for Northern Ireland, known as the Quigley Report, proposed government incentives and support, combined with increasing political stability and the reduction of political violence as strategies for attracting international investment to stem the rise of unemployment in Northern Ireland's manufacturing sector.[28] Quigley's recommendations were adopted as central strands in the Callaghan government's 'framework and strategy for the future of industry in Northern Ireland'.[29]

Callaghan and Mason's enthusiasm and ostensible confidence in the transformative potential of the economic and social instrument were clearly marked by their distinctive politics and experience in British Labourism. In his September 1977 speech, Mason talked about his 'genuine concern and determination' to overcome unemployment and deprivation and to push forward with 'wide-ranging improvements in the fields of education, health and the social services'.[30] His assertion that he was pursuing a strategy that was 'compassionate and that cares' can only be understood in the moral framework of the distinctive Labour position, in which politicians like himself, Callaghan and many of his Cabinet colleagues had been formed.[31] This vision had been expressed since 1945 in terms of a commitment to a mixed economy, guided through government intervention and 'Keynesian' economic policies, to ensure full employment, growth and rising living standards. The ideals of Britain's post-war consensus were underwritten by the social, economic and institutional settlement initially laid down by the Attlee government and consolidated in the 1950s. The social settlement of Britain's welfare state rested on high levels of public expenditure and taxation along with other measures of social reform designed to reduce social and economic inequality and expand opportunity. Above all, this version of 'democratic socialism' was firmly rooted in British parliamentary democracy and the constitutional status quo.[32]

Mason's economic strategy failed to deliver on its rhetorical promises, most notoriously in the DeLorean car factory debacle. Designed to create over 1,000 jobs in an unemployment blackspot in nationalist West Belfast, it exemplified the danger of attaching the government's normalising agenda to the rational business of economic decision-making. This extraordinarily risky 'inward investment' swallowed up £85 million in government subsidies at no risk or cost to the DeLorean company. Without creating a single permanent job, the whole enterprise ended up as nothing more than a Potemkin village vainly trying to project an image of successful stability and peaceful normality on the international stage. Underneath the PR hyperbole, this 'back to the future' vision of a partnership between the entrepreneurial state and international business sat uncomfortably with the sound and solid objectives of job creation and social improvement outlined in the government's economic plans.[33]

While the spectacular failure of DeLorean might be attributed to Mason's tendency to play the viceroy in the absence of any effective regional accountability, it is better attributed to the political structures of direct rule itself. One of the unforeseen consequences of mobilising economic development as a tool for delivering political stability in Northern Ireland was the destabilisation of economic planning and decision-making in ways that frequently mitigated against the long-term goals of normalisation. For example, the government's decision to take the Harland & Wolff shipyard into full public ownership in 1975 had largely been motivated by the imperative of averting the 'serious political, social and security consequences' of forcing the East Belfast-based company into liquidation.[34] By seeming to promise economic investment as an incentive for political cooperation, the government found itself more and more drawn into Northern Ireland's zero-sum game of resource competition and special pleading.

Further contradictions arising in the field of fair employment challenged the 'colour blind' rationale that underpinned Britain's post-war settlement. The principle of universal provision of public goods relies on understandings of shared citizenship and trust in an impartial state machinery. The universal ideal invoked an often 'unspoken inscription of a singular set of patterns of life, values and needs' that defined a shared political community.[35] Although formally modelled on the British system, the organisational structures of Northern Ireland's post-war social and economic settlement had rested unstably upon a contested idea of citizenship and an oppressive and divisive system of governance in which Unionist patronage and partiality had become endemic. The adverse effects of anti-Catholic discrimination had become most acute in areas of the public sector and the economy, which were dominated by Unionist interests. The Fair Employment Agency (FEA) was set up in 1976 to address the resulting problems of discrimination and disadvantage. Lacking the political momentum of earlier responses to demands for civil rights, the FEA focused on institutional rather than structural change by monitoring the religious composition of the workforce and investigating individual complaints of direct discrimination. Operating through a colour-blind commitment to equality of opportunity, facilitated by economic and social development at the macro level, the FEA demonstrated the even-handedness of the direct rule government, while failing to address the structural patterns of segregation and discrimination that were still endemic in the state and civil society in Northern Ireland.[36]

ONLY BREASTING THE TIDE[37]

In his historic visit to the Bogside in Derry in the early days of the Troubles, Callaghan, speaking from an upstairs window of a small terraced house to the assembled crowds, made an emotional commitment to right historical wrongs and to intervene on the side of the oppressed and excluded: 'I am not neutral. I am on the side of those, whoever they may be and in whatever community they live, who are deprived of justice and of freedom.'[38]

Callaghan's oft-expressed commitment to reform in Northern Ireland in the late 1960s is frequently contrasted with his government's 'world-weary resignation' in the late 1970s.[39] Building on this understanding of his individual frustration, Callaghan's critics talk of an abdication of leadership, whether through its 'abject spinelessness' in the face of the Unionists or its recourse to repression and military force.[40] This weighing up of Callaghan's leadership and policies in

Northern Ireland took on a more dramatic form in the closing hours of his government. On 28 March 1979, encircled by mortal enemies from all sides, who threatened the verities and decencies of the world that Labour had built since 1945, Callaghan's fate was sealed by the intervention of a Northern Irish MP, Gerry Fitt from West Belfast.[41] For three years, the minority Labour government had resorted to all sorts of expedience and deal-making just to keep going. So tenuous was their grip on power that they had even attempted a political understanding with Ulster Unionist MPs in Westminster.

During the long debate, the Belfast West MP explained why he was not going to support the government in the vote of no confidence. Reflecting the view of many nationalists in Northern Ireland, he began by accusing the government of negotiating deals with Unionist MPs to increase Northern Ireland's parliamentary representation. The bitter tone conveyed his sense of personal and political betrayal about Labour's pursuit of a military solution based on repression and the ill-treatment of prisoners. Accusing Mason of being a 'Unionist Secretary of State' in a government committed to 'consolidating Unionist supremacy in Northern Ireland', Fitt attributed Labour's capitulation to a lack of resolution. Referring to the 1974 UWC strike, he argued that

> [t]hat strike terrified the Labour government. Since then the Labour government have been running away. They have not stood up to Unionist and Loyalist extremists as they should have done … the sheer ingratitude of that crowd knows no bounds. The Northern Ireland Unionists have used the Labour government for their ends, and tonight they will try to bring about their downfall … They are not concerned about what happens in other parts of the United Kingdom.[42]

The Belfast West MP ended by saying that Labour's betrayal would bring about a loss of faith and a withdrawal from constitutional politics by nationalists in Northern Ireland. This intrusion of the peripheral concerns of Northern Ireland into the centre of the British political system, at that moment of the highest drama, revealed much more than the particular failings of Callaghan's government.

The frustrations of the Callaghan and Mason years show that the British post-war social democratic model adopted as a standard for the administration of direct rule in Northern Ireland had simply proven unworkable. In terms of inequality, social deprivation and unemployment, Belfast might have appeared to be as British as Barnsley, but its structural problems were grounded in an altogether different historically conditioned political economy. Northern Ireland's distinctive experience as a site of communal conflict around different claims to national sovereignty marked it out as a place apart from the rest of the United Kingdom. If understood as an integral part of the Union, Northern Ireland was experiencing a temporary breakdown in social order that had disrupted the normal working of liberal democracy and the market economy. Britain's role, therefore, was to restore order by instituting reforms, rebuilding the economy and defeating the criminal elements that were threatening life and property in the region. On the other hand, Northern Ireland's exceptional history of civil conflict and contested sovereignty meant that Britain could not unequivocally assert its authority to govern impartially, but only act to democratise and rebuild the state in a partnership with a new imagined Northern Ireland political community.

Callaghan's policy for normalisation reflected these two contradictory understandings of Northern Ireland, either as a problem that could be resolved through reform, investment and the re-establishment of a pre-existing rule of law or as a crisis that necessitated the restructuring of the state itself. The critique that Callaghan acted as if he were 'in office, but not in power' does not reflect his lack of attention to the region, but simply describes the nature of the British state and the dilemmas it faced governing in Northern Ireland.[43] Moreover, in talking about a possible loss of faith in constitutional politics, Fitt was describing a problem that extended far beyond the streets of West Belfast or even the Palace of Westminster. It was a growing sense of disenchantment and exhaustion that would contribute to the dramatic reshaping of society, politics and the state from the 1980s onwards. In July 1981, Callaghan would express this tired mood as he reflected on the failures and frustrations of British policy in Northern Ireland since the late 1960s. Perhaps he too sensed that politics and society in Britain and Northern Ireland would drift ever further away from the social democratic vision that he had embraced and embodied throughout his political career.[44]

NOTES

1   Hansard, HC Deb, 2 July 1981, vol. 7, col. 1046.

2   J. Callaghan, *Time and Chance* (London: Collins, 1987), p. 500.

3   For an overview of the debate on 'the crisis of the 1970s' see L. Black, H. Pemberton and P. Thane (eds), *Reassessing 1970s Britain* (Manchester: Manchester University Press, 2013).

4   K. McNamara, 'Reflections on aspects of Labour's policy towards Northern Ireland, 1966–70: a personal narrative', in L. Marley (ed.), *The British Labour Party and Twentieth-Century Ireland: The Cause of Ireland, the Cause of Labour* (Manchester: Manchester University Press, 2015). Kevin McNamara was one of a small number of backbench Labour MPs who consistently raised questions about Northern Ireland in the House of Commons and in the 1960s drew attention to the civil rights abuses of the Unionist government at Stormont.

5   J. Callaghan, *A House Divided: The Dilemma of Northern Ireland* (London: HarperCollins, 1973).

6   The Downing Street Declaration August 1969, Callaghan, *A House Divided*, p. 191.

7   This view on the causes of unrest was widely shared by media commentators and critics of the Stormont regime in the late 1960s. Even as impeccable an 'establishment' source as the Cameron *Report into Disturbances in Northern Ireland* cited social deprivation and housing issues as contributory factors in the outbreak of political violence in 1968. See: https://cain.ulster.ac.uk/hmso/cameron.htm

8   This assumption is still an important theme in both academic analysis and policy-making globally in relation to the causes of political violence. See, for example, the range of analyses discussed in J. Horgan and K. Braddock (eds), *Terrorism Studies: A Reader* (London: Routledge, 2012).

9   P. Neumann, *Britain's Long War: British Strategy in the Northern Ireland Conflict, 1969–98* (Basingstoke: Palgrave, 2003), pp. 35–8.

10 *Ibid.*, p. 36.

11 The Downing Street Declaration August 1969, Callaghan, *A House Divided*, p. 191.

12 Communiqué issued at the end of the visit of the Home Secretary to Northern Ireland, 29 August 1969, Callaghan, *A House Divided*, p. 202.

13 The National Archive, CAB 164/334.

14 Private conversation, 1991, with Stan Orme, former Minister of State for Social Security 1976–79.

15 HMSO, 'The Future of Northern Ireland' (London: HMSO, 1972), Annex 3, note 7.

16 The Sunningdale Agreement December 1973 in M. Elliott (ed.), *The Long Road to Peace in Northern Ireland* (Liverpool: Liverpool University Press, 2007), p. 223.

17 T. Benn, *Against the Tide: Diaries 1973–76* (London: Arrow, 1989), pp. 137–8.

18 https://www.theguardian.com/uk/2005/jan/01/past.nationalarchives6

19 N. Ó Dochartaigh, 'The Longest Negotiation', *Political Studies* (2015), vol. 63, no. 1, pp. 202–20.

20 The Conservative government discussed the crisis and the nature of the dilemma it posed during a series of Cabinet meetings held in February and March 1972, CAB 128/48/1, 5, 6, 1972.

21 R. Mason, 'Press Release of Speech, 13 September 1977', Public Records Office Northern Ireland (PRONI): proni_CENT-1-6-1_1977-09-13.pdf

22 *Ibid.*

23 R. Mason, *Paying the Price* (London: Robert Hale, 1999), p. 161. For just two representative examples of critical assessments of Roy Mason's period in office as Secretary of State for Northern Ireland, see B. O'Leary, 'Northern Ireland', in A. Seldon and K. Hickson (eds), *New Labour, Old Labour: The Wilson and Callaghan Governments, 1974–9* (London: Routledge, 2004) and 'Rest in Peace, Roy Mason, and Good Riddance', *New Statesman*, 23 April 2015.

24 O'Leary, 'Northern Ireland', p. 244.

25 'Mason Opts for Defeating Terror and Creating Jobs', *Irish Times*, 27 December 2007.

26 O'Leary, 'Northern Ireland', p. 249.

27 Lord Mason of Barnsley obituary, *The Guardian*, 20 April 2015: https://www.theguardian.com/politics/2015/apr/20/lord-mason-of-barnsley; Gerry Fitt is famously quoted attacking Mason as 'that wee f****r … He put things for us back ten years. Fifteen.'

28 M. Cunningham, *British Government Policy in Northern Ireland, 1969–89: Its Nature and Execution* (Manchester: Manchester University Press, 1991), pp. 125–27.

29 'Economic and Industrial Strategy for Northern Ireland (Quigley Report)', Hansard, HC Deb, 28 October 1976, vol. 918, cols 676–9.

30 Mason, Press Release, 13 September 1977.

31 *Ibid.*

32 R. Miliband, *Parliamentary Socialism: A Study in the Politics of Labour* (London: George Allen & Unwin, 1961), pp. 318–77.

33 Cunningham, *British Government Policy in Northern Ireland*, pp. 127–8.

34 CAB/128/55.

35 J. Clarke and J. Newman, *The Managerial State: Power, Politics and Ideology in the Remaking of Social Welfare* (London: SAGE, 2004).

36 Cunningham, *British Government Policy in Northern Ireland*, pp. 132–3.

37 Callaghan, *Time and Chance*, p. 500. In his memoir Callaghan describes the limited impact of his Northern Ireland policies: 'At no time did I feel we were doing more than breasting the tide.'

38 Film: *James Callaghan Visit and Battle of the Bogside 1969*: https://youtu.be/lelufdmP_EQ

39 O'Leary, 'Northern Ireland', p. 243.

40 *Ibid.*, p. 242.

41 'The Party's Over', *The Guardian*, 22 March 2009: https://www.theguardian.com/politics/2009/mar/22/james-callaghan-labour-1979-thatcher

42 Hansard, HL Deb, 28 March 1979, vol. 965, col. 516.

43 O'Leary, 'Northern Ireland', p. 241.

44 Hansard, HC Deb, 2 July 1981, vol. 7, col. 1046.

13

CALLAGHAN AND EUROPE

Jasper Miles

JAMES CALLAGHAN BECAME PRIME Minister ten months
after the June 1975 referendum in which Britain had voted to remain
a member of the European Economic Community (EEC). The vote
in favour of remaining a member of the 'Common Market' was prem-
ised on the renegotiated terms, negotiated by Callaghan as Foreign
Secretary. From the outset, he 'negotiated to succeed', success being
measured in terms of keeping the United Kingdom in the Community.
His renegotiation allowed the government to present new terms to the
British people as a 'success' and justified the Labour government campaigning to remain. Interestingly, he played only a limited role in the
referendum campaign, keeping a lower profile than other Cabinet ministers on either side of the debate. Regardless, Callaghan had played
a critical role in keeping the United Kingdom within the Community.

On becoming Prime Minister, Callaghan 'wished to keep the focus
away from European questions',[1] repeatedly telling colleagues that
British membership of the Community was no longer an issue. However, Europe dogged the Callaghan government. The Labour Party

remained divided and the British people displayed little enthusiasm for the Community. This was despite the two-to-one margin of victory for remaining in the Community and, at the time, the apparent settling of the European question in British politics. The Callaghan government had to deal with three important aspects of membership: direct elections to the European Parliament (or Assembly, as it was then known), the Common Agricultural Policy (CAP), which was the flagship policy of the Community in the 1960s and '70s, and the European Monetary System (EMS), the critical feature of which was the Exchange Rate Mechanism (ERM). These three matters caused the government significant problems, exposing the divisions within the Parliamentary Labour Party (PLP) and the broader labour movement and straining relations with European neighbours, all of which was exacerbated by minority government and underlying economic difficulties.

This chapter will assess Callaghan's attitude towards Europe and European integration, revealing how his 'middle of the road' scepticism meant he belonged to neither the pro- nor anti-Europeans in the PLP. The chapter will then move on to consider how Callaghan and his government responded to calls for direct elections, attempts to reform the CAP and discussions over whether to join the EMS. Throughout, the chapter will consider the domestic environment and pressures in which he operated. The conclusion will stress that although Callaghan disappointed his pro-European contemporaries, the emphasis he placed on national parliaments and the British national interest as distinct from the Community interest amounted to his 'own avuncular version of Gaullism'.[2] His Gaullism allowed him to prioritise the unity of the Labour Party and the survival of the government over lofty ambitions of 'ever closer union' at a time when the labour movement was riven with divisions over Europe and his government was in a precarious parliamentary position. Firstly, let us turn our attention to Callaghan's attitude towards European integration.

CALLAGHAN AND EUROPEAN
INTEGRATION

A common theme among those who have written on Callaghan is the idea that he was sceptical about Europe and reluctant on European matters. Alan Watkins, the political columnist, considered Callaghan to be a 'Commonwealth man first, an Atlanticist second, and not a European at all'.[3] Watkins's first two points contain some merit, whereas the final assertion requires clarification, and others have put forward more nuanced observations contextualising Callaghan's scepticism. Peter Hennessy wrote that Callaghan's respect for institutions did not fully extend to Europe, suspecting 'an old patriot's ambivalence that vied with a realist's appreciation of the price that would be paid if Britain found itself on the edge of an integrating community'.[4] Callaghan's biographer Kenneth Morgan asserts: 'Like Churchill, he saw Britain's world role as consisting of three concentric rings, the North Atlantic alliance, the Commonwealth, and a relationship with western Europe, but the last of these was also last in importance.' Callaghan's naval background, wartime service and relationships with Commonwealth leaders all fostered a deep attachment to the Commonwealth. He also looked to America, believing that 'when Britain was truly in crisis, the Americans would help out'. Furthermore, 'by political outlook, legal conventions, and ties of culture and sentiment, Britain had a more natural affinity to the United States than to the motley array of European nations'.[5] *The Guardian* noted that he much preferred Americans to Europeans, sticking firmly to surnames with his European colleagues, but engaging in hearty first-name badinage with Americans at NATO meetings.[6]

Callaghan belonged neither to the 'euro-fanatics' nor the 'anti-Europeans' within the PLP. Instead, he belonged to the grouping within the Labour Party that viewed the matter dispassionately, and with cool-headed realism. For Callaghan, Europe was not an article of faith or a matter of high theology, yet David Owen felt that Callaghan suspected that the pro-Europeans had made Europe a political religion.[7] Rather, Europe was an issue that needed to be viewed through the prism of whether it would advance or hinder the British national interest. In 1975 Callaghan stated what he thought were the limits of membership and how 'Europe' aroused no sense of emotion among the British people:

> I know that there are many people whom I like and respect, who really have a vision about Europe. I'm sorry to say I don't share it. It is a useful and convenient way of organising our relations with Europe, and in matters of commerce and trade it is obviously a worthwhile instrument. But it is not a vision in the way that the Empire was a vision, the way the people hoped that the Commonwealth would be.[8]

His comments on the renegotiation process in his autobiography are revealing, and the attitude remained apparent during his time as Prime Minister: 'I shared neither the conviction of the pro-Marketeers that it would result in a vast improvement in our economic performance nor the deep despair of the anti-Marketeers that membership would ruin Britain.' Economic salvation 'depended upon ourselves; whether we were in or out of the Community was marginal to the result'.[9] This is in distinction to the anti-Europeans, for whom membership was a drag on economic growth and an attack on political and economic sovereignty, and for the pro-Europeans, for whom social and economic life outside of the Common Market would have been even worse. Consequently, Callaghan's approach put him at odds with both the anti-Europeans in Cabinet – Peter Shore, John Silkin, Tony Benn and Michael Foot – and the pro-Europeans like Roy Jenkins (who became President of the European Commission in 1977), Bill Rodgers, Shirley Williams and Harold Lever, as he had neither the inclination nor the political room to manoeuvre to satisfy either grouping. To some extent, Jenkins's move into European politics and the sacking of Barbara Castle eased Cabinet tensions over Europe, but it remained deeply divided.

In a letter to the General Secretary of the Labour Party at the start of the British presidency of the Community in 1977, Callaghan outlined his government's stance on Community affairs. Firstly, the maintenance of the authority of national governments and parliaments; secondly, democratic control of community business; thirdly, the necessity of common policies recognising the need for the national governments to attain their economic, industrial and regional objectives; fourthly, reform of the Common Agricultural Policy; fifthly, the development of a Community energy policy compatible with national interests; and sixthly, enlargement of the Community. Callaghan desired reform so that the policies of the Community reflected both the interests of other member states and British interests, importantly complementing British industry and revitalising the British economy. In a forthright manner in late 1977, Callaghan reminded European leaders that the seas around Britain were not only full of fish but also endowed with energy in the form of North Sea oil, and a common energy policy had to take account of Britain's status as an oil producer. He continued:

> In this spirit we do not believe that the Community can develop into a federation. It is our view that Europe will make most progress if the rights of national governments and Parliaments are upheld. Nor will Europe move forward together if any individual member feels its own economic, industrial, and social objectives are being overridden. Progress will be most firmly rooted when there is consensus on major issues.[10]

However, as mentioned, he was 'sympathetic to closer cooperation with our European neighbours',[11] and he supported the applications

of Greece, Spain and Portugal to join the Community. Regarding
Portugal, Callaghan was concerned about the strength of the Communist Party as the country moved towards democracy. As such, he
sought to help the Socialist Party which was committed to the fledgling democratic system. While their accession would raise problems,
Britain's support for their application, according to Callaghan, was
designed to strengthen the representative character of the Community, not to dilute it. Others, of course, viewed widening membership
as a method of slowing down European integration, evidenced by
a Cabinet review of EC policy in June 1976 that saw expanding the
Community as a way of weakening moves towards supranationalism.[12]
Callaghan also saw the advantages of pursuing the Joint European
Torus (JET) programme – research into nuclear fusion – arguing for
it to be based in Britain and displaying the practical benefits of membership to a sceptical electorate.

Underpinning Callaghan's stance was the concern that with British economic and political decline in a world of superpowers, Britain
was losing influence on the world stage. The method to correct this
was by exerting influence over world developments via a stronger
European voice. For Callaghan, there was no credible alternative
to membership, and it entailed political benefits that would be lost
should Britain withdraw. Indeed, membership was a reality which
the electorate had supported in the 1975 referendum. He regularly
informed European political leaders that he had no intention of
leading Britain out of the Common Market. Therefore, the question
was how to balance the British interest with the Community interest.
The competing approaches within Cabinet, the PLP and National
Executive Committee (NEC) shaped this uneasy path to European
integration. Yet Callaghan's ability to balance disparate views on European integration, as shown below, should be viewed as a success of
his leadership.

DIRECT ELECTIONS TO THE
EUROPEAN ASSEMBLY

The Treaty of Rome had made provisions for direct elections to a European Parliament, but it was not until Harold Wilson had agreed to direct elections to a European assembly as part of the renegotiation process to appease the French that the matter started to become a reality. In July 1976, the French argued that there must be reciprocity, and a commitment was reached by all member states to endeavour to hold direct elections in the spring of 1978. The domestic political situation hampered the government, and Wall considers the subject to have been the dominant European issue facing the Callaghan government in 1977, as it exposed Labour's deep European divisions.[13] Moreover, it revealed something of Labour's attitude towards electoral reform and proportional representation, a constitutional matter that also caused division.[14] Anti-Europeanism appeared to be in the ascendency, as there was a majority against membership on the NEC, and Labour Party conference in 1976 had voted by a majority of two to one against the introduction of direct elections. A significant number of Labour MPs intended to vote against any form of direct elections – after all, there was the fear that direct elections would legitimise, grant more power to and push the Community towards a federal destination. Additionally, there was the self-interested concern that if direct elections were held under first-past-the-post (FPTP) the Conservatives would win a large majority of seats. On the other side, the emergence of the Lib–Lab Pact, based on the government's commitment to introduce legislation for direct elections to the European assembly, meant Callaghan had to appease the pro-European Liberals. This forced Callaghan into a balancing act.

At a Cabinet meeting on 25 February 1977, Callaghan deemed that 'there were strong arguments for the arrangements being made by the present government rather than being left to a possible future Conservative Administration'.[15] Callaghan opposed proportional representation – 'an animal of a very different colour, for the Party was against it and so was I'[16] – and there was no Community requirement for a proportional electoral system. Nevertheless, he took full account of the Liberal Party's commitment to a system of proportional representation, and maintaining the Lib–Lab Pact and keeping the Labour Party in government took precedence. In June 1977, the government introduced a Bill implementing direct elections, with provision for proportional representation. The government allowed a free vote, including for ministers, and the Commons rejected proportional representation in December 1977 by 319 votes to 222. Callaghan voted in favour, but a majority of Conservative and Labour MPs voted against. This meant that the boundary commission had to devise constituencies based on FPTP, forcing Callaghan to inform his European partners that Britain would be unable to hold direct elections by 1978. In turn, the Community had to delay until June 1979, reinforcing a perception that Britain was a reluctant partner. Gowland and Turner write that the government's tactics were 'evidently not out of tune with the instincts of the British electorate, the large majority of whom did not vote in the first direct elections for the European Parliament'.[17]

THE COMMON AGRICULTURAL POLICY

The CAP had been agreed by 'the six' prior to Britain's entry into the Community, and as a latecomer Britain had not had the opportunity to shape the CAP to meet its needs. Upon becoming a member, Britain had to accept the CAP as a key element of membership, although this challenged 'deeply held British attitudes towards food prices and loyalty to traditional Commonwealth exporters of food'. Also, Britain was a major importer of both industrial and agricultural products, on which the Community had placed levies and charges, and this, along with a relatively small but efficient agricultural sector, meant the UK would contribute more than other members and receive little in return.[18] As such, Callaghan's government was concerned with the impact that the CAP was having on prices, alongside its wider attempts to tackle inflation in the economy. In addition, by the end of the transition period in 1979, Britain would be expected to pay the full costs of membership, a problem exacerbated by Britain being one of the poorer members of the Community, and the budget was driven up by the costs of the CAP. Consequently, the CAP and budget contribution became increasingly contested, a problem that would occupy the thoughts of subsequent governments. The CAP also had a knock-on effect on attitudes towards the EMS, specifically the acceptability of the ERM, as initially the government considered that it could leverage resource transfers during the negotiations.

In September 1976, Callaghan replaced the agricultural minister Fred Peart, earlier a Eurosceptic but at this time a committed pro-European, with John Silkin, a staunch anti-European. This represented a change in tone and direction, as Peart had sought to compromise and build relationships with other member states, whereas Silkin 'saw his role in Brussels as one of open opposition to the EC'.[19] Matters came to a head during the British presidency of the EEC in the first half of 1977. When Cabinet had discussed the British presidency the year prior, Callaghan took inspiration from the French approach to Community matters. He suggested that they 'make the Community dimension part of our departmental thinking and pursue this with the same determination as the French: but in so doing we should also remember the need sometimes to cloak a hard position in suitably "Communautaire" doctrine and phraseology'. The Cabinet agreed that the presidency was an opportunity to 'demand major reforms of the Common Agricultural Policy'.[20] After some debate over whether

Jenkins should attend, Wall writes that 'the British government's objectives for the Presidency were in fact quite modest', avoiding 'targets for "the building of Europe"'. Ambitions included changes in the Common Fisheries Policy (CFP), a CAP price-fixing which discouraged surpluses; resolving unemployment; a decision to locate JET at Culham; a cautious lead on enlargement, and to avoid trouble with direct elections.[21] In other words, the presidency was seen as an opportunity to pursue British interests in the Community. When Silkin chaired the Council of Agricultural Ministers, he was deliberately confrontational without gaining much, delaying an agreement of the ministers to obtain a small rise in the subsidy of butter granted to the UK to compensate for price increases.[22]

As for Callaghan, he had developed friendly relations with Schmidt. West Germany was also a net contributor to the CAP, and while they would often criticise the workings, they did little to reform it. At a meeting between Callaghan and Schmidt in October 1978, Schmidt invited Callaghan to send him a 'non-paper' setting out his ideas for improving the CAP. The paper outlined the achievements of the CAP and its problems, focusing on how the policy encouraged surpluses, increased costs to the budget and hampered development of other policies. Callaghan reiterated British insistence on a 'realistic price policy', and national aids to help farmers in hardship. He repeated that the UK 'benefited very little from the budget because of the CAP and was due to become a net payer to the budget'.[23] Callaghan continued to complain about the wastefulness and inefficiency of the CAP into 1979, arguing that unless it was reformed and stronger nations made a greater contribution, there would be a European tax revolt. Once the budget had been reformed, Callaghan considered that the Community could focus on more pressing issues, such as narrowing the gap between richer and poorer members.[24] Callaghan's attempts to persuade Schmidt failed, as his attention had turned to EMS.

THE EUROPEAN MONETARY SYSTEM

In Europe there developed an idea of a European-type Bretton Woods system. In two speeches in late 1977 Roy Jenkins, the President of the European Commission, fleshed out ideas around European monetary union. It was considered that closer economic and monetary union was vital in bringing about closer political cooperation. However, it was the following year when the idea had been taken up by Schmidt, and supported by Giscard d'Estaing, that the European Monetary System started to take shape. The key component of EMS was the Exchange Rate Mechanism (ERM), a method of tying European currencies to the powerful Deutschmark.

Callaghan writes, 'I could not travel fast.' There remained significant opposition within the Labour Party towards membership of the Community, and there was hostility at the 1978 Labour Party conference as EMS represented an attack on economic sovereignty, perceived as a step on the road towards a federal Europe. This was 'coupled with my own and the Treasury's belief that sterling was standing too high to make our entry advantageous'.[25] Throughout, Callaghan was intent on postponing a decision and playing the matter long. In part, this was due to the general election on the horizon, and he wished to avoid further divisions within the Cabinet and PLP over Europe. On the other side, he feared that by not joining the ERM there would be a run on the pound; understandable, considering the recent 1976 sterling crisis and the 1967 devaluation, the latter of which he presided over as Chancellor. Consequently, it was essential to act in a way that would not 'spook' the market. According to Edmund Dell, who was then Secretary of State for Trade, the Cabinet were aware of the politics of the EMS, and the anti-Europeans understood Callaghan's strategy and 'appeared ready to play his game with him'.[26]

Few within and without the PLP and government were prepared to make a case for membership. Within Cabinet, Lever argued in favour,

considering that full membership of the EMS would provide stability, prevent exposing sterling to speculators and that, in time, there
could be the concession of resources. Later, Sir John Hunt, then
Cabinet Secretary, and Michael Franklin, then Head of the European
Secretariat in the Cabinet Office, both admitted to favouring membership.[27] Elsewhere, Denis Healey noted that by this time the Foreign Office favoured anything that included the word 'European', a
view shared by Silkin who added the Cabinet Office had become 'an
instrument of appeasement' with Brussels.[28] Other pro-Europeans
such as Dell believed that, on balance, the disadvantages outweighed
the advantages. Without, most economists and experts, along with
industrialists, were against membership, arguing that the ERM would
not stabilise exchange rates or Britain would join at too high a level.
The lack of a body of opinion in favour of membership hampered the
pro-Europeans. Moreover, the refusal of the Community to commit
to the government's initial decision to make British entry conditional
upon transfer of resources, including a reduction in the contribution
to the European budget, did little to convince moderates that membership entailed benefits.

When Schmidt and Giscard d'Estaing decided to appoint a 'secret
committee' to begin preparations for a monetary system, Callaghan
chose to send Sir Kenneth Couzens, Second Permanent Secretary
for Overseas Finance at the Treasury, as his representative. Dell wrote
that Couzens 'brought to the party a sceptical mind', and 'Callaghan,
in appointing Couzens to this role, gave him strict instructions not
to agree to anything'. The first evaluation Couzens produced contained eight 'cons' and two 'pros'. Appointing Couzens allowed
Germany and France to shape the basic character of the EMS, but
Callaghan 'knew exactly what he was doing. So far as was possible,
given the close relationship between Schmidt and Giscard, he was
keeping track of what was going on without allowing himself to be
committed.'[29]

In a Cabinet meeting on 6 July 1978, Callaghan outlined that his approach at the Bremen Conference would be in favour of greater stability, but if a durable solution was to be found, certain principles had to be accepted: firstly, symmetrical obligations on stronger countries; and secondly, the transfer of resources from richer to poorer countries of the Community. He summed up by agreeing to further studies of the conditions that would have to be satisfied before agreement could be reached.[30] At the Bonn Summit later in July, Schmidt explained to Callaghan in private his idea of fixing currencies against a European Unit of Account. Yet, prior to the Summit, Callaghan had devised a 'five-point plan': commitment to growth; the maintenance of world trade; currency stability; the long-term use of capital surpluses; and conservation of energy.[31] For Callaghan, the revival of the Western economy relied on a combined European–American effort, something that could be hampered by a European monetary bloc. Callaghan did not wish to act in such a way that excluded America, and did not wish to strengthen the Deutschmark to the disadvantage of sterling.

In the same month, Callaghan set up a special ministerial group on European Monetary Co-operation (GEN136) under the chairmanship of the Chancellor, Denis Healey, who had already laid down preconditions for membership. As Chancellor, Healey played a critical role during the EMS debates, sharing many of Callaghan's concerns and wishing to play the issue long. In his autobiography, Healey says that he began by being fairly agnostic but then turned against the idea, concluding that the way it would work in practice would only serve to help Germany keep the Deutschmark competitive.[32] At the final meeting of GEN136 on 10 October, Callaghan took the chair. The Treasury paper stated that while Britain may have less influence by remaining out of the EMS, there were strong economic arguments not to join. Healey provided a cover note, concluding that if it proved impossible to shift the German position, he could not advise membership. Callaghan summed up: 'the group by a large majority felt that it was clearly not in our interests to join the proposed European Monetary System in the form it was likely to emerge', though there should be 'no advance disclosure' and for tactical reasons they should 'continue to play a part constructively'.[33]

Callaghan was receptive to the idea of monetary stability, something that was in the interests of Britain as a trading nation, but criticised the EMS in detail. Morgan writes that he 'became somewhat more enthusiastic about joining a European monetary system than were his Cabinet colleagues, although not by a great margin', whereas Franklin considered he moved in the opposite direction, showing interest at the beginning but gradually cooling towards it.[34] Callaghan's response is best understood as sceptical. While the proposal held out the prospect of more order in the European currency market, his view was shaped by domestic political and economic constraints, memories of previous British devaluations, and recent attempts to link currencies in the early 1970s through 'the snake', of which Britain had been a member for all of six weeks. Indeed, the EMS prompted the same questions as 'the snake' had: namely whether sterling could afford an arrangement with the Deutschmark, which in turn would only strengthen the highly competitive West German economy, which was disciplined by low inflation. Dell later wrote that Callaghan understood that this had little to do with European economic integration, 'but a great deal to do with Schmidt's worries about German competitiveness'.[35]

Following on from the Cabinet discussion in late 1978, it was formally decided that sterling would be withheld from the ERM. However, it was possible to join the EMS without signing up to the ERM, and while Callaghan welcomed the scheme in principle, he could only commit Britain to associate with the development of a European Currency Unit, a partial pooling of gold and foreign reserves. When Britain did join the ERM in October 1990, it would join at too high an exchange rate, the fear expressed by Callaghan and the Labour government in 1978. When Britain crashed out in September 1992, having raised interest rates from 10 per cent to 12 per cent and then 15 per cent, and having spent billions on buying up the sterling being sold on the currency market, it arguably vindicated the Callaghan government's reluctance fourteen years before to join a mechanism that operated in the interests of others.

CONCLUSION

It is always popular in the academic literature on Britain's relationship with Europe to criticise British reluctance on European issues as a 'missed opportunity'. Broadly, the argument continues that if only British governments, whether Labour or Conservative, would realise that the British interest was the same as the European interest, then the UK could take a seat at the top table with France and Germany and effectively shape the direction of travel in the Community to suit its own ends. The same analysis could be applied to the Callaghan government, with its delay in legislating for direct elections, the consistent demands to reform the CAP, and the scepticism and then withholding of membership of the ERM. Consequently, Callaghan disappointed his pro-European contemporaries. Heath considered that Callaghan's failure to incorporate Britain into all aspects of the EMS had diminished Britain's influence and lost the country hundreds of millions of pounds. In addition, Callaghan had dragged his feet on every development in the European Community since he took office. Jenkins welcomed the victory of Margaret Thatcher in 1979 due to Britain's poor standing in the Community, confirming Callaghan's suspicion that the pro-Europeans had turned European integration into a political religion that trumped social democracy at home. Franklin wrote that the EMS episode confirmed our reputation as a semi-detached member, losing out on the opportunity to enter an equal partnership with France and Germany.[36]

However, Callaghan never shared the enthusiasm of some of his contemporaries towards their grandiose vision of 'ever closer union', and he understood the limits of their argument. He had an instinctive sense of the mood of the party and country and preferred common sense and practical judgement over high-minded intellectualism. This served him well given the domestic political and economic constraints over Europe, and by the end of the 1970s, the electorate was becoming increasingly sceptical about membership. Butler and Kitzinger wrote that support for membership in 1975 'ran wide, but did not run deep', meaning the electorate's attitudes were fluid, not fixed, and if there was a change in circumstances, their opinion would duly change.[37] As such, Callaghan was not prepared to split the Labour Party and government as it had been in recent years over European matters. Instead, as Prime Minister, Callaghan charted a different course, emphasising that membership of the Community was an important reality, and one that should be shown to be important to the British people and their European neighbours, but it was not the panacea to the nation's ills. After all, certain aspects of membership caused specific problems, such as the CAP and its budget mechanism, and the ERM, which was mostly about maintaining and expanding German industrial competitiveness. He was happy to delay, argue for reform or ultimately reject opportunities if they did not align with British interests. As such, he denounced federalist ambitions, consistently stated the importance of national parliaments, and reiterated the need for the Americans to be involved in the revival of the Western economy.

On reflection, Callaghan's 'avuncular Gaullism' offers a pleasing contrast to what Peter Shore referred to as the 'euro-travelling'[38] of subsequent Labour leaders and luminaries, for whom European integration became an end in itself.

NOTES

1 J. W. Young, 'Europe', in A. Seldon and K. Hickson (eds), *New Labour, Old Labour: The Wilson and Callaghan Governments, 1974–9* (London: Routledge, 2004), p. 147.
2 'Callaghan spells out his Gaullism', *The Guardian*, 15 November 1977.
3 See 'Happy go lucky Jim', *London Daily News*, 23 April 1987.
4 P. Hennessy, *The Prime Minister: The Office and Its Holders Since 1945* (London: Allen Lane, 2000), p. 392.
5 K. Morgan, *Callaghan: A Life* (Oxford: Oxford University Press, 1997), p. 393.
6 'A keen nose for the winds of change', *The Guardian*, 6 April 1976.
7 D. Owen, *Personally Speaking* (London: Pan Books, 1988), p. 114.
8 Quoted in *The Observer*, 'Assets of Sunny Jim', 8 June 1975.
9 J. Callaghan, *Time and Chance* (London: Collins, 1987), p. 305.
10 Quoted in *The Guardian*, 'Callaghan spells out his Gaullism'.
11 Callaghan, *Time and Chance*, p. 305.
12 Young, 'Europe', pp. 147–8.
13 S. Wall, *The Official History of Britain and the European Community, Volume III: The Tiger Unleashed, 1975–85* (London: Routledge, 2019), p. 70.
14 See J. Miles, 'The Labour Party and the Westminster Electoral System', PhD thesis, University of Liverpool, 2017.
15 Wall, *The Official History of Britain and the European Community, Volume III: The Tiger Unleashed*, p. 77.
16 Callaghan, *Time and Chance*, pp. 455–6.
17 D. Gowland and A. Turner, *Reluctant Europeans: Britain and European Integration, 1945–98* (London: Routledge, 2014), pp. 222–3.
18 K. Seidel, 'Britain, the Common Agricultural Policy and the Challenges of Membership in the European Community: A Political Balancing Act', *Contemporary British History*, 34/2 (2020), p. 180.
19 *Ibid.*, p. 190.
20 CC (76) 9th Conclusions, Cabinet, Conclusions of a Meeting of the Cabinet held at 10 Downing Street on Friday 11 June 1976 at 10.30 a.m., TNA, CAB 128/59/6. Quoted in *ibid.*, p. 191.
21 Wall, *The Official History of Britain and the European Community, Volume III: The Tiger Unleashed*, pp. 64–5.
22 Seidel, 'The Common Agricultural Policy', p. 192.
23 *Ibid.*, pp. 194–5.
24 *Irish Times*, 'Callaghan says farm policy will lead to tax revolt', 13 March 1979.
25 Callaghan, *Time and Chance*, p. 493.
26 E. Dell, 'Britain and the Origins of the European Monetary System', *Contemporary European History* (1994), vol. 3, no. 1, p. 32.
27 M. Franklin, 'Could and Should Britain have Joined the European Exchange Rate Mechanism in 1979? A Personal Memoir', *Journal of Contemporary European Research* (2013), vol. 9, no. 5, p. 760.
28 D. Healey, *The Time of My Life* (London: Michael Joseph, 1990), p. 439; J. Silkin, *Changing Battlefields: The Challenge to the Labour Party* (London: Hamish Hamilton, 1987), p. 189.
29 Dell, 'Britain and the Origins of the European Monetary System', p. 4.
30 *Ibid.*, pp. 35–6.
31 Callaghan, *Time and Chance*, pp. 489–92.
32 Healey, *The Time of My Life*, p. 439.
33 Quoted in Franklin, 'A Personal Memoir', p. 762.
34 Morgan, *Callaghan*, p. 615; Franklin, 'A Personal Memoir', p. 763.
35 Dell, 'Britain and the Origins of the European Monetary System', p. 32.
36 *The Guardian*, 18 April 1979; R. Jenkins, *European Diary, 1977–81* (London: Macmillan, 1989), p. 374, 400. Quoted in Young, 'Europe', p. 150; Franklin, 'A Personal Memoir', p. 764.
37 D. Butler and U. Kitzinger, *The 1975 Referendum* (London: Macmillan, 1976), p. 280; See P. Ludlow, *The Making of the European Monetary System* (London: Butterworth, 1982), p. 154.
38 K. Hickson, J. Miles and H. Taylor, *Peter Shore: Labour's Forgotten Patriot* (London: Biteback, 2020).

14

LABOUR'S DEFENCE AND FOREIGN POLICY, 1976–79[1]

Martin S. Alexander, Eric Grove, R. Gerald Hughes
and Kristan Stoddart

DEFENDING THE REALM
WHEN MONEY TALKED

THIS CHAPTER CONSIDERS THE record on defence and
foreign affairs of James Callaghan's government of 1976–79,
arguing for a positive but not complaisant view of its policies and
the government's achievements. The contour lines around the major
external and defence questions of the era were contested, and yet in
the end their shape was settled with a broad consensus. Matters generally remained as they had been when Labour held office previously
(under Clement Attlee, 1945-51, and Harold Wilson, 1964-70 and
1974-76).

To alter the metaphor, surface choppiness over defence was caused
in the mid-1970s by the Labour left, the unilateral disarmers whose

greatest influence would come in the post-Callaghan era.[2] Beneath the waves, however, Britain's foreign and defence policies sailed on. Much of the credit for this lay with Callaghan himself – a patriotic politician and Royal Navy veteran of 1939–45.[3] He remains the last British Prime Minister to have served in the armed forces and the only one to have served in the Royal Navy. As a politician, Callaghan's demeanour, exemplified by the nickname 'Sunny Jim', belied his guile and his determination.

Labour defence policy had been set out and then robustly defended by Roy Mason, Defence Secretary under Wilson and then Callaghan from February 1974 to September 1976 – not least against the Treasury's budget-cutters and Denis Healey (the Defence Secretary from 1964 to 1970, who from February 1974 was Chancellor of the Exchequer). Britain's armed forces were buffeted by economic gales, but sheltered from ideological cross-winds once Callaghan entered No. 10. Mason was a tough Yorkshireman and ex-miner, who had been minister of defence (equipment) under Healey from 1967 to 1968.[4] Mason fought the corner of the armed services to good effect, steering a coherent Defence Review into policy in 1975 while conceding that some cuts were unavoidable owing to Britain's parlous finances.

> I laid down the principle that we intend to maintain a modern and effective defence system while reducing its cost as a proportion of national resources ... We also indicated in the manifesto that we would look at the GNP figure compared with NATO and try to bring the figures into line with those of our major European allies. That is still the commitment.[5]

Reshuffling Mason to the Northern Ireland office in September 1976, Callaghan replaced him at the Ministry of Defence with Fred Mulley, a former sergeant in the Worcestershire Regiment who had been captured at Dunkirk.[6] He was well-travelled, and formerly minister for the Army (1964–65), minister for disarmament (1967–69) and minister of state at the Foreign and Commonwealth Office.

As the 1974–75 Defence Review began, Healey warned that the UK government might be facing the worst peacetime economic crisis in its history.[7] Furthermore, the defence budget was costing the UK taxpayer some £1 billion in foreign exchange payments per annum.[8] By Callaghan's prime ministership, Labour was operating as a minority government (which led to a pact with the Liberal Party from 1977 to 1978).[9] This impacted upon all areas of policy. In October 1976, when discussing Britain's contribution to NATO, Callaghan warned about the possibility of the UK being 'pushed into a position where we would have to make a choice between whether we carry on with these responsibilities or we have to say "sorry", our economic position demands that we put our own position first'.[10]

Healey wished to bring defence spending down from 5.5 per cent of GDP to c.4 per cent over ten years.[11] In response, the Chief of the Defence Staff (CDS) of 1973 to 1976, Field Marshal Sir Michael Carver, decided that the best option for the services was to cooperate with the Defence Review. Learning from their self-defeating disunity in the face of Healey's own 1966 Defence Review,[12] the military chiefs collectively decided to establish a 'critical level of forces', below which they could demonstrate that 'the resultant reduction in our contribution to NATO would call into question our support of the alliance, and … risk the cohesion of the alliance itself'.[13]

Nuclear Weapons (I): Strategic

Nuclear weapons had long constituted an extremely divisive issue for the Labour Party. Callaghan therefore excluded the full Cabinet from the policy process, minimised parliamentary debate on the issue, and sought to keep Labour's annual conference away from the matter.

It was an article of faith for those of Callaghan's stamp that the nuclear deterrent 'gave [the UK] a lever on world peace'.[14] The

technologically advanced Chevaline modification to Polaris, designed to allow Polaris to circumvent Soviet anti-ballistic missile
(ABM) defences, was ongoing when Callaghan became Prime Minister. Chevaline's funding was classified, not least for fear of the Labour
left's reaction. In the event, the project's cost rose to an estimated
£1 billion by 1980.[15] This was deemed a price worth paying because
British nuclear weapons betokened 'top table' power in international
politics, and were greatly prized by the UK's NATO partners.[16]

The urgency of the question of the British deterrent's future was
underlined in meetings between Callaghan, Healey, Mulley, and Foreign and Commonwealth Secretary David Owen.[17] A replacement for
Polaris was essential because the UK could one day be isolated in
facing 'Soviet political pressure or military threats. In this situation,
a British deterrent would provide us with the basis for resistance.'[18]
The new US missile, the Trident C4, was top of Callaghan's preferred
options, with US cruise missiles second-favourite. Callaghan's meeting at Guadeloupe in January 1979 with US President Jimmy Carter
saw the Prime Minister request that the UK purchase the Trident C4
– a proposition that Carter accepted.[19]

Callaghan advised Carter that he wanted to 'put on record what
I told you privately in Guadeloupe about the future of our nuclear
deterrent ... the option which at present seemed to me most likely
to meet British requirements was the Trident C4'.[20] Carter accepted
this and assured Callaghan that the US was prepared to defer matters
until after the impending general election.[21] On 4 May 1979, on his
last day as Prime Minister, Callaghan instructed that the 'incoming
Prime Minister should be briefed on the need for replacing Polaris
(or otherwise as she thinks!) and should decide whether to make her
own approaches to President Carter'.[22]

Nuclear weapons (II): 'Tactical'

In 1963, John Profumo, then the war minister, informed the House of Commons that 'the use of all tactical nuclear missiles in Europe, including those held by the British Army of the Rhine [BAOR], is governed by arrangements with the United States concerning the custody of the warheads'.[23] The BAOR had nuclear-capable artillery that could fire US nuclear shells. With regard to battlefield nuclear-tipped missiles, 50 Missile Regiment Royal Artillery operated, from 1976, a battery of twelve Lance missiles with US-held warheads. By this time, the 'independent' tactical nuclear armoury of the United Kingdom consisted of variants of the WE.177, an air-dropped weapon. Types of WE.177 were carried by a number of RAF and Royal Navy aircraft as either bombs or depth charges.[24]

When Callaghan became Prime Minister there was a rough parity in such forces between NATO and the Warsaw Pact on the Central Front, the heavily militarised territory stretching south from Denmark down the frontier between the Federal Republic (West Germany) and the German Democratic Republic (communist East Germany). This was not the case with Long-Range Theatre Nuclear Forces (LRTNF), where the military balance had been upset by the deployment of Soviet SS-20 missiles.[25] The Callaghan government was at the heart of debates as to how NATO should respond to this threat.[26] These were enmeshed with various proposed counters to Warsaw Pact conventional force superiority. A suspicion circulated that the US wished to deploy 'neutron bombs' (enhanced radiation weapons [ERW]).[27] In the event, this weapon was not proceeded with – a decision supported by Callaghan's government.[28]

It was widely believed NATO could not long resist an attack at a conventional level. The use of tactical nuclear weapons in the European theatre was therefore an accepted part of NATO strategy and known as 'flexible response'.[29] In October 1977 West German Chancellor Helmut Schmidt, who had been rapturously applauded after addressing the Labour Party special conference in December 1974,[30] called for the modernisation of NATO's European theatre nuclear capabilities in response to SS-20.[31] While the UK was due to deploy the Tornado to replace the Vulcan in the sub-strategic role, the Callaghan government was advised that US cruise missiles represented a better option.[32] This modernisation was urged on Carter by Callaghan and Schmidt at Guadeloupe in January 1979.[33] This represented the basis of the so-called 'twin-track approach' whereby NATO would deploy new missiles while offering to desist if the USSR removed their SS-20s.[34] This decision was finalised by NATO on 12 December 1979.[35]

THE ROYAL NAVY: CUTS, CRUISERS AND CARRIERS

In 1966, Wilson's government dismayed the Royal Navy (RN) by cancelling the two proposed replacement fixed-wing aircraft carriers (CVA01 class).[36] When asked during a tri-services seminar at the time of the Heath government if a plan existed to convert HMS *Eagle* – paid off in 1973 – into a commando carrier like HMS *Albion* and *Bulwark*, the commodore representing the RN replied, 'No, that would take too many skilled matelots "simply to drive it about".'[37] When the final deployment of HMS *Ark Royal* in the autumn of 1978 was followed by its decommissioning, Britain had no aircraft carrier. Accompanied by the band of HM Royal Marines, the *Ark Royal*'s crew recorded a cover version – with a measure of commercial success – of Roger Whittaker's popular song 'The Last Farewell'. Was this the funeral lament for British naval air power?

No, for replacement ships and aircraft were at hand. Three new *Invincible*-class light carriers were under construction and would embark Fleet Air Arm (FAA) Sea Harriers.[38] These developments were applauded in the then-authoritative annual *Jane's Fighting Ships* by the editor, Captain John Moore, RN (Retired):

The need for embarked aircraft, both fixed-wing and rotary, is proved in exercise after exercise. The continuation of the A/S [anti-submarine] cruiser [i.e. the *Invincible* class] programme in the Royal Navy is one way of achieving this, particularly since the decision to provide a force of twenty-five naval [FAA Sea] Harrier aircraft was at last announced on 15 May 1975.[39]

In December 1978, Vice-Admiral Sir Desmond Cassidi declared, 'With the Ark Royal going ... some people seem to envisage the end [of the FAA]. On the contrary, we are very much alive and kicking ... The Navy is being re-shaped to take advantage of new ideas and resources and we are confident that in techniques and quality we are second to none.'[40]

The new carrier programme remained alive – not least thanks to the cunning designation of them as 'anti-submarine cruisers' sometimes,[41] and at other times employing the euphemism 'through-deck cruiser', that term itself 'subsequently changed to "command cruiser"' (felt to be 'a reasonable title' given *Invincible* being 'above all ... a flagship, having effective control of submarines and surface ships').[42] This sleight-of-hand was abetted by a crafty and determined naval staff under Admiral Sir Edward Ashmore (First Sea Lord, 1974–77).[43] The Callaghan government was fortunate to inherit exceptionally talented senior RN officers who included Ashmore himself (appointed Chief of the Defence Staff in 1977) and his successor, Admiral Sir Terence Lewin, later a robust leader during the Falklands War.[44] In addition, the junior navy minister, Patrick Duffy (MP for Sheffield Attercliffe), was a former RN officer with the enthusiasm, intelligence and strength of character to preserve the new warship programmes.

As part of the 1975 Defence Review, the Ministry of Defence defined four minimum 'pillars' of defence: the Central Front, the Eastern Atlantic and Channel, the UK homeland and the nuclear deterrent.[45] Three of these pillars included the Royal Navy and the other could only be put into effect if command of the Atlantic were retained; albeit the effective abandonment of the Mediterranean flank did reduce Britain's amphibious ambitions.[46] Core naval programmes remained unscathed. Besides the new carriers, the RN's number of SSN nuclear attack submarines rose and, while some projected ships were cancelled, construction continued at a level close to shipyard capacity. Even for the Labour left, these were vital job schemes. Each carrier meant employment for 4,000, plus hundreds more working for subcontractors. Here were echoes of the debate in December 1974 when the Labour left was dissecting Roy Mason's draft Defence Review and 'a government spokesman defended the policy, especially the naval spending involved, not on grounds of an ostensible naval threat but on the grounds of the redundancies which would result if the cuts went further'.[47]

It was the fleet bequeathed by Callaghan that ensured victory in the South Atlantic in 1982. The commando carrier HMS *Hermes* was converted to a Sea Harrier role in 1978 and formed, with HMS *Invincible*, the core of the RN carrier task group in the Falklands War (the Sea Harriers performing superbly).[48] The Callaghan era left the RN a legacy of five new Type 42 destroyers (criticised, however, for inadequate armament),[49] three new Type 22 frigates, two *Invincible*-class carriers, three new SSNs and two minehunters. 'We are proceeding as rapidly as we can', Mulley told the Commons, 'with the modernisation of the Royal Navy. All three specialist warship-building yards of British Shipbuilders are fully occupied with naval orders and a large number of workers at three other yards … We have plans for ordering seven major warships in 1978–79 compared with three in 1977–78.'[50] Late in the Callaghan government, Duffy looked to the future:

With the introduction into service of [its new] ships the Soviet Navy will undoubtedly continue to improve its anti-submarine and anti-surface shipping capability. However, the threat that they pose can be countered by a concerted response from land-based aircraft, together with Royal Navy missile-armed warships and SSNs and, in due course, the Sea Harrier. The Royal Navy ... will be able to rely on the support of NATO [and] I am glad to be able to inform [the House] that HMS *Invincible* will be engaged in sea trials this spring and that we shall embark the Sea Harrier for further trials next year.[51]

By the end of the 1970s the head of the Soviet fleet, Admiral Sergey Gorshkov, had built, as he put it, 'a powerful ocean-going navy'.[52] Callaghan understood that maintaining a strong Royal Navy was vital: 'The Soviet Union could survive without sea power – the Western World could not.'[53] The Callaghan government's record on the Navy was a good one (especially compared with the readiness of Margaret Thatcher and her Defence Secretary, John Nott, to eviscerate the fleet in their 1981 review, 'The UK Defence Programme: The Way Forward', Command Paper No. 8288).[54]

THE THREAT TO THE FALKLAND ISLANDS

Menacing noises over the Falklands Islands by Argentina's President Juan Perón in the early 1950s led Churchill's government to deploy naval units to the South Atlantic to demonstrate British resolve.[55] This show of force was repeated in November 1977 after fifty Argentine 'scientists' landed on Southern Thule, prompting fears of an Argentine invasion of the Falklands. Under the codename 'Operation Journeyman', the SSN HMS *Dreadnought*, two frigates and two support vessels moved to the South Atlantic.[56] Callaghan's official biography states that Maurice Oldfield (head of SIS/MI6) ensured that the Argentines were aware of the deployment when Ted Rowlands, a junior minister at the FCO, began negotiations with Buenos

Aires on 13 December 1977.[57] The official history of the Falklands
War records that, after the Argentine government engaged positively
with Rowlands, the RN force was withdrawn on 20 December 1977,
'with no publicity about its mission'.[58]

On the eve of the Argentine invasion of the Falklands in 1982, Callaghan revealed the 1977 deployment to Parliament: 'On a very recent
occasion, of which I have full knowledge, Britain assembled ships
which had been stationed in the Caribbean, Gibraltar and in the
Mediterranean, and stood them about 400 miles off the Falklands in
support of HMS *Endurance*, and that when this fact became known,
without fuss and publicity, a diplomatic solution followed.'[59] Callaghan was more circumspect in his memoirs: 'I informed the head of
MI6 of our plan before the ships sailed and it is possible, as I hoped,
some information reached the Argentinean armed forces.'[60]

This version of the events of autumn 1977, however, may now be
doubted. Hugh Bicheno, then the deep-cover SIS officer in Buenos
Aires, has written that, since the Argentines did not know about the
'Operation Journeyman' deployment, 'the gesture served no deterrent purpose whatever'.[61] And, continues Bicheno, 'in 1982 Callaghan
alleged he had used SIS channels to let the Argentines know about it
in 1978. He lied.'[62] David Owen admitted, years later, that there was
'no trace of any such action on file'.[63]

Opinions on the usefulness of 'Journeyman' naturally differed according to political affiliation. Healey opined that 'the deterrent was
sufficient. There was no invasion.'[64] Conversely, Lord Carrington,
Conservative Foreign Secretary when the Falklands were invaded in
1982, saw no evidence that the existence of 'Journeyman' was ever
communicated to Buenos Aires.[65] The Royal Navy had the capacity to take devastating counteraction in late 1977; but the Argentinians did not know it, and did not act then because they were not
ready to.

THE ARMY: MAKE DO AND MEND

The two chief challenges for the Army's senior officers in 1976–79 were manpower and equipment. A British Army overly 'manpower intensive' and saddled with obsolete equipment would undermine its NATO allies in a war and most probably suffer heavy casualties and defeat. But an Army over-invested in high-tech weapons and equipment, yet short on manpower, would be over-stretched, unable to meet many simultaneous calls in the late 1970s for British boots on the ground. Ongoing commitments for the Army included Germany, Northern Ireland, Belize, Hong Kong and Cyprus.[66]

From the Army's standpoint, global overstretch would risk upsetting the careful balance between the four 'core' priorities agreed in the 1975 Defence Review. With regard to the Falklands, rapid reinforcement if a crisis occurred would be impossible, as the runway at Port Stanley was too short. 'Were the Argentinians to occupy the islands, their recovery by military means, though far from impossible, would be a major operation.'[67] In his 1976 report on the Falkland Islands, Lord Shackleton recommended upgrading the airport at a cost of £2 million, but this was rejected on cost grounds.[68] Although Mason warned the Cabinet that the re-conquest of the islands, if invaded, would require 5,000 troops and a substantial naval force,[69] spending on their security did not happen. Callaghan, meanwhile, presciently observed that Britain and Argentina were 'now on a collision course'.[70]

The Army's priorities remained with maintaining BAOR's combat power in North Germany and with battling to keep law and order, in support of the RUC (Royal Ulster Constabulary), in Northern Ireland – a mission absorbing more than an infantry division equivalent.[71] Callaghan had been Home Secretary when the troops first went into Northern Ireland in 1969 – an experience that caused him to grant Merlyn Rees, Secretary of State for Northern Ireland, relative autonomy.[72] In September 1976, Rees was replaced by Mason, who intensified anti-terrorist activities by the security forces, such as deploying the Special Air Service (SAS) to South Armagh.[73] Indeed, Martin McGuinness, a former Provisional IRA chief of staff, later testified that Mason 'beat the shit out of us'.[74]

One TA (Territorial Army) officer recalled that 'Callaghan was a good man struggling to control his fractious party which was deeply divided and dominated by the trade unions... People of centre right political persuasion thought the country was going to the dogs and this group would include many Army Officers.' The reasons for this were clear:

> A Lieutenant-Colonel in the mid-1970s would have been in the army for twenty to twenty-five years and seen nothing but a steady reduction in the size of the force during that time and more recently Aden, Singapore, Malta ... handed over, even Gibraltar soon to be deprived of an Army garrison. This inexorable process, accompanied by regimental amalgamations and disbandments ... affected their morale and sense of worth.[75]

The BAOR was organised in three divisions and two artillery brigades and was based at Joint Headquarters (JHQ) Rheindahlen, along with the Royal Air Force Germany (RAFG).[76] It lived under constant political scrutiny. When Conservative leader Margaret Thatcher requested an undertaking that there would be 'no reduction in our forces in BAOR', Callaghan defensively retorted that 'as a matter of policy it is certainly not the Government's desire to reduce such forces'.[77] The army's professional head from 1976 to 1979, the Chief of the General Staff, was Field Marshal Sir Roland Gibbs. 'Primarily a front-line soldier rather than a "Whitehall warrior"', in the words of one obituary – a mixed kind of compliment when his army was fighting the fights of peacetime.[78] More positively, the minister for the Army, Robert C. Brown, expressed satisfaction 'that the British Army of the Rhine has the equipment it needs to perform its role. Our aim is to ensure that BAOR can continue to meet the threat as it develops, and there is a major re-equipment programme under way to achieve this aim.'[79]

Yet the BAOR's effectiveness remains debateable in the Mason–Mulley years. One commentator observed that 'they are Micawber's Army pretending to be Nato's Praetorian Guard. Britain's Rhine Army, nominally 55,000, rarely exceeds 40,000.' Though the worsening sterling–Deutschmark exchange rate was compensated by a Local Overseas Allowance – and higher when serving in Germany – Army pay was comparatively low.[80]

For the TA, the 1970s saw modest expansion from a low starting point, although the basis for some of the reorganisation challenged anyone seeking its logic or consistency. At least, as Major Paul Bradburn has said, 'I don't, to be fair, recall us being made to economise on things like vehicle fuel or ammunition – the things governments do when money is tight.'[81] Another senior officer, a Regular Army Royal Engineer who spent nearly twenty years serving in Germany, remembers training being 'always subject to periodic restrictions, often changing on a yearly basis as it was the one available variable against mostly fixed costs'. Despite 'the distractions of Northern Ireland, training was good and morale was high certainly in the RE'. One highlight of the Callaghan–Mulley era was the parade of the entire British 4th Armoured Division (under Nigel Bagnall, a talented commander who became Chief of the General Staff in 1985) for the Queen's Silver Jubilee Review at Sennelager in June 1977.[82]

However, by 1978–79 problems were apparent even with what were long-regarded as the Army's strengths. British Chieftains performed poorly in NATO tank gunnery competitions. BAOR 'used to say that Chieftain was the best tank in the world as long as it broke down in a good fire position … Its armour protection was good, its 120mm rifled gun powerful and accurate, but its automotive systems let it down.'[83] The 105mm-armed West German Leopard demonstrated better mobility and reliability, while the Chieftain was outmatched by the Soviet adversary's T-64 and T-72 tanks which had self-loading 125mm guns.[84]

Despite further global retreats, including the closure of the Malta naval base in 1979,[85] BAOR's shortcomings seemed set to worsen, with quantities of guns and tanks going into reserve for want of crews.[86] In central Europe the Warsaw Pact already outnumbered NATO by 2.5 to 1 in tanks and 2 to 1 in aircraft, and it had at least 40 per cent more troops.[87] Of the three military services, the British Army had the biggest question mark against it by 1979 as regards its combat-power relative to size.

THE ROYAL AIR FORCE

The RAF, too, had problems. The Heath government had insisted on stretching aircraft lifespans and had cut support elements, spares and stockpiles. One officer, then a young Army captain, recollects the alarm at how little ammunition BAOR and RAF Germany disposed of in the 1970s. He was attending a study session when someone 'asked a question of an Air Commodore, about the RAF's munitions. The picture was very depressing, he replied, as they had only enough for SIX days "at intensive rates". This was in the early '70s, but that was quite a shock.'[88]

Shortly afterwards, Mason's 1974–75 Defence Review eliminated 17,000 RAF personnel, plus transport aircraft and aircrew, and logistics.[89] Brushing this aside, Mason claimed that 'no significant reductions will be made in front-line combat aircraft, and all the major re-equipment programmes affecting the front line will go ahead'.[90]

In June 1976 the RAF Under-Secretary of State for Defence, James Wellbeloved, stated:

> The savings made have been largely in ... support helicopters and training and communications aircraft. Reductions in our overseas commitments and the RAF withdrawal from [East of Suez] have allowed us to make the Transport Force smaller. At home, the RAF has given up a number of stations and is regrouping on larger, more cost-effective sites ... by and large, everyone now accepts that, in the situation we were faced with, the outcome of the Defence Review was both timely and right.[91]

The RAF had held Labour in suspicion since Healey's cuts in the 1960s: most notably of the TSR-2,[92] and its (supposed) replacement, the F-111K.[93] Killing these programmes signalled for many a big reduction in, respectively, the British aircraft industry and the RAF as a front-rank air force.[94] Instead of the F-111K, the RAF had been supplied with the Blackburn Buccaneer as a supposedly interim measure in 1969. Periodic updates to the Buccaneer culminated in 1979, when the RAF obtained the US AN/AVQ-23E Pave Spike laser designator pod for Paveway II laser-guided bombs.[95] The Buccaneer's flexibility and its longevity in service underlined how fortunate the RAF had been to have possessed such an outstanding aircraft.

Global operations had been much reduced after the RAF Far East Air Force had been disbanded on 31 October 1971.[96] 'Out of area' operations thereafter became very limited, as when airpower contributed to the Sultanate of Oman's suppression of the Dhofar Rebellion.[97] By 1976 the RAF's primary role was Western Europe's defence against the Warsaw Pact, its main bases being RAF Brüggen, RAF Gutersloh, RAF Laarbruch and RAF Wildenrath (the latter the sole air defence base of the RAFG). The deployment of the RN's strategic nuclear deterrent had freed the RAF from that responsibility, leaving the last 'V-bomber', the Avro Vulcan, assigned to the tactical nuclear strike role as part of the British contribution to NATO.[98]

The RAF understood it must fight for scarce funds. In 1974 Air Chief Marshal Sir Andrew Humphrey stated that, as the East Bloc's threat increased, the West was constrained by 'the hard facts of financial life: [especially] the effects of inflation and the rising costs of manpower and equipment'.[99] Matters were exacerbated when Mason's Defence Review instructed the air marshals and accountants to cut £1.4 billion from the RAF as part of economies totalling £4.4 billion over eight years.[100] As ever, the downsizing was discussed in the same breath as an insistence that compensatory gains from high-tech new weapons and support equipment were imminent. Crucial to this was the British–German–Italian multirole combat aircraft (MRCA), the Panavia Tornado which would, boasted the RAF minister James Wellbeloved, bring a 'substantial improvement' to 'qualitative strength'.[101]

The Callaghan years heralded a period of stability for the RAF. The defence of UK air space was the domain of the Lightning and the US F-4 Phantom.[102] These aircraft had both entered service in 1960,[103] and Mulley announced that they were to be replaced. 'We are pressing ahead with the development of the air defence variant [ADV] of the Tornado with its Sky Flash medium-range air-to-air missiles and AIM 9L short-range air-to-air missiles. Its important new air intercept radar will bring a new dimension to our ability to control the airspace above this country and the seas around.'[104]

The Nimrod maritime reconnaissance aircraft was upgraded (from MR1 to MR2), although the force shrank from forty-six to thirty-five by 1979.[105] The Nimrod had replaced the venerable Shackleton. It seemed logical that it repeat the trick in the airborne early warning (AEW) role. Mulley declared that 'the radar detection which is so essential to ... air defence will be immeasurably improved by the introduction of the new Nimrod airborne early warning aircraft, on which full development is under way'.[106] And just days before the end of the Callaghan government, Wellbeloved stated that the 'design work [was] well in hand'.[107] Unfortunately, this turned into a long and sorry saga. The Nimrod AEW3 became an expensive flop: it was cancelled, and the US E-3 Sentry was bought in its stead.[108]

The RAF held its own under Callaghan. As one contemporary opined, however, while it remained 'a large and formidable force', it was 'neither as large nor as formidable as the situation warrants or the spend on it should have produced'.[109]

RHODESIA

Though defence was heavily focused in the later 1970s on NATO–Europe and, for the Royal Navy, on the Eastern Atlantic and Channel, some residual overseas issues remained. Never long absent from the Callaghan Cabinet's deliberations, or from the spotlight of the press, was Rhodesia. There a Unilateral Declaration of Independence (UDI) in 1965 by the white minority government of Ian Smith created a problem familiar to Callaghan (as it had dogged Wilson's governments).[110] Rhodesia was embroiled in a bitter guerrilla war by 1976.[111] The Smith regime's ability to defy British-led international sanctions had been greatly reduced with the end of Portuguese East Africa (Mozambique) in June 1975.[112] On the ground, Rhodesia's armed forces maintained a clear military edge over the guerrillas,[113] but Smith now found that even his South African ally was urging him to compromise.[114] One of Smith's main opponents, Joshua Nkomo, came to London and asked Callaghan to press B. J. Vorster, the Prime Minister of South Africa, and Henry Kissinger, the US Secretary of State, to warn Smith that he must negotiate so as to 'avoid dangerous guerrilla activity'. Callaghan agreed to do so.[115]

With Callaghan as Prime Minister, Tony Crosland took over the

Foreign and Commonwealth Office until his untimely death in 1977. Crosland reported to Cabinet that Kissinger and Vorster were both working on persuading Smith to accept negotiations. On 19 September 1976, Kissinger met Smith and proposed that, within two years, his government should accept black majority rule. For Crosland this was crucial, as 'nothing can be done until and unless the principle of majority rule is accepted' by Smith.[116]

As is commonplace with insurgencies, politics rendered the military successes of the Rhodesian state irrelevant. On 3 March 1978, a power-sharing deal (the so-called 'Internal Settlement') was reached between Smith's government and the moderate African nationalists.[117] This was not acceptable to Britain and the international community. Callaghan believed Smith might be willing to negotiate although, supported by President Carter, he would not be used to mediate anything that avoided black majority rule. With that in mind, in November 1978 Callaghan despatched the MP for Anglesey, Cledwyn Hughes, a long-time political ally and chairman of the PLP, to Rhodesia as envoy; he did not persuade Smith to open discussions but his mission renewed contacts that led to more success a year later.[118] Hughes 'recommended that [Callaghan] should be ready to call a conference at once if developments should indicate a better prospect of success than would be the case today'.[119] The Prime Minister expected little from Smith's attempt to cooperate with the moderate nationalists.

> The fears that we expressed at the time [of the signing of the 'Internal Settlement'], I think, would not have been removed if that settlement had been recognised by the British Government. The situation would have continued to deteriorate, in our view, but that is a matter of judgment. However, rather than justifying ourselves before the bar of history, I prefer to look forward.[120]

Smith held elections in April 1979 and Bishop Abel Muzorewa was elected Prime Minister.[121] The name of the country was changed to Zimbabwe Rhodesia, with whites guaranteed a third of the seats in Parliament and control of the police, armed forces and judiciary. But it was clear that this was not a permanent solution.

Callaghan appeared to have failed over Rhodesia, as Wilson and Heath had before him.[122] But it is now clear that, as with other areas we have examined, Callaghan was not without achievements. He had approached the Rhodesia problem in a realistic and nuanced fashion, and brought Carter into the process.[123] Cyrus Vance (Kissinger's successor) observed that Callaghan and Owen had paved the way for the eventual solution brokered in 1979–80.[124]

TIME AND CHANCE IN DEFENCE AND FOREIGN POLICY

On defence matters, Callaghan's government could be quietly satisfied. Rationalised 'core' commitments had been accompanied by armament modernisation programmes, especially benefiting the RN and the RAF. Fred Mulley rightly reaffirmed in the House of Commons, when he moved the 'Statement on the Defence Estimates 1978' (Command Paper No. 7099), Labour's 'determination to make a full and effective defence contribution to NATO as well as to seek, in conjunction with our allies, realistic measures of arms control and disarmament by international agreement'. When pressed by Conservative MPs Michael Mates and Patrick Cormack about the Warsaw Pact's numerical superiority, Mulley skewered the challenge by reminding the House that 'what simple figures and charts cannot, of course, show is the quality of the forces they depict'.[125] In general, the Labour left, HM Treasury and the Tory opposition were outflanked, out-argued and out-fought.

Between 1974 and 1978, UK defence spending fell from 5.5 per cent to 4.7 per cent of GDP.[126] At times, it had been an uneasy process. Tony Geraghty wrote that 'the spending forecasts contained in the 1974 review … were rooted in the false assumption that Britain's economic situation would not deteriorate'. There was a sense of 'uncontrolled disarmament by inflation' going on.[127] Particularly problematic was the failure of service pay to keep up with the rest of the public sector. By 1979 there was real dissatisfaction at this state of affairs and recruitment suffered. An opportunistic Conservative Party promised to rectify this situation.[128] Two days before the election, Thatcher pledged 'that as soon as possible after the election, we will restore service pay to the full and fair levels recommended by the Armed Services Pay Review Board'.[129]

Yet in most respects, the years 1976–79 saw greater 'punch' generated for the pounds spent on defence, thanks, not least, to well-specified new technologies. Otherwise put, the coat of defence was tailored to the cloth available. In 1979, since only 2 per cent of the electorate thought that defence was a major issue,[130] this was plainly not where Callaghan lost the election. In any case, as Fred Mulley told the Cabinet, 'it was not possible to please both those who thought we spent too much on defence, and those who thought we spent too little'.[131] The Callaghan government had, given its operating constraints, done well.

NOTES

1   This chapter is dedicated to the memory of David Steeds (1938–2020).
2   K. Morgan, *Callaghan: A Life* (Oxford: Oxford University Press, 1999), p. 726.
3   J. Callaghan, *Time and Chance* (London: Collins, 1987), pp. 55, 57–9; Morgan, *Callaghan*, pp. 46–8.
4   'Lord Mason of Barnsley – obituary', *Daily Telegraph*, 15 April 2015; B. Jackson and D. Bramall, *The Chiefs: The Story of the United Kingdom Chiefs of Staff* (London: Brassey's, 1992), p. 378.
5   Hansard, HC Deb, 21 May 1974, vol. 874, col. 170.
6   Jackson and Bramall, *The Chiefs*, pp. 381–2.
7   R. Mason, *Paying the Price* (London: Robert Hale, 1999), p. 124.
8   D. Healey, *The Time of My Life* (London: Michael Joseph, 1989), p. 412.
9   P. Hennessy, *The Prime Minister: The Office and Its Holders Since 1945* (London: Allen Lane, 2000), pp. 392–3.
10 L. Freedman, 'British Foreign Policy to 1985. II: Britain's Contribution to NATO', *International Affairs* (1978), vol. 54, no. 1, p. 30.

11 Jackson and Bramall, *The Chiefs*, p. 378.
12 C. Taylor, *A Brief Guide to Previous British Defence Reviews*, International Affairs and Defence Section, SN/IA/5714 (London: House of Commons Library, 2010), pp. 5–6.
13 M. Carver, *Out of Step: The Memoirs of Field Marshal Lord Carver* (London: Hutchinson, 1989), p. 448.
14 The National Archives: Public Record Office (hereafter TNA: PRO): PREM 16/1181, Bryan Cartledge to Martin Vile, 20 July 1977.
15 P. Hennessy and J. Jinks, *The Silent Deep: The Royal Navy Submarine Service Since 1945* (London: Allen Lane, 2015), pp. 467–8.
16 TNA: PRO: PREM 16/1977, David Owen to Callaghan, 31 July 1978.
17 D. Owen, *Time to Declare* (London: Michael Joseph, 1991), p. 381.
18 TNA: PRO: PREM 16/1978, Cabinet, 21 December 1978.
19 Callaghan, *Time and Chance*, pp. 552–8; Morgan, *Callaghan*, pp. 620–21.
20 TNA: PRO: PREM 16/1978, Callaghan to Carter, 27 March 1979.
21 TNA: PRO: PREM 16/1978, Cartledge to Hunt, 6 April 1979.
22 P. Hennessy, *The Secret State: Preparing for the Worst 1945–2010*, 2nd edn (London: Penguin, 2010), p. 317.
23 Hansard, HC Deb, 13 February 1963, vol. 671, col. 1280.
24 D. Campbell, *Nuclear Facts: A Guide to Nuclear Weapons Systems and Strategy* (London: Hamlyn, 1984), p. 167.
25 US Department of Defense (DOD), *Soviet Military Power* (Washington DC: US Government Printing Office, 1983), pp. 35–7.
26 K. Stoddart, *The Sword and the Shield: Britain, the USA, NATO and Nuclear Weapons 1970–76* (Basingstoke: Palgrave, 2014), pp. 192–202.
27 G. Smith, 'The SS-20 Challenge and Opportunity: The Dual-Track Decision and its Consequences', in L. S. Kaplan (ed.), *American Historians and the Atlantic Alliance* (Kent, OH: The Kent State University Press, 1991), p. 123.
28 Morgan, *Callaghan*, p. 604.
29 J. S. Duffield, 'The Evolution of NATO's Strategy of Flexible Response: A Reinterpretation', *Security Studies* (1991), vol. 1, no. 1, p. 132.
30 R. G. Hughes, '"Don't Let's Be Beastly to the Germans": Britain and the German Affair in History', *20th Century British History* (2006), vol. 17, no. 2, p. 277.
31 H. Schmidt, 'The 1977 Alastair Buchan memorial lecture', *Survival* (1978), vol. 20, no. 1, pp. 2–10.
32 TNA: PRO: DEFE 68/240, J. D. Sutton, 7 November 1978.
33 C. Bluth, *Britain, Germany and Western Nuclear Strategy* (Oxford: Clarendon Press, 1995), pp. 234–5.
34 Morgan, *Callaghan*, p. 619.
35 Bluth, *Britain, Germany and Western Nuclear Strategy*, p. 235.
36 E. Hampshire, 'The Battle for CVA01', in T. Benbow (ed.), *British Naval Aviation: The First 100 Years* (Farnham: Ashgate, 2011), pp. 177–96.
37 Maj. (Retd) Paul Bradburn, by email (6 June 2020).
38 C. Chant (ed.), *The World's Navies* (London: David & Charles, 1979), p. 203.
39 Foreword, John Moore (ed.), *Jane's Fighting Ships 1975–76* (London: Macdonald & Jane's, 1975), p. 97.
40 'We're flying High!', *Navy News*, December 1978.
41 *Jane's Fighting Ships 1975–6*, p. 348.
42 *Conway's All the World's Fighting Ships 1947–1982* (London: Conway Maritime Press, 1983), pp. 148–9.
43 Jackson and Bramall, *The Chiefs*, p. 380.
44 T. Heathcote, *The British Admirals of the Fleet 1734–1995* (Barnsley: Pen & Sword, 2002), p. 16, p. 159.
45 Jackson and Bramall, *The Chiefs*, p. 379.
46 The main source here is E. Grove, *Vanguard to Trident; British Naval Policy Since World War Two* (Annapolis, MD: Naval Institute Press, 1987).

47 K. Booth, *Navies and Foreign Policy* (New York: Holmes & Meier, 1979), p. 200 and p. 215 (referencing *The Times*, 17 December 1974).

48 J. Moore 'The Lessons of the Naval War in the Falklands', in J. Moore (ed.), *Jane's Naval Review* (London: Jane's, 1982), p. 18.

49 Chant (ed.), *The World's Navies*, p. 203.

50 Hansard, HC Deb, 13 March 1978, vol. 946, col. 55.

51 Hansard, HC Deb, 20 March 1979, vol. 964, cols 1291–2.

52 J. E. Moore, 'The Modern Soviet Navy', in R. Bonds (ed.), *The Soviet War Machine* (London: Salamander, 1980), p. 99.

53 I. Parsons (ed.), *The Encyclopaedia of Sea Warfare: From the First Ironclads to the Present Day*, foreword by Lord Mountbatten (London: Salamander, 1977), p. 250.

54 J. Nott, *Here Today, Gone Tomorrow: Recollections of an Errant Politician* (London: Politico, 2002), pp. 203–15, pp. 228–40.

55 TNA: PRO: CAB/195/11/14, CC6(53), Cabinet, 3 February 1953; TNA: PRO: CAB/128/26, C.C. (53), Cabinet, 1 April 1953.

56 L. Freedman, *The Official History of the Falklands Campaign*, 1, *The Origins of the Falklands War* (London: Routledge, rev. edn 2007), pp. 76–88.

57 Morgan, *Callaghan*, p. 59.

58 Freedman, *The Official History of the Falklands Campaign*, 1, p. 86.

59 *Hansard*, HC Deb, 6th Series, 30 March 1982, vol. 21, col. 168.

60 Callaghan, *Time and Chance*, p. 375.

61 H. Bicheno, *Razor's Edge: The Unofficial History of the Falklands War* (London: Phoenix, 2007), p. 25; R. G. Hughes, *The Postwar Legacy of Appeasement: British Foreign Policy Since 1945* (London: Bloomsbury, 2014), p. 96; email from Bicheno, 3 March 2013.

62 Bicheno, *Razor's Edge*, p. 25(n).

63 Owen, *Time to Declare*, pp. 349–50.

64 Healey, *The Time of My Life*, p. 494.

65 Lord Carrington, *Reflect on Things Past: The Memoirs of Lord Carrington* (London: Collins, 1988), p. 351; Hennessy and Jinks, *The Silent Deep*, p. 392.

66 C. Chant (ed.), *The World's Armies* (London: David & Charles, 1979), p. 154.

67 TNA: PRO: FCO 16/743, MoD, 'Defence of the Falkland Islands', 21 February 1975.

68 TNA: PRO: FCO 16/743, Reg Prentice to Foreign Secretary James Callaghan, 9 March 1976. After the 1982 war, a large runway was constructed at RAF Mount Pleasant.

69 TNA: PRO: 128/58/11, CC76(11), Cabinet, 18 March 1976.

70 TNA: PRO: 129/188/8, G76(33), Callaghan memo, 'The Falkland Islands: Future Policy', 16 March 1976.

71 Lt. Col. Michael Dewar, *The British Army in Northern Ireland* (London: Guild, 1985), pp. 147–58.

72 S. C. Aveyard, *No Solution: The Labour Government and the Northern Ireland Conflict, 1974–9* (Manchester: Manchester University Press, 2016), p. 135.

73 P. R. Neumann, 'Winning the "War on Terror"? Roy Mason's Contribution to Counter-Terrorism in Northern Ireland', *Small Wars & Insurgencies*, 14/3 (2003), pp. 45–64.

74 Aveyard, *No Solution*, p. 135.

75 Email from Maj. (Retd) Paul Bradburn, 12 April 2020.

76 A. Mallinson, *The Making of the British Army* (London: Bantam, 2009), p. 440.

77 Hansard, HC Deb, 25 January 1977, vol. 923, cols 1176–7.

78 Field Marshal Sir Roland Gibbs obituary, *Daily Telegraph*, 4 November 2004.

79 Hansard, HC Deb, 27 June 1978, vol. 952, col. 1200.

80 T. Geraghty, 'A Cloud over Defence', *The Spectator*, 26 March 1977; more generally see P. Johnston, *British Forces in Germany: The Lived Experience* (London: Profile Editions, 2019).

81 Email from Maj. (Retd) Paul Bradburn, 12 April 2020.

82 Email from Maj.-Gen. (Retd) Mungo Melvin, 14 June 2020.

83 Lt. Col. (Retd) Stuart Crawford, 'Challenger2 – the wrong tank for the British Army?', *UKDJ*, 23 August 2018: https://ukdefencejournal.org.uk/challenger-2-the-wrong-tank-for-the-british-army/

84 US DOD, *Soviet Military Power*, p. 38. Hope for the Royal Armoured Corps later came in the shape

of the main battle tank replacement, Challenger 1. This had originated as an export model, Shir II, for the Shah of Iran – an order that was cancelled because of the Iranian Revolution in 1979.

85 R. Dannatt, *Boots on the Ground: Britain and Her Army Since 1945* (London: Profile, 2017), p. 154.

86 *Ibid.*, pp. 152–3; W. M. E. Hicks, 'The Maintenance of Operational Standards', *British Army Review* (1977), vol. 36, pp. 6–15; Jackson and Bramall, *The Chiefs*, p. 382.

87 Mason, *Paying the Price*, p. 124.

88 Email from Maj. (Retd) Paul Bradburn, 6 June 2020.

89 I. Watson, *Fading Eagle: Politics and Decline of Britain's Post-War Air Force* (Stroud: Fonthill, 2013), p. 165.

90 *Statement on the Defence Estimates 1975*, Cm 5976 (London: HMSO, 1975); Hansard, HC Deb, 6 May 1975, vol. 891, cols 1234–5.

91 Hansard, HC Deb, 10 June 1976, vol. 912, col. 1708.

92 S. Straw and J. W. Young, 'The Wilson Government and the Demise of TSR-2, October 1964 – April 1965', *Journal of Strategic Studies* (1997), vol. 20, no. 4, pp. 18–44.

93 C. Gardner, *British Aircraft Corporation: A History* (London: B. T. Batsford, 1981), p. 116.

94 J. Hamilton-Paterson, *Empire of the Clouds: When Britain's Aircraft Ruled the World* (London: Faber & Faber, 2011).

95 R. Chesneau, *Blackburn Buccaneer S Mks 1 and 2* (Suffolk: Ad Hoc, 2005), p. 16.

96 I. Proctor, *The Royal Air Force in the Cold War, 1950–1970: Rare Photographs from Wartime Images* (Barnsley: Pen & Sword, 2014), p. 83.

97 J. Buckley and P. Beaver, *The Royal Air Force: The First One Hundred Years* (Oxford: Oxford University Press, 2018), p. 191.

98 H. Wynn, *The RAF Strategic Nuclear Deterrent Forces: Their Origins, Roles and Deployment, 1946–1969 – A Documentary History* (London: HMSO, 1997), p. 462.

99 Air Chief Marshal Sir Andrew Humphrey, 'More for your money', *Royal Air Force Yearbook 1974* (London: RAF, 1974), p. 7.

100 Watson, *Fading Eagle*, p. 168.

101 Hansard, HC Deb, 10 June 1976, vol. 912, col. 1712.

102 D. Hobbs, 'British F-4 Phantoms', *Air International* (2008), 7, no. 5, pp. 30–31.

103 P. R. March, *Freedom of the Skies: An Illustrated History of Fifty Years of NATO Airpower* (London: Cassell/RAF Benevolent Fund, 1999), p. 63.

104 Hansard, HC Deb, 13 March 1978, vol. 946, col. 55.

105 Buckley and Beaver, *The Royal Air Force*, p. 175.

106 Hansard, HC Deb, 13 March 1978, vol. 946, col. 55; M. Streetly, *World Electronic Warfare Aircraft* (London: Jane's, 1983), p. 20.

107 Hansard, HC Deb, 3 April 1979, vol. 965, col. 365.

108 March, *Freedom of the Skies*, p. 118; 'Very reluctantly I have decided that the time has now come to cancel the project', *The Times* (London), 19 December 1986.

109 C. Chant (ed.), *The World's Air Forces* (London: David & Charles, 1979), p. 177.

110 K. Maxey, 'Labour and the Rhodesian Situation', *African Affairs* (1976), vol. 75, no. 299, pp. 152–62.

111 Callaghan, *Time and Chance*, p. 530.

112 P. Baxter, *Bush War Rhodesia, 1966–1980* (Birmingham: Helion, 2014), p. 23.

113 I. F. W. Beckett. 'The Rhodesian Army: Counter-insurgency, 1972–1979', in I. F. W. Beckett and J. Pimlott (eds), *Counter Insurgency: Lessons from History*, 2nd edn (Barnsley: Pen & Sword, 2011), pp. 185-7.

114 I. Smith, The Great Betrayal: *The Memoirs of Ian Douglas Smith* (London: Blake, 1997), p. 186.

115 TNA: PRO: 128/58/4, CC76 (4), Cabinet, 5 February 1976.

116 TNA: PRO: 129/192/5, CP76 (80), Tony Crosland, 'Rhodesia', 21 September 1976.

117 D. Kenrick, *Decolonisation, Identity and Nation in Rhodesia, 1964–1979: A Race Against Time* (Basingstoke: Palgrave, 2019), p. 51.

118 D. L. Jones, 'Hughes, Cledwyn, Baron Cledwyn of Penrhos (1916–2001), politician', in National Library of Wales, *Dictionary of Welsh Biography* at: https://biography.wales/article/s8-HUGH -CLE-1916#?c=0&m=0&s=0&cv=6&manifest=https%3A%2F%2Fdamsssl.llgc.org.uk%2Fi-iif%2F2.0%2F1490010%2Fmanifest.json&xywh=1283%2C1544%2C3184%2C2749 (accessed 28 June 2020); Callaghan, *Time and Chance*, pp. 530–31.

119 Hansard, HC Deb, 17 January 1979, vol. 960, col. 1712.

120 Hansard, HC Deb, 17 January 1979, vol. 960, col. 1716.

121 Beckett, 'The Rhodesian Army', p. 166.

122 Morgan, *Callaghan*, p. 598.

123 Callaghan, *Time and Chance*, p. 531, p. 541.

124 Owen, *Time to Declare*, p. 381.

125 Hansard, HC Deb, 13 March 1978, vol. 946, col. 47.

126 NATO, 'Financial and economic data relating to NATO defence', M-DPC-2(78)20, 5 December 1978.

127 Geraghty, 'A Cloud over Defence'.

128 H. Leach, *Endure No Makeshifts: Some Naval Recollections* (London: Leo Cooper, 1993), p. 190; Jackson and Bramall, *The Chiefs*, pp. 382–5.

129 Margaret Thatcher Archive, Churchill College Cambridge: 'Speech to Conservative Rally in Bolton', GE800/79, 1 May 1979. Thatcher kept her word. Leach, *Endure No Makeshifts*, p. 190.

130 M. Heseltine, 'The United Kingdom's Strategic Interests and Priorities', *RUSI Journal* (1983), vol. 128, no. 4, p. 3.

131 TNA: PRO: 128/61/4, CC77(4), Cabinet, 3 February 1977.

PART THREE
PERSPECTIVES

15

INSIDE NO. 10

David Lipsey

J IM CALLAGHAN WAS A proper Prime Minister, in both meanings of the word. He was proper in that he followed the proprieties of the British constitution. His was Cabinet government, though with the civil service playing its vital role, and he expected his ministers to behave properly. My previous boss, the Foreign Secretary, Anthony Crosland, discovered this when he turned up inappropriately dressed to greet a visiting dignitary, enraging Callaghan. A greater contrast with Harold Wilson, his predecessor, and his No. 10, is hard to imagine.

But he was proper in the more important sense that he saw his overriding duty to do his best for his country. That, for him, trumped personal glory or party popularity.

I joined No. 10 after the death of Crosland, to whom I was a devoted special advisor. I took on a bits-and-pieces sort of a role. I was a political speechwriter; I advised him on opinion polls; I was a member of the first-ever policy unit headed by Bernard Donoughue; and I helped out with the political office under Tom McNally. When

Tom, perhaps Jim's closest advisor, left to fight a Labour seat, I some-
how found myself faute de mieux running the political office and later
coordinating Jim's team in the disastrous 1979 general election.

Jim was a competitive man. He had to be, having fought his way
to the top from a humble background. He once asked Crosland what
degree he would have got had he gone to university. Crosland, probably accurately but not tactfully, replied, 'a 2:1'. In those days when
Labour politics was stuffed with brilliant men – Healey, Crosland,
Jenkins – Callaghan used common sense to trump intellect. His handling of the controversial IMF loan of 1976 was a classic of turning an
initial minority in Cabinet into a unanimous decision.

That made him in some ways a tough man to work for. The first
time I went into his first-floor study to discuss a speech, I nervously
mistook which of the two doors I had come in by and found myself
in the Prime Minister's lavatory. Trying to laugh off my gaffe, I said,
'I expect lots of people do that, Prime Minister.' 'No,' he replied. 'You
are the only one.'

In truth, I wasn't really his type. Though I had always been a
party member, and had worked for a trade union after Oxford, my
relationship with the labour movement was always more intellectual,
while his was instinctive. I was overawed in his presence, and that in
turn inhibited any closeness, such as I had enjoyed with Crosland.
At least once he nearly fired me after I had written him a speech he
disliked, only saving myself by a breakneck rewriting. On another, he
delivered a speech to a Coop gathering which went down a storm.
When I congratulated him, he said, 'You are only saying that because
you wrote it.'

Callaghan preferred more grounded folk – McNally, his press
secretary Tom McCaffrey and his personal secretary Ruth Sharp.
He had a close and supportive family: a wonderful wife Audrey;
and his daughter Margaret, who decades later went on to become a

distinguished Leader of the House of Lords. When the 1979 election took place, his son Mike joined his little team.

The 1979 election is the reason Callaghan's premiership is underrated. After a rough patch, by the autumn of 1978 we were level-pegging with the Tories in the polls. Most of his team thought he would outgun Margaret Thatcher during a campaign. Indeed, one of our team leaked to the *Daily Mirror* that an election would take place then. But Callaghan thought it over and decided not to go.

He was full of good reasons to delay. He cited a poll by Labour's pollster Bob Worcester, showing the party behind in the marginal it needed to win for a majority. I pointed out that the sample sizes were too small to pronounce this with confidence. He understandably asked who he should believe: Britain's most famous pollster or a whippersnapper of thirty.

But it seems to me, years later, that really he postponed going to the country for a quite different reason. The trade unions were getting ready for a tremendous fight over pay over the winter. Callaghan wanted modest settlements. I remember going to see him with McNally when he was contemplating setting a 5 per cent limit on rises. We thought this would be politically disastrous. Jim turned to us and half-snarled, 'What are you two saying? That 5 per cent wouldn't be best for the country?' Of course, we were not saying that at all. We retired licking our wounds.

I believe he set this course because he felt that, if the election was still pending, he would have a strong negotiating hand with the trade unions. They, after all, no more than he wanted a Tory government under Mrs Thatcher. They surely would acquiesce, albeit sullenly, in his 5 per cent limit.

This turned out to be wrong – the unions and their members precipitated the Winter of Discontent. But what I believe motivated Callaghan was what he said to us: that 5 per cent would be best for the country. That was more important to him than any advantage that would accrue to Labour from a more generous set of settlements.

Callaghan's toughness showed over the election manifesto. He eventually rejected the Bennite draft that emerged from Transport House. So Tom McNally wrote the foreword and I did the policies – overnight. Then Jim showed his guile. 'Call over Lena Jeger,' (a left-wing member of the National Executive) 'put her in a room with the draft and a bottle of whisky and don't let her out until she says it's fine.' Some hours later, Lena emerged the worse for wear and declared her support, which helped the manifesto go through.

It was not the manifesto that caused our defeat. It was a turn of sentiment in the country. At times we looked to be closing the gap, but bright morning soon turned to black night. Ultimately, Callaghan had to chew the lemon of political defeat. But he did so for his country.

16

A LABOUR BACKBENCHER'S VIEWPOINT

Austin Mitchell

I'VE SERVED SEVEN PARTY leaders since first elected to Parliament in the Grimsby by-election in 1977. Jim Callaghan was not only the best but the most genuinely Labour of all of them, and the one I was happiest to work for. As far as we humble foot-soldiers in Labour's army were concerned, Callaghan was the most open and accessible; indeed, the only one who didn't consider himself too important to mix with the pioneer corps of politics and tell them what was going on without hiding behind puff pastry, empty promises and pandering protectors. As a product of the age of duty rather than ego, he was more interested than most of his successors in the responsibilities of power rather than its trappings.

This first struck me when he came to talk to us at Nuffield College just after he'd been shunted from the Chancellorship to the Foreign Office. No sulking, no resentment: just open and honest conversation about what the government was doing, and a display of figures when I criticised his long failure to devalue which had undermined the Labour government.

He had a quiet sense of self-satisfaction and the pride of an ordinary man who'd mastered the money trade and done it better than the intellectuals, an attitude which showed in the way he treated Sir Donald MacDougall, our top economist, like an office boy there to produce the figures.

In my by-election I happily defended his policies – basically incomes policy to bring down inflation, plus high benefits and public spending to boost the economy. More importantly, Grimsby approved too, electing me with a narrow majority – the first sign that the tide had turned for an embattled Labour government. I shouted, 'We did it for Jim!' from the town hall balcony to a bemused crowd of at least seven down below.

I'd like to say that that was the start of a beautiful friendship. It wasn't. Backbenchers don't have much contact with the leaders they serve and usually leaders like their troops to be seen and not heard. Jim did, too, though it's fair to say that the average backbencher in his day had more contact with their leaders than any counterpart since, as politics moved on from team management of the party to manipulating the media, while leaders prefer being supermen rather than ordinary blokes.

Taking your seat in Parliament means taking the oath, then a quick trip to the leader's office and a short meeting. In ours, so far as I recall, Jim asked me about Grimsby and fishing, I thanked him for making us a development area (which the Tories shortly rescinded) and that was it. However, unlike his successors, Jim did mix with the troops and actually knew who they were. He would come into the dining room unheralded and unescorted, where later leaders preferred a place prepared and an awestruck group waiting and would have liked the corpus of heralds were it possible. Callaghan joined me several times, but it was more depressing than enlightening as he lamented the passing of the days when backbenchers were loyal, trade unions cooperative and fewer intellectuals aired their egos. He seemed to feel that he was drifting out of touch with a PLP that had fewer genuine workers and trade unionists, more graduates and far too many intellectuals. As one of the latter, I kept quiet.

Jim was a hardworking Prime Minister. His PPS, Roger Stott, used to come back exhausted after a day at No. 10 commenting that his boss was a 'driven man'. Yet he was more approachable than any Prime Minister has been since and he spent more time around the House, which kept him in touch with the moods of his quixotic party better than his more aloof successors. Unlike them, Jim never developed delusions of grandeur. Rather he was a man of common sense who never hesitated to express it, or to call an intellectual a twerp. This made him seem rude when he was just being honest – as when he came to my house in Grimsby and I showed him a wonderful John Hopkinson painting of Grimsby, of which I was very proud (it was rumoured that Elton John also bought one). 'How much did you pay for it?' asked Prime Minister Jim. I told him. 'You were robbed.'

The usual view is that Callaghan was right on the little problems but disastrously wrong on major ones, and the timing of the 1979 election is usually given as the prime example. It may well be that had he gone to the country in autumn 1978, he would have won with a small majority, but at the time (as a new chum) I certainly agreed with both his decision to leave the TUC waiting at the church and the 5 per cent pay policy with which he hoped to struggle on until the economic revival changed the mood. In a sane world, with a sane trade union movement, he might have been right. The economy was recovering and the mood brightening.

But that wasn't the world he lived in. It was now a different world with egotistical and irresponsible union leaders, particularly in the public services, uncontrollable shop stewards, a union membership tired of the disciplines of incomes policy and the most powerful among them, such as the car workers, determined to do better under the law of the jungle known as free collective bargaining. So, Jim's gamble failed, destroyed by the militant idiocy of the Winter of Discontent, then by the parliamentary turkeys determined to vote for Christmas. Jim, an honourable man, was fed up with clinging to power and determined not to fiddle and manoeuvre to keep it, despite what his critics claimed. He refused to do dirty deals of the type both Theresa May and Boris Johnson later did, and wouldn't countenance the gas pipeline to Northern Ireland, which Roy Hattersley was urging to buy Ulster Unionist support. So, he went down to an inevitable defeat, betrayed by the union movement he'd defended and nurtured for so long.

Having destroyed their own government, the unions got what they deserved in the shape of Margaret Thatcher. Jim's reward was a chorus of sarcastic complaints that 'Jim fixed it for me', and a clamour for radical left policies and institutional changes to weaken the power of both leader and MPs by putting them under the control of party members, conference and the National Executive. At which point Jim seemed to me to give up, like Canute unable to check the tide of lunacy. No recriminations, no regrets, no blame and no resistance. He stood down and handed the mess to Michael Foot, resulting in the longest suicide note in history, the breakaway of the SDP and a recovery process which took eighteen years.

Occasionally he warned me that I had become far too cynical in my writings about the party we both loved. He certainly never did. His autobiography is modest and there was an air of sadness about his person that the party could be so foolish and so ready to reject the achievements of a great Labour government which had, after all, saved the nation from the worst economic crisis since the war. Instead he took refuge in pride at his own achievement in rising from humble trade unionist to the highest offices in the land, and in becoming Prime Minister to lead the nation through its most desperate days.

I remember both the sadness and the pride. Both stood out the last time I saw him for a chat on his farm after retirement. His beloved wife Audrey was dying of Alzheimer's disease, the farm was silent, and he was happy to reminisce about our party and the past. It was a sad experience as he said goodbye over the farm gate like a noble Farmer Jim. He was a great man from Labour's greatest era.

17

A TORY BACKBENCHER'S
VIEWPOINT

Jonathan Aitken

To a newly elected Conservative backbencher serving in the 1974–79 parliaments, Jim Callaghan seemed a formidably impressive Foreign Secretary and Prime Minister.

With Harold Wilson's star waning, for health reasons no one knew about at the time, and Denis Healey mired in belligerent battles with the hard left of his party over his policies at the Treasury, Callaghan's canny, comfortable style at the despatch box made him appear head and shoulders above anyone else in the Labour Cabinet.

I came to know Jim as a result of a small but revealing incident in 1975. As Foreign Secretary, he was attending a banquet given by Crown Prince Fahd of Saudi Arabia at the end of his state visit to Britain. As the meal concluded, ceremonial speeches began. But there was a snag. A three-line whip vote was due to take place at 10 p.m. in the Commons. At that particular moment of bitter hostilities between the parties, a wafer-thin government majority, and allegations of cheating in the division lobbies a few days earlier, all 'pairing' was strictly forbidden. Normally the Foreign Secretary of the day would always be paired if fulfilling a nationally important engagement, but not on this occasion. So just before 10 p.m., a greatly embarrassed Jim Callaghan began explaining that he would have to leave the banquet without delivering his official speech of thanks to his Saudi hosts.

I was present at this dinner. I knew enough about Saudi Arabian culture and protocol to realise that a walk-out by the Foreign Secretary would look insulting to the de facto Saudi king. So I sent a note to Mr Callaghan saying that I would 'pair' with him. He gave me a thumbs up sign, delivered an exemplary speech in honour of Crown Prince Fahd and preserved all the correct diplomatic niceties.

Jim gave me a lift back to Westminster in his car. 'Decent of you to help out,' he said. 'I hope you won't be in too much trouble with your whips.' 'I probably will,' I said. 'But I wasn't doing a favour for you. I was doing it because I thought it was in the national interest.' 'You're right. It was,' said the Foreign Secretary. 'The national interest should always come first.'

The rapport created by this episode continued in small ways. One of the hottest topics on the Foreign Secretary's agenda at that time was Rhodesia. Jim Callaghan was a master of his brief on arcane topics in the country such as African A and B voting rolls, the divisions between the Shona tribes and the protection of white farmers. I was a fairly assiduous attender at Foreign Office Questions. I once asked what I thought was a sharpish Parliamentary Question about the role of the RAF fighter squadron based in nearby Zambia at Lusaka. Jim skilfully took the wind out of my sails by saying, 'I seem to remember the Honourable Member's father was a distinguished and gallant RAF Spitfire pilot, so the Hon. Member will surely know...'

A little flattery goes a long way in the House of Commons. Yet in one way the exchange was typical of Jim. Having served in the Royal Navy, he took a great interest in people's military records. He revered those on both sides of the House who were thought to have had 'a good war'. It was an important ingredient in his simple, sturdy patriotism.

As Prime Minister, Jim Callaghan quickly shone in the House of Commons, partly just by not being Harold Wilson, and partly because, to some surprise, he established a well-acknowledged supremacy over the new Leader of the Opposition, Margaret Thatcher. In my 2014 biography, *Margaret Thatcher: Power and Personality*, I wrote a chapter headed 'Outmanoeuvred by Jim Callaghan'. It contains this passage:

> [Thatcher] lost clash after clash with Callaghan. His technique was to don the mantle of a wise elder statesman brushing aside the clamourings of an over-eager challenger. His condescension infuriated her. 'I am sure that one day the Right Hon lady will understand these things a little better' was one of his patronising put-downs when she tried to interrogate him about government borrowing.

As Callaghan's authority in the House increased, Thatcher had great difficulty in penetrating his armour. On one occasion she attacked him for his 'avuncular flannel', but he genially brushed her aside. 'I have often thought of the Hon. Lady in many ways, but never as my niece.'

Jim's genial flannelling was far more effective than Margaret's shrill flailings, for throughout the 1977–78 period the Conservative parliamentary party was growing restive about their leader's failure to lay a glove on the Prime Minister in the House of Commons. By October 1978, this mood had taken root in the country, for all the polling data suggested that the electorate trusted Callaghan more than Thatcher. Labour even had a slight edge in most marginal seats. So, it remains a mystery why the Prime Minister did not call a general election that autumn.

I offer one clue to solving this mystery. In that brief conversation with Jim Callaghan coming back from the Saudi dinner when he was Foreign Secretary, I mentioned that I had worked as a junior speechwriter for Sir Alec Douglas-Home. 'Decent, upright man, Alec,' responded Callaghan.

> Good on foreign affairs. Unlucky to have such a short time in No. 10. As it was, he nearly won the '64 election. If he'd had another six months to consolidate his position he might have held on to power. And if he'd lost, well, 'PM from '63 to '65' would have looked better in the history books than his eleven-month stint – '63 to '64.

Looking back on it, I wonder if the same thought about dates in the history books nudged Callaghan into staying on to be a '1976 to 1979' Prime Minister. But, unfortunately for him, the Winter of Discontent intervened and sank his chances of re-election. He knew it himself. Sailor Jim had sniffed the wind of change correctly. He lost the election by some forty seats.

Seen with the benefit of hindsight, Jim Callaghan deserves a high rating both as a man and a statesman. Forced by the Conservative government's 'Geddes Axe' to leave education at seventeen, he rose via the Navy and through assiduous hard graft as a parliamentarian to serve competently in all three great offices of state. He was an honourable and effective Prime Minister despite his non-existent majority. In a period of extreme political volatility and trade union unrest, he held the ship of state steady until the last three months of his premiership. He was a better character and abler politician than several of his predecessors and successors. Not a bad epitaph for a Prime Minister.

18

THE LIB–LAB PACT

Duncan Brack

IN NOVEMBER 1976, THE Labour government's tiny majority in the House of Commons was wiped out by by-election losses and defections, and the government became increasingly prone to defeat in Parliament. In the wake of soaring inflation and the financial crisis that forced the government to apply for a massive loan from the IMF, there was a real fear that Britain was becoming ungovernable. Matters came to a head in March 1977, when the opposition leader Margaret Thatcher tabled a motion of no confidence.

While the Labour whips tried to do deals with the other minority parties (they were eventually to persuade three Ulster Unionists to abstain), the Liberal Party was the obvious target. After a number of contacts, the Liberal leader David Steel met Jim Callaghan on Monday 21 March, two days before the vote was due. Steel made it clear that he was not interested in an agreement just for a single debate; he wanted a longer-term framework for cooperation. Callaghan agreed that he would recommend to his Cabinet 'the idea of general consultation in return for general support'.[1] After intense discussions over the following two days, an agreement was reached and announced by Callaghan and Steel in their speeches in the debate. The no-confidence motion was defeated by 322 to 298; if the thirteen Liberal MPs had voted with the opposition, the government would have lost by two.

The joint statement issued by the two leaders set out a framework for cooperation between the parties. Later extended, it eventually encompassed a joint consultative committee and regular meetings between Labour ministers and their counterparts in the 'Shadow Administration', as the Liberal MPs and peers involved came to call themselves. Liberal proposals on devolution, worker participation, homelessness and small businesses were to be given a serious hearing, and the introduction of proportional representation (PR) both for elections to the proposed devolved assemblies in Scotland and Wales and for direct elections to the European Parliament was to be put before the Commons, subject to free votes.

For Callaghan, the main reason for entering the pact was obvious: avoiding an election. A Gallup poll in March had seen the Conservatives lead Labour by 16.5 per cent. The Liberals' reasons were more complex. While they were suffering less than Labour in the polls, the prospect of a Tory majority government was distinctly unappealing. The pact offered stability for the nation at a time of economic crisis on terms at least partly determined by the Liberals, and it would help to demonstrate the party's responsibility in bringing to an end the previous six months of legislative stalemate in the Commons.

Perhaps most importantly, it would demonstrate the practicality of the sort of cooperation entailed by the electoral reform promoted by the Liberal Party and, particularly for Steel, would show that the Liberals were more than just a party of protest and permanent opposition. Steel had long supported the idea of cooperation between parties in addressing the critical economic challenges facing the country. During the Liberal leadership election in 1976 he had observed that 'there are occasionally small "l" liberals to be found on particular issues outside the Liberal Party, and we should never fear to co-operate with them effectively to promote some part of our cause'.² Eighteen months later, at the height of his party's unhappiness over the pact, he quoted these remarks to Liberal candidates and added, 'no one can say they did not know where I stood'.³

The questions were how long the cooperation should continue and at what price, and it rapidly became clear that Steel would accept a lower price for a longer agreement than many of his colleagues. As the Liberal MP John Pardoe put it, 'David was determined to do a deal at all costs.' Labour ministers seemed to agree; one source reported that 'the "terms" were heard with some incredulity by the Cabinet' and 'the [Labour] Party had simply undertaken to do what it had anyway intended to do and desist from what it could not do'.⁴ Callaghan's claim, in his memoirs, that some of his Cabinet ministers had argued that 'some of the provisions were humiliating' is hard to credit, given that the pact placed them under no obligation to do anything about Liberal proposals other than listen to them.⁵

The full story of the pact, which in the end lasted for seventeen months, has been told elsewhere.⁶ It went through three distinct phases. The first, from March to December 1977, was one of relative harmony within and between the partnered groups; the government's legislative programme got back on track (though the Liberals occasionally voted against individual measures), inflation slowly began to fall and a few Liberal policies were given a fair wind by government ministers. Liberal support in the polls sank almost immediately into single figures, however, and the party lost three-quarters of its seats in the county council elections in May.

During the winter, the pact was tested to destruction. On 13 December, the vote for PR in the European elections was lost by 319 to 222. Conservative whipping against the Bill did damage, but more significant for the Liberals was Labour's lukewarm response.

Although a majority of Labour MPs voting – 147 to 122 – supported the Bill, fewer than half of the Parliamentary Labour Party voted for it, and eleven ministers, four of them Cabinet members, voted against it. This was hardly the 'best endeavours' of the government that Liberals had been promised. An immediate meeting of Liberal MPs decided to continue with the pact by only six votes to four. To achieve this, Steel was obliged to pretend that Callaghan was going to see the Queen to call an election, a prank which made some of his colleagues feel physically sick.[7]

Astonishingly, Callaghan does not even mention the vote in his memoirs, simply listing the Bill as one of those that 'caused most trouble' during that parliamentary session.[8] Later, when free votes on proportional representation for the proposed Scottish and Welsh assemblies went the same way, he observed merely that 'fortunately, David Steel was satisfied that Michael Foot [Leader of the House] and I had fully discharged the undertakings we had given him'.[9] In fact Callaghan and Foot had steadfastly refused to whip their colleagues into supporting PR, and in practice by then the Liberals had lost much of their leverage; bringing down the government and fighting an election on the basis of electoral reform for institutions that either did not yet exist or that the electorate knew nothing about was hardly a realistic prospect.

The pact was now doomed. Although a special Liberal Assembly in January 1978 granted Steel the freedom to continue it for the remainder of the session, most delegates regarded this as allowing the pact a dignified demise in preference to administering a lethal injection. In May, Steel announced his intention to end the pact in the summer, and in August the party gave notice that all joint meetings were at an end. The government limped on for a further seven months until, in March 1979, it was defeated by one vote on a motion of no confidence, which all Liberal MPs supported.

For the Liberal sceptics, the experiment in cooperation was costly and largely fruitless. In electoral terms, as well as losing hard-won council representation, the Liberals lost ground at every parliamentary by-election during the pact, losing over 10 per cent of the vote in half of the contests between April 1977 and May 1978. The tangible rewards in terms of policy were at best thin, although a handful of Liberal demands, particularly on employee share ownership, made their way into legislation and some Labour proposals for extending state control were dropped; in addition, the economic situation improved markedly during the pact's lifetime.

Whether Steel could have achieved more through tougher negotiation is debatable; but for the Liberal leader the concrete outcomes of the pact were probably secondary. In his eyes, it had demonstrated both in general that parties were capable of cooperating in the national interest and in particular that the Liberal Party was able to affect the direction of government, as well as providing political and economic stability. And in the longer term, it helped to lay the foundations of the Liberal–SDP alliance, Steel's second, and much more sustained, attempt to break the mould of British politics. As Tom McNally, head of Callaghan's political office during the pact, later observed, the success of the pact partially lay 'in loosening the cement of the old two-party system and improving the prospects for cross-party cooperation. It gave the social democrat wing of the Labour Party a place to go when this was later needed.'[10]

Whatever its legacy, one conclusion seems clear: at the heart of the pact stood the positive relationship between the party leaders who agreed it. Before March 1977, Steel and Callaghan hardly knew each other; they were of entirely different backgrounds and generations. Yet, as Steel recounted, 'we established an easy rapport'.[11] Callaghan explained in his memoirs that 'I had been predisposed to like him from the start … First impressions were lasting.'[12] The two men trusted and came to understand each other, and Callaghan took Steel into his confidence over a much wider range of issues than their formal agreement had contemplated. If the two parties had been led by Callaghan's predecessor Harold Wilson, and Steel's leadership opponent John Pardoe, it is inconceivable that any kind of pact could have come into existence. Steel was right, as he later acknowledged, that 'it's fair to describe it as a Steel/Callaghan Pact'.[13]

NOTES

1   J. Callaghan, *Time and Chance* (London: Collins, 1987), p. 455.

2   D. Steel, *A House Divided: The Lib–Lab Pact and the Future of British Politics* (London: Weidenfeld & Nicolson, 1980), p. 22.

3   David Steel, letter to Liberal candidates, 16 December 1977; cited in M. Cole, 'Breaking the Mould (1974–1988)', in R. Ingham and D. Brack (eds), *Peace, Reform and Liberation: A History of Liberal Politics in Britain, 1679–2011* (London: Biteback, 2011).

4   P. Whitehead, *The Writing on the Wall: Britain in the Seventies* (London: Michael Joseph, 1985), p. 259.

5   Callaghan, *Time and Chance*, p. 457.

6   As well as the other references cited here, see A. Michie and S. Hoggart, *The Pact: The Inside Story of the Lib–Lab Government, 1977–78* (London: Quartet, 1978) and J. Kirkup, *The Lib–Lab Pact: A Parliamentary Agreement, 1977–78* (Basingstoke: Palgrave, 2015).

7   Cole, 'Breaking the Mould', p. 279.

8   Callaghan, *Time and Chance*, p. 498.

9   *Ibid.*, p. 508.

10   G. Lippiatt, 'Working with Others: The Lib–Lab Pact', *Journal of Liberal History* (2003), vol. 60, p. 23.

11   Steel, *A House Divided*, p. 155.

12   Callaghan, *Time and Chance*, pp. 465–6.

13   Quoted in M. Oaten, *Coalition: The Politics and Personalities of Coalition Government from 1850* (London: Harriman House, 2007), p. 193.

19

THE LABOUR LEFT
UNDER CALLAGHAN

Simon Hannah

BY THE END OF Callaghan's government, the Labour left felt only bitter disappointment: a mood that paved the way for the climatic battles of the 1980s between left and right.

To understand the disappointments of the Callaghan years we have to examine the trajectory of politics during this time. The Wilson government of 1964–70 had achieved some significant successes but ultimately the left of the party had been frustrated – most notably over the spectacular disaster of the 'In Place of Strife' policy which sought to shackle the trade unions.

During Labour's years in opposition from 1970 to 1974, Britain was rocked by serious clashes between unions and government, leading to a near general strike in 1972 and then the three-day week as the miners walked out.[1] This struggle had emboldened the Labour left, and radicalised it. Tony Benn in particular, who had started his career as an entitled son of nobility and a moderate in Wilson's very moderate Cabinet, moved rapidly left during this time, seeing in the class struggles wracking Britain the need for a new popular democracy out of the hands of the 'political class'.

Likewise, new radical left initiatives like Ken Coates's Institute for Workers' Control were having a profound effect on the left, bringing back socialist ideas that had been buried since the 1930s. The Alternative Economic Strategy developed by Stuart Holland was championed by the left, briefly informing both the economic policies of Labour and the TUC.[2] The AES took various forms, but the more radical version pioneered by Holland argued for more state control of the mesoeconomic sector – nationalisation of twenty to twenty-five of the largest private companies. Certainly, the AES was counterposed to the classical Keynesian policies that were favoured in Labour, but it often composed a system of state control and a degree of economic isolation (around import controls, for instance) that appeared to draw some inspiration from the Communist Party of Great Britain's manifesto *The British Road to Socialism*.

The February 1974 election had seen Labour run and win (narrowly) on its most radical programme in generations, calling for a fundamental and irreversible transfer of power and wealth from the rich to the poor. The red flag was flying high.

The Labour right tried to spin this period as one of left insurgency. Disgraced MP Reg Prentice and others decried the taking over of Labour by Marxist extremists.[3]

However, by the time Callaghan became leader in 1976 after Wilson's two years of premiership, the left was already deeply disillusioned. The radical proposals of the manifesto had been ignored or watered down by Wilson, including state ownership of the economy, and a much vaunted National Enterprise Board was gutted of its radical intention.[4] The EU referendum had gone badly wrong for the Bennite wing of the left, leading to Benn's demotion from a ministerial position that was of strategic importance to the left programme.

The Callaghan government was one of perpetual crisis due to the economic chaos of that decade. The 1973 oil crisis accelerated a general decline of the economy towards what appeared to be an almost terminal point – introducing the theoretically impossible (according to the leading economists) phenomenon of 'stagflation'. Callaghan saw his job as the keeper of the domestic peace, primarily through forcing wage restraint on the unions in exchange for some social policies that never materialised – the 'social contract'.

It was the social contract and its consequences that formed the backdrop to the 1970s battles within Labour. Tribune's primary concern was that Britain had historically low levels of investment and only state-led intervention into the economy would save the nation. Militant advocated breaking the social contract with trade union action and nationalising the top 250 companies in the country as a step towards socialism.

In Parliament, the Tribune group of MPs was the main thorn in the side of the Callaghan government. Labour's majority was so slim that any backbench rebellion of more than a handful of people would result in legislative defeat – the Tribune Group had around eighty MPs affiliated at its height. While the left in the wider party could still cause some inconveniences with troublesome motions to conference, in Parliament groups like Tribune were caught in the eternal Catch-22 conundrum: they could rebel, but only up to a point, or risk the downfall of the government. They could sit on the back benches and criticise freely, but have no real influence, or they could accept a position in the Cabinet. This meant more influence but also collective responsibility for Cabinet decisions. Benn opted for the latter approach, but it meant his silence on crucial controversies. From Callaghan's position it meant he had Benn by the leash of his career, telling reporters, 'I've got him on the end of a rope, and occasionally I give a sharp jerk on the noose.'[5] As such, PLP discipline meant that the parliamentary left's 'bark was worse than their bite'.[6] The unions' reluctance to organise extra-parliamentary opposition hamstrung any retaliation.

The IMF loan and the capitulation of social democratic policies to the diktats of international financial organisations run by people utterly unsympathetic to the cause of the left were the sites of a significant battle within the party. It was also Benn's last real fight within the Cabinet from his position as minister for energy. The acceptance of the loan by most of the PLP, with all the austerity and right-wing economics that came as strings attached, was a bitter blow for the aspirations of the left, and finally buried the 1974 manifesto pledges for good. Benn admitted in his diary, 'It is the moment of defeat and we have to recognise it.'[7]

The AES was dead and buried as a programme for government long before the 1979 defeat. The Labour right criticised it as autarkic and isolationist, and Healey famously derided the Labour left as being 'out of their Chinese minds'[8] – comparing their economic strategy to communism in China.

Looking back on defeat, Ken Coates claimed in 1980, 'Callaghan had presided over what has been fundamentally, as well as in name, a Liberal–Labour coalition, covering for the International Monetary Fund.'[9] The book he edited, *What Went Wrong*, gives voice to the disillusioned left in its grim post-mortem. Coates argues that party members remained against corporatism and patronage and for full employment – but at the government level these principles were 'abandoned without a fight'.[10] The Labour Party had promised an irreversible shift in the balance of power and wealth from the rich to the poor, but during its time in office the opposite had occurred, and in introducing monetarist economic logic around the IMF loan and subsequent Healey budgets, the government had in fact paved the way for Thatcher's own economic revolution.

It was this that formed the impetus for the Campaign for Labour Party Democracy (CLPD) which waged partially successful reform campaigns after 1979.[11] The demand to empower the members over the MPs – the NEC over the PLP – was the organisational response of the left, a battle that is still going on to this day.

This period deserves important examination for advocates of the Labour left as it was a period in which the left was well-organised, politically confident and theoretically developed with economic strategies and well-known leaders like Benn. The failure of the left during this time began a 35-year period of retreat until Corbynism, but arguably most of the fundamental problems of party democracy and the limitations of electoralism for facilitating radical change were never overcome, and perhaps never could be.

NOTES

1   D. Sandbrook, *State of Emergency: The Way We Were: Britain, 1970–1974* (London: Penguin, 2011), Chapter 3.

2   Holland's books elaborating the AES include *Strategy for Socialism: The Challenge of Labour's Programme* (London: Spokesman, 1975) and *The Socialist Challenge* (London: Quartet, 1975).

3   *The Times*, 2 March 1978.

4   The left had hoped that the National Enterprise Board would be used to take over private companies and expand state control of industry. It was badly underfunded and underpowered, and ended up not doing very much.

5   *Sunday Times*, 29 January 1978, p. 10.

6   P. Norton, 'Parliament', in A. Seldon and K. Hickson (eds), *New Labour, Old Labour: The Wilson and Callaghan Governments, 1974–1979* (London: Routledge, 2014), p. 194.

7   T. Benn, *The Benn Diaries: 1940–1990* (London: Hutchinson, 1995), p. 387.

8   *The Times*, 24 February 1976, p. 1.

9   K. Coates (ed.), *What Went Wrong? Explaining the Fall of the Labour Government* (Nottingham: Spokesman Books, 2008), p. 8.

10 *Ibid.*, p. 28.

11 S. Hannah, *A Party with Socialists in It: A History of the Labour Left* (London: Pluto, 2018), pp. 156–7.

20

HOW JAMES CALLAGHAN SOWED THE SEEDS OF HIS OWN DOWNFALL[1]

Polly Toynbee

CALL IT POETIC JUSTICE, or perhaps just a bitter irony that in the end James Callaghan's fall in 1979 came as the direct result of his own devious opportunism back in 1969. The trade unions he had wooed to win power in the party eventually brought him down too. It was not just he who fell; but he took with him the Labour Party too, casting the country into eighteen long years of Thatcherism as a result. If, in his ambition, he presented himself as defender of the power of trade unions, instead he ushered in an era that demolished their strength, leading to a steep rise in the inequality gap between incomes at the top and bottom of society, from which Britain has never recovered. His legacy bears the heavy burden of the significant part he played in the rise of Margaret Thatcher.

Barbara Castle, newly appointed by Harold Wilson to the Department of Employment, was seen – and saw herself – as a valiant defender of the left and the unions. Surveying the chaos of industrial relations, she set about drawing up a White Paper, 'In Place of Strife', that she firmly believed to be a socialist plan to cement in law the rights of trade unions for the first time and to ease out an incomes policy that had become unpopular. But, in exchange, she proposed the imposition on unions of some modest responsibilities to put their own house in order. She began as a whole-hearted enthusiast for the unions, and saw resolving dispute mechanisms as the way to best preserve them, especially against putative future Conservative government action. A distressing disillusionment followed.

Wild-cat strikes – spontaneous walk-outs without union backing – were the main problem. They had doubled in the past decade, mainly in ship-building, engineering and the docks, industries that account- ed for a third of export earnings. The 1966 seamen's strike and the 1967 dock strike had done the government serious economic and reputational damage. Inter-union disputes were notorious, where minor infringements by one worker touching the machinery belong- ing to another craft union led to instant downing of tools, which both management and the TUC council seemed powerless to resolve. When the rail unions devised a new weapon, the work-to-rule, this organised bloody-mindedness drove commuters to distraction with pettifogging excuses to delay trains running on time.

It was not the total number of days nor the actual damage done to production that was the main problem. Cambridge academic Profes- sor H. A. Turner estimated the total cost was only one thousandth of the annual national product; many more days were lost to sickness. Germany, the Netherlands and Sweden all had far better records for industrial relations, but UK newspapers would have surprised their readers had they reported that the US, Italy, France and Japan all lost more days to strikes than Britain.

But here was the important difference: while other countries lost days to organised strikes, negotiable with unions, Britain had many more wild-cat walk-outs, beyond restraint of their own unions, which felt impossible to deal with. These sudden down-tool events became notorious abroad, damaging Britain's reputation, with jokes about tea-break walk-outs circulating round the globe as the I'm-alright-Jack 'English sickness'. Just as British design was in demand, fear of unreliable delivery was turning clients to Germany or Sweden. Girling, the brake manufacturer, had fifty-seven strikes in eighteen months, with the knock-on lay-off of 5,000 car workers waiting for parts. Other workers were often the chief victims of industrial disorder elsewhere.

'In Place of Strife' was designed not to ban strikes but to establish the right to organise, the right to join a union and protection from unjust dismissal – a feudal sacking had just seen a worker dismissed for parking in front of a director's car. Castle meant to regularise the conduct of strikes, proposing a 28-day cooling-off period for negotiations where the minister could be summoned to help, a Commission for Industrial Relations that could resolve inter-union disputes, and a compulsory ballot before a strike. Fines could be levied as an ultimate penalty. As the row developed with the unions, Castle and Wilson were prepared to abandon fines if the TUC itself toughened its own rule-book with its own sanctions and discipline to ensure unions obeyed them.

In the spirit of those times, this policy might have been enough to show voters, as Wilson had always claimed, that Labour was indeed best placed to deal with trade unions through amicable and reasoned agreement. Had Labour held together to pass the legislation, had the senior unions settled and agreed that they themselves would put their house in better order, that might have been the beginnings of a better industrial relations culture. Castle pleaded for the social democratic cause of unity and agreement between government and unions. In promising to ease the prices and incomes policy introduced to curb inflation, she thought a positive blending of interests was possible. There would always have been rejection by the left-most part of the party and some unions, but TUC leader Vic Feather and others were at first not outright opposed.

Here is where Callaghan saw his opportunity. Wilson, Roy Jenkins, Richard Crossman and Tony Crosland represented most of the senior Cabinet backing the Castle plan, but many were angry that the White Paper had been sprung on them without coming to Cabinet first. The reason for that was Callaghan: Wilson and Castle didn't trust him not to leak it to the unions before it was presented to them. Callaghan was the most senior minister to oppose and to rally the unions as their champion, to the fury of Castle, who saw herself and her plan as their true long-term saviour. He took the chance to become the voice of trade unionism against the government of which he was a leading member. He put his own leadership intentions ahead of both party and country. 'Honest Jim' was a far more duplicitous, resentful and ambitious politician than his carefully nurtured public persona suggested. Enemies muttered the rhyme on the back of Force cereal packets: 'High o'er the fence leaps Sunny Jim, Force is the food that raises him!'

He had reason for his resentments: as Chancellor he had faced a severe buffeting, and together with Wilson had delayed too long in devaluing sterling, so when it happened, it had too little effect. He offered to resign, and Wilson moved him to the Home Office when he hankered after the Foreign Office. That was a demotion in the protocol of that government from third to seventh in rank. Besides, he felt himself a victim of snobbery from a Cabinet of intellectuals all of whose leading members were Oxbridge men, plus Castle, an Oxford woman. He adopted a bluff, philistine, man-of-the-people manner to defend his non-university background. A clever man denied the education he deserved, those who worked with him saw the intelligent speed with which he grasped a brief, but, with a chip on his shoulder about his lack of a degree, he adopted common-man affectations, opposing Roy Jenkins's liberal reforms with PC Plodisms such as 'some of us old fuddy-duddies…' As Home Secretary he rejected the Wootton Report on easing cannabis penalties laws and was tough on immigration.

He was even snobbishly mocked for the very sensible action of going to Oxford for economics tuition on becoming Chancellor: they should all do that. Although he was known patronisingly as the Keeper of the Cloth Cap, a rare Cabinet member who had come up through union ranks, he was not quite regarded as a real union man by unions, as he was from the white-collar tax inspectors' union. Other former workers, George Brown, a fur salesman, and Ray Gunter, ticket collector, had already left the Cabinet.

As party and unions increasingly swung against the Castle plan, Callaghan, from the right, was uniting with the left to seize the party's commanding heights: as party treasurer he sat on the National Executive Committee ex officio, where eighteen out of twenty-five seats were trade unions, as was 80 per cent of the card vote at party conference. Castle lost in the NEC by three to one, despite her reputation as the constituency party's favourite, regularly topping the NEC poll.

At this point Wilson was surrounded by plotters. The abysmal failure of Crossman's Parliament Act to reform the House of Lords was a humiliation, brought down by an unholy combination of left and right in Parliament. But the struggle over 'In Place of Strife' was causing a full-blown leadership crisis in which many expected him to fall. In beer-and-sandwiches meeting after meeting in Downing Street, the unions used their best weapon, sheer grinding boredom, and monotonous minutiae yielding no movement. Wilson told them, 'We can be destroyed economically and politically if we have no answer to unofficial strikes.' But the unions would neither agree to fines, nor to imposing their own new sanctions on those who broke union rules. As other members of the Cabinet slid onto the fence, away from Castle and Wilson, Callaghan, in backing this destructive union intransigence, made himself natural heir.

Talks collapsed. The Chief Whip, Robert Mellish, told the PM there was 'not a hope' of getting it through Parliament with scores of Labour rebels. As a result, a 'solemn and binding agreement' was drawn up, a toothless instrument that was a plain climb-down by the Prime Minister: 'not a victory for either side, a victory of good industrial relations', Wilson pretended. It was greeted with as much baying from his own side of the House as from the benches opposite. Edward Heath remarked pointedly that 'power resides elsewhere', meaning Labour was controlled by its union paymasters.

It became known contemptuously as Solomon Binding when, time and again over the years, strikers ignored it. But Wilson weathered the storm: 'I know what's going on, I'm going on,' he said, and he did, at least until the 1970 election was lost. But Wilson had defied the often unjust image of a man without principle who bent with every wind to hold his party together. Here was a key occasion on which he stuck to his guns and stood by Barbara Castle to the very last, even looking political death in the eye as enemies growled around him, because he believed 'In Place of Strife' was vital for the survival of the party, and the good of the country. The policy was always popular with the public, reaching 70 per cent support. Not only the middle-class but working-class voters too wanted the chaos contained: it was other workers who often lost pay and were laid off as a result of a small number of strikers elsewhere. Wives were even more strongly in favour than husbands, according to Gallup. The Tories had secretly feared that if the Castle plan passed, it would spike their guns and keep Labour in power for many more years.

Nonetheless, the 1970 election defeat was a shock, with Labour leading in the polls until the last minute. There were many causes, but without doubt the collapse of the Castle–Wilson plan for establishing order in unofficial strikes was an important reason. The Labour leader couldn't even push his own policy through his own party and his own trade union backers. Callaghan had done serious damage by joining those with whom he usually had little in common, such as Michael Foot, who had denounced the Bill as 'a war on the unions' in *Tribune*.

Would it have made a great difference to industrial relations? Some said it would have no effect: wild-cat strikers would have paid no attention to either legal sanction by government, or sanctions and threats of expulsions from the TUC. It might, they claimed, have only inflamed matters. That's one of history's 'what ifs'. But a Labour movement that managed to come together sufficiently to acknowledge there was a problem, ready to set about trying to solve it would have been an infinitely better electoral proposition than a party and its paymasters rebelling en masse against not only their leader but the clear wish of the electorate expressed in opinion polls. It looked like a party more concerned with the working of its own intestines and peculiar power plays than in the world beyond.

Callaghan was the man who knew best how this particular digestive system worked, and he used that knowledge unscrupulously to position himself as Wilson's successor. It was a curious act of betrayal, for he was the law and order man, the avuncular upholder of a regular man's common sense – and 'In Place of Strife' was a modest piece of prudence and sound judgement.

There was a brutal justice in his own dethronement in 1979. Stepping off the plane from a summit in Guadeloupe in the pleasing social democratic company of Jimmy Carter and Helmut Schmidt, followed by a few days' holiday in Barbados, he had lost touch with the ugly mood of the country when he didn't quite say 'Crisis? What crisis?' He had landed back into the coldest winter with strikers piling up rubbish in public parks and – that abidingly fatal image – some Liverpool gravediggers refusing to bury bodies. Would that Winter of Discontent have been as severe and chaotic as it seemed, had he not sabotaged 'In Place of Strife' a decade earlier? Edward Heath was brought down by mishandling the unions in his ill-conceived 'who governs?' election. Callaghan, too, was brought down by industrial disorder.

What followed was, as Castle had warned, the systematic ideological destruction of trade unions, whose power and numbers have declined ever since, to the great detriment of all working people. Instead, a culture has been allowed to arise entirely devoid not only of organised labour but of the very principles fought for by earliest trade unions – zero hours, gig economy jobs, instant dismissal, chronic low and irregular pay, institutionalised bullying in 'fulfilment' warehouses, care workers unpaid for travelling between jobs in their own cars. None of these would have been tolerated in the days when unions were strong. But by failing to channel that strength into productive and effective German-style collaborative power, they precipitated their own downfall. James Callaghan, through sheer ambition, played a key part in that tragic trajectory.

NOTES

1   For this article I have drawn heavily on my late husband Peter Jenkins's 1970 book, *The Battle of Downing Street*, chronicling Barbara Castle and Harold Wilson's failed attempt at trade union reform.

21

THE PRIME MINISTER OF DOCK GREEN: JAMES CALLAGHAN IN HISTORY

Dominic Sandbrook

I F T H E R E I S O N E image that captures Jim Callaghan's political persona, it is surely the photograph of him laying the foundation stone for a new building at Ruskin College, Oxford, on 14 October 1976.

Callaghan had been Prime Minister for only a few months, and was already immersed in the gruelling saga of Britain's bailout by the International Monetary Fund. But this was an occasion that meant a lot to him. As an institution dedicated to the education of working men, Ruskin College held a cherished place in left-wing hearts. And as a self-made man from a working-class background, Callaghan was passionately committed to education. As a boy, he had not been a high achiever; as he recalled, his reports at Portsmouth Northern Secondary School had been 'indifferent, if not downright bad'.[1] But he was convinced that schools were the route to working-class opportunity, and was determined to restore classroom discipline, high standards and accountability to parents after years of dreadful headlines about supposed progressive anarchy.

At the time, the press focused entirely on the content of his speech, which is now remembered as a first step towards the education reforms of the Thatcher government. But the picture tells a broader and, frankly, more richly enjoyable story. In the foreground stands Callaghan, soberly bespectacled in his conservative suit, with the engraved Ruskin foundation stone. Behind him, though, is a forest of placards: 'Cut Arms', 'No Cuts Jim'. There are a lot of badges, and several wispy beards. One placard reads sternly: 'This Stone Was Laid by a Tory.'

Since Callaghan had spent his adult life in the Labour Party, and is remembered as the soul of 'Old Labour' – whatever that might mean – the notion that he was actually a Tory might sound laughable. Indeed, the occasion was rich with comic potential. During the Prime Minister's speech, Callaghan's policy chief Bernard Donoughue noted that he was jeered by 'student Trot militants protesting about education cuts', and relished the irony that 'these were the *privileged* students' interrupting a speech meant to benefit 'the underprivileged in education'. Even the girls, Donoughue remarked, had beards. And the foundation-stone-laying was even more excruciating, as Ruskin's student union president introduced the guest of honour by accusing him of 'dancing to the tune of the International Monetary Fund'. The Prime Minister had the last laugh, though. When the protesters struck up the 'Internationale', they soon tailed off because they did not know the words. Only just suppressing a smirk, Callaghan asked if they would like him to finish it for them.[2]

It may be testament to Callaghan's stamina and self-confidence that although he is remembered as the only man to have held all four major Cabinet offices, many of his most resonant moments involved him being jeered, abused or generally embarrassed. Perhaps the most familiar image of his tenure as Chancellor in the 1960s, for example, was a shot of him being driven away from 11 Downing Street, his face drawn and exhausted, after the devaluation of the pound. The abiding image of his time as Foreign Secretary was his awkward press conference with the formidable figure of Idi Amin in Uganda in 1975, after he had effectively begged for the release of the imprisoned teacher Denis Hills. Four years later, the moment that defined his tenure as Prime Minister was his press conference after returning from Guadeloupe during the Winter of Discontent, when reporters badgered him about the 'mounting chaos' in Britain's towns. And his final, unhappy months as Labour leader after the 1979 election were characterised by the sight of Callaghan sitting glumly on various platforms while angry activists lined up to harangue him. '"Jim'll fix it," they said,' yelled the former MP Tom Litterick at the party conference that autumn, to applause from the delegates. 'Aye, he fixed it. He fixed all of us. He fixed me in particular!'[3]

Callaghan was not, of course, the first or the last Labour leader to find himself without honour in his own party. Few Labour leaders are ever forgiven for wielding power. But Callaghan drew such opprobrium from middle-class activists not just because of what he did, but because of who he was. In the 1976 Labour leadership contest, which saw him triumph over such self-consciously bookish, clever figures as Roy Jenkins, Michael Foot and Denis Healey, he was the only candidate who had never been to university. 'There are many cleverer people than me in the Labour Party,' he told an aide, 'but they're there and I'm here.'[4] With characteristic snobbery, Jenkins remarked that there was 'no case I can think of in history where a man combined such a powerful political personality with so little intelligence'.[5] But if Callaghan was so stupid, what did that say about the beaten Jenkins?

It is a cruel irony that in the public imagination, Callaghan has come to personify the economic failures of the 1970s. To people who are not very interested in political history, which is to say most people, he belongs to the world of Harold Wilson, Michael Foot and Tony Benn: the bleak, broken landscape of British Leyland and the National Enterprise Board, endless pay disputes and double-digit inflation, bin bags in the streets and publicly funded factories making both car radiators and orange juice. But in many ways, this was not really Callaghan's world at all. As the archival and diary evidence for the 1970s shows, he consistently argued against Benn's vision of a state holding company propping up lame, dead and dying ducks. He regularly urged Wilson to get a grip on inflation, and as Prime Minister he famously used his first conference speech to pronounce the death rites of incontinent Keynesianism. He presided over the most extreme public spending cuts since the war, as well as the highest levels of unemployment since the Depression. And it was even Callaghan who launched Whitehall's drive to get computers into schools, which became one of the lasting symbols of Margaret Thatcher's enthusiasm for economic change and technological modernity. He would not have taken kindly to being called a proto-Thatcherite, of course. But perhaps it is not such a stretch to see him as the bespectacled John the Baptist to her handbag-wielding Messiah.

What makes it hard to picture Callaghan as a harbinger of change, though, is the fact that his public persona was so thoroughly backward-looking. Even in his very first broadcast as Prime Minister in 1976, he looked backwards, promising to restore family values and asking his audience, 'Do you, like me, sometimes feel that we have been slipping?'[6] Indeed, everything about him suggested nostalgia, from the thick glasses and dark suits to the slow, deliberate speaking style and rounded Hampshire vowels. As the proud son of a Chief Petty Officer, and as someone who saw active service himself during the Second World War, he loved the Royal Navy's ethos of patriotic solidarity, and decorated his Sussex farm with naval prints, even using an old ship's rope ladder to get up to the attic. Any criticism of the police, the armed forces or the trade unions was guaranteed to provoke him, and he nursed a profound admiration for the Queen and the Boy Scouts. Not for nothing did the Conservative politician Kenneth Baker call him 'the Prime Minister of Dock Green'.[7]

Like many Labour politicians born and brought up in the early decades of the twentieth century, Callaghan was steeped in the culture of religious nonconformity. Not only was his mother a strict Baptist, but he had attended Sunday school every week and learned passages of the Bible by heart. In Donoughue's words, his values were those of a 'nonconformist Victorian'.[8] He hated any suggestion of moral and sexual permissiveness, and for a nominally left-wing politician he could be astoundingly conservative. He told his aides that he had been 'completely unaware of homosexuality until well into adult life', and still could not bring himself to watch any scenes of sex or nudity beside his children, on television or the stage, even though they were now adults and had children themselves.[9] And his handling of Margaret Thatcher in the Commons was, in its way, a masterpiece of chauvinist condescension, as if he were permanently amused to find himself opposite, of all things, a woman. His only true competitor as the personification of British values in the late 1970s, Roger Moore, could hardly have done it better.

So it is easy to see why, at a moment of deeply unsettling cultural and economic change, Callaghan was consistently one of the most popular politicians in the country. Most people never regarded themselves as permissive, had never been to university and, unlike the protesters at Ruskin College, did not even have beards. Between the activists who jeered Callaghan at Labour conferences and the ordinary people who put their cross in the Labour box, a great gulf was already opening up. But Callaghan's sympathies were very clearly with the latter. Like them, he was instinctively suspicious of the cause of European integration, telling an audience at Southampton that if French was to be the language of the European Community his answer would be 'Non, merci beaucoup'. He threw himself enthusiastically into the Silver Jubilee celebrations in 1977, later writing of how his spine tingled after the naval review at Spithead. During the Falklands War five years later, he was notably sympathetic to the Thatcher government and made a point of wishing Britain's fighting men 'God-speed' before the landings on the islands. ('He is just an old Tory warmonger,' fumed Tony Benn.[10]) And perhaps above all, he never lost his sense of what really mattered to ordinary people, and of the concrete reality of their daily lives. When, a week after the 1979 election, Benn insisted that Labour hold an inquest into the reasons for their defeat, Callaghan remarked that the reasons were perfectly clear. 'I'll tell you what happened,' he said. 'We lost the Election because people didn't get their dustbins emptied, because commuters were angry about train disruption and because of too much union power. That's all there is to it.'[11]

So, did all this make him a Tory? Of course not. The truth is that it was Callaghan, not Benn, who was closer to the founding traditions of the Labour Party. As the historian Martin Pugh has shown, the party began as a much more conservative (and even capital-c Conservative) institution than is often remembered. At the very first meeting of the Independent Labour Party in 1893, Ben Tillett, the future TUC President and MP for Salford, warned that if it was to be called 'the Socialist Party, he would repudiate it'. 'The great mass of British workmen', the meeting agreed, 'do not understand Socialism and have rather a prejudice against it.'[12] And as the Labour MP turned SDP enthusiast David Marquand later remarked, many of the party's founding figures actually 'drew on a long line of working-class Toryism: a rollicking, rambunctious, fiercely patriotic and earthy tradition, at odds both with the preachy nonconformist conscience that saturated the culture of provincial liberalism and with the patronising, "we-know-best" preconceptions of metropolitan intellectuals'.[13]

Callaghan only partly fits that definition, since he was hardly 'rollicking' and was no stranger to the nonconformist conscience. But he was certainly earthy and patriotic, and he had no time for patronising metropolitan intellectuals. In this respect he was the true heir to Ernest Bevin, another working-class patriot from southern England who said that his foreign policy was to 'take a ticket at Victoria Station and go anywhere I damn well please', and who insisted that Britain have its own nuclear deterrent with a 'bloody Union Jack on top of it'. Indeed, Callaghan is the obvious link between Bevin and later figures such as David Blunkett, another conspicuous patriot who, like Callaghan, won public applause for a firm line as Home Secretary. Blunkett, too, was no fan of the party's condescending middle-class intellectuals. Even as the young leader of Sheffield Council, he hated the idea that 'people should be told and given what is good for them'. That sounds like Sunny Jim talking.[14]

Oddly, perhaps the most evocative piece written about Callaghan was published after he had stepped away from the limelight. The author was Frank Johnson, *The Times*'s brilliant sketchwriter, who decided to spend a day with the former Prime Minister during the June 1983 election. So, one morning in the final days of the campaign, Johnson found himself in the post-war council estate of Llanrumney, in the heart of Callaghan's Cardiff constituency. In suitably elegiac style, the place was almost totally deserted. 'Rain beat down in straight lines,' wrote Johnson. 'Big puddles formed in the undulations of the pavement. Mr Callaghan stood bare-headed in a light plastic raincoat.' But for Johnson, it was perfect: 'as great a contrast as possible with the old statesman's time of grandeur'.

Callaghan and Johnson duly set off, accompanied with a handful of activists with stickers and a Special Branch man who refused an umbrella with the explanation that he preferred 'to keep both hands free when I'm working', which Johnson found mildly chilling. Callaghan's progress, he thought, was like that of a 'territorial magnate among his tenants'. People recognised him immediately, and treated him with immense respect. And as Callaghan talked, the effect, thought Johnson, was that of 'a proletarian or lower-middle class version of the Third Marquess of Salisbury – wary, experienced, loathing ideological fervour'.

At one point, the conversation turned to the alienation of people living on the new estates. They felt 'uprooted', Callaghan said. Like so many people in Britain in the 1980s, they felt unsettled by change, with their status, their communities, their very identities threatened by economic and cultural upheaval. 'Often these people live in the past,' Callaghan said thoughtfully. 'Perhaps it is not for me to say it, but they see me as part of that past.'[15]

He was, of course, quite right. Appeals to the past were not very fashionable among the Labour activists of the 1980s, and no doubt the protesters at Ruskin College would have seen Callaghan's words as conclusive proof of his shameful crypto-Toryism. But the record of history – not just in Britain, but in almost every other major industrial democracy – suggests that appeals to the past, to community, order, identity and place, are often remarkably effective. And for Callaghan, such nostalgia was not a prison but an inspiration: a starting point, not an end point. For him, as for Labour's founding fathers, this sense of a shared past was the wellspring from which his politics came, giving him the determination to improve people's lives in concrete, tangible ways without destroying the values they held dear or the world they loved. There is, after all, no shame in looking backwards; for if you do not know where you have come from, how do you know who you are, or where you are going?

And if Callaghan's heirs could bring themselves to learn that lesson, then one day they might actually win an election.

NOTES

1   J. Callaghan, *Time and Chance* (London: Collins, 1987), pp. 34–5.
2   B. Donoughue, *Downing Street Diary, Volume Two – With James Callaghan in No. 10* (London: Jonathan Cape, 2008), p. 84; *The Times*, 19 October 1976.

3 *Daily Mirror*, 2 October 1979; *The Guardian*, 2 October 1979.

4 K. Morgan, *Callaghan: A Life* (Oxford: Oxford University Press, 1997), p. 474; P. Hennessy, *The Prime Minister: The Office and Its Holders Since 1945* (London: Allen Lane, 2000), pp. 378–9.

5 R. Crossman, *The Diaries of a Cabinet Minister, Volume Three: Secretary of State for Social Services, 1968–1970* (London: Holt, Rinehart & Winston, 1978), p. 62.

6 *The Times*, 6 April 1976.

7 *Daily Express*, 6 April 1976.

8 B. Donoughue, *The Heat of the Kitchen: An Autobiography* (London: Politico, 2003), p. 234.

9 Donoughue, *Downing Street Diary*, pp. 244, 363, 435–6.

10 T. Benn, *The End of an Era: Diaries 1980–1990* (London: Arrow, 1994), pp. 217–8.

11 T. Benn, *Conflicts of Interest: Diaries 1977–80* (London: Arrow, 1990), p. 499.

12 M. Pugh, *Speak for Britain! A New History of the Labour Party* (London: Vintage, 2010), pp. 37–8.

13 *New Statesman*, 2 April 2010.

14 On Blunkett, see *The Times*, 5 April 1984; *The Guardian*, 9 April 1981, 25 July 1984.

15 F. Johnson, *Frank Johnson's Election Year* (London: Robson, 1983), pp. 175–6.

INDEX